RUGBY LEAGUE
HALL OF FAME

RUGBY LEAGUE

HALL OF FAME

ROBERT GATE

TEMPUS

First published 2003

Tempus Publishing Ltd
The Mill, Brimscombe Port
Stroud, Gloucestershire GL5 2QG
www.tempus-publishing.com

British Library Cataloguing in Publication Data.
A catalogue record for this book is available from the British Library.

ISBN 0 7524 2693 1

Typesetting and origination by Tempus Publishing.
Printed and bound in Great Britain.

CONTENTS

ACKNOWLEDGEMENTS

I am indebted to many people for help in compiling this book. Most are the usual suspects – those who regularly rally round whenever I decide to try to produce another work celebrating the history of the game and the men who made it. Without their assistance it would be so much harder to produce and so much poorer in content. If I have omitted anyone who has contributed, I apologise unreservedly.

Special thanks go to Raymond Fletcher, who has kindly and expertly proofread my manuscript and pointed out the error of my ways where necessary. I have said it before and doubtless will again: no one has a better eye for detail in matters pertaining to rugby league facts and figures than Raymond.

I am equally grateful to Stuart Smith for providing me with the paintings of the thirteen Hall of Fame players, which so enrich the book.

Curtis Johnstone, Chris Park and Alex Service have been particularly helpful in providing photographic material from their excellent personal collections, while David Gronow was most generous in loaning material on Huddersfield's Team of all the Talents.

Others who should be acknowledged are: Tony Capstick, Tony Collins, Ernie Day, Trevor Delaney, the late Harold Farrimond, Charles Gate, Myfanwy Gate, John Jenkins, Michael Latham, David Middleton, Alan Moore, Mike Rowan, Roger Shackleton and Henry Skrzypecki.

Thanks are extended to Richard Lewis, Executive Chairman of the Rugby Football League, for providing the foreword. Many of the images in this work have come from private collections and scrapbooks and their origins are unclear. If any photographic copyrights have been breached it has been unintentional.

INTRODUCTION

The Rugby League Hall of Fame was the brainchild of David Howes, the Public Relations Officer of the Rugby Football League. Its establishment was first mooted in 1987 and a year later, on 24 October 1988, the first nine entrants were inducted. The purpose of the exercise was, of course, to honour, celebrate and commemorate the game's greatest players. Election to the Hall of Fame was to be restricted to the most elite, *la crème de la crème*. There was to be no higher accolade to which any rugby league player could aspire. The idea was beautiful but flawed in practice.

It is doubtful if any rugby league enthusiast was against the concept of a Hall of Fame, but some felt that it should not be housed in a restaurant/public house. A purpose-built museum would have been preferable to the Bentley Arms in Oulton, near Leeds, spacious though it was. However, the fact that Whitbread, the brewing giants, were injecting around a quarter of a million pounds into the project (which would otherwise not have got off the ground) was enough to override other considerations. Moreover, the contract with the RFL was for ten years. Sam Whitbread, the company chairman, officially opened the Hall of Fame.

As a publicity vehicle the project was a great success. For over a year there was newspaper speculation as to the entrants, competitions for the public to make their nominations and when the first nine were named there was even more high-profile publicity. The induction ceremony, in a marquee in the grounds of the Bentley Arms, was a supremely dignified, decorous and moving event – which drew extremely complimentary press reviews. The tone was set when Jim Sullivan's widow Eve, a very frail figure on a Zimmer frame who had been virtually housebound, was called upon to receive Jim's medal. Alex Murphy, the sorcerer's apprentice to the great Welshman, immediately leapt to his feet and led the applause, shaking with emotion and tears streaming down his cheeks. If it meant that much to the hardbitten, voluble Murphy then how could anyone doubt that this was the supreme honour?

There were four living members of the Hall of Fame present to receive their medals (struck by Garrards, the Crown Jewellers) from the RFL's president, the Earl of Derby – Brian Bevan, Billy Boston, Alex Murphy and Gus Risman. Relatives of the remaining five deceased members received medals on their behalf – the widows of Jim Sullivan and Jonty Parkin, the sons of Billy Batten and Harold Wagstaff, and the daughter of Albert Rosenfeld. There was hardly a dry eye in the marquee. Peter Wilson wrote in the *Daily Star*: 'It could have been tacky and plastic. Instead it was an occasion for hard heads to show soft hearts. There were gold medals and glowing tributes, a recital of great exploits – and now a permanent reminder of the golden days of the game.'

A special Hall of Fame Challenge Match, Great Britain versus the Rest of the World, took place at Headingley on 29 October 1988, when players from Australia, France, New Zealand and Papua New Guinea were brought over and participated in an entertaining match, which was won 30-28 by the British. Among the Great Britain team were Garry Schofield, Martin Offiah, Shaun Edwards, Andy Gregory and Ellery Hanley – all, surely, prime candidates for inclusion in the Hall of Fame in future years.

In 1995 the centenary of rugby league was celebrated – I use the term loosely, as the officials running the game at the time seemed more interested in ignoring the game's past. However, they were not running the postal services, thank heaven. The British Philatelic Bureau did the game proud and chose to commemorate the game's history by featuring the sport's greatest icons, Hall of Famers, on their centenary postage stamps, covers and assorted philatelic memorabilia – a wonderful tribute to the game's great men.

The members of the Hall of Fame were to be selected by a panel of five. They were David Oxley, Chief Executive of the RFL; Bob Ashby, Chairman of the RFL; David Howes, Raymond Fletcher, co-editor with Howes of the *Rothmans Rugby League Yearbook*, and this author, the RFL's official archivist. However, many people were consulted by the panel members before the final decisions were made. It was decided that nominees would have to have played the vast majority of their careers in England and that no one would be admitted who had played the game within the last ten years.

It was realized that nine was an extremely odd number of entrants. No number had been laid down and the nine who were selected had absolutely impeccable credentials. No one, in fact, ever contested their right to be admitted. The problems arose, of course, with the omissions. Most notable was the omission of any forwards. Logically, there is no doubt that there should have been forwards, but the reality is that before any forwards were inducted there were even more backs whose legendary status warranted consideration and who may have got preference. It was a question of where to stop. Provision was made for future admissions and that problem would eventually be resolved. Neil Fox, who incidentally had played the latter part of his career in the pack, was an obvious entrant to the Hall of Fame but had not been retired ten years. He became the tenth member of the Hall of Fame on 29 August 1989 – ten years after his retirement.

Within a couple of years of the opening of the Hall of Fame it was increasingly obvious that the location was wrong. Contractual obligations could not be ignored, however, and physically the Hall of Fame remained at Oulton for the full ten years of its duration. In the meantime, changes of personnel within the RFL and the creation of Super League diverted all attention in other directions. History, tradition and celebration of past heroes were not even in the power brokers' lexicon. It was not until a decade after Neil Fox's elevation that thoughts of adding to the Hall of Fame were seriously addressed. A new selection committee was formed and in 2000, on the occasion of the World Cup final at Old Trafford, three more legendary figures were inducted – Vince Karalius (the first forward proper), Roger Millward and Tom van Vollenhoven.

With a more enlightened leadership at Red Hall and a capable catalyst in Tony Collins, the RFL's official archivist, it is hoped that the Hall of Fame, currently housed at Red Hall, will be afforded the status to which it is entitled. Plans are afoot to make regular additions to this pantheon. If this book, first contemplated fifteen years ago, can contribute something to the sense of pride in and gratitude for the sport's heroic figures, it will have been worth the wait.

FOREWORD

Ever since the sport came into existence in 1895, rugby league has been creating heroes for its followers and it is fair to say that even among that elite there have been players who have combined exceptional talent with a charisma that has transformed them into legends. In 1988 the Rugby Football League decided to recognize the contribution that these legendary athletes had delivered to the sport by creating a Hall of Fame. Initially there were nine inductees and their lives and careers were duly celebrated. Since then the Hall of Fame has expanded to thirteen members and we are always reviewing the process of delivering further inductees.

The debate about who should be in the Hall of Fame is constant because rugby league as a sport attracts passionate support from each of its followers. More often than not the discussion focuses upon who has been omitted from the Hall of Fame rather than who has already been inducted and this we regard as a healthy situation because it stimulates interest in the sport's qualities and past both immediate and long term.

I am delighted that Tempus Publishing has undertaken the publishing of a volume devoted to the Hall of Fame and its residents. It will enhance rugby league's growing library and gives the kind of public recognition that all thirteen of these players deserve. Tempus have played a major role in the expansion of the number of league-based titles and I hope that their investment in rugby league is rewarded in not only sales terms but also the gratitude of the reading public.

Very few people understand the significance of rugby league's history and its relevance to our club's communities more than Robert Gate, who has made the study of our sport into a virtual art form. It is, therefore, appropriate that he should be writing of the sport's superheroes. As I write we are again reviewing the candidates for possible induction into the Hall of Fame. It is an enjoyable and yet taxing task as the people charged with deciding who will eventually be inducted are aware of the impact their selection will have on so many people and communities. The benchmark such future inductees must seek to emulate is ideally illustrated by the thirteen existing members. I would urge you to read on to discover whether your favourites would measure up to the standards established by the 'immortals'.

Richard Lewis
Executive Chairman
Rugby Football League

SOURCES

Although the essays in this work concern thirteen of the most famous men in the sport of rugby league, there are in fact very few substantial secondary sources relating to most of them. Obituaries, newspaper and periodical articles, scrapbook material and oral history are generally the main sources of information available. Listed below are the substantial sources consulted:

Billy Batten – none.

Brian Bevan – Robert Gate's *The Great Bev* (London League Publications, 2002) is the only substantial work.

Billy Boston – Jack Winstanley's *The Billy Boston Story* (Wigan Observer, 1963) is an excellent account of Boston's career up to 1962. Less good is V. Peacock's *Living Legends of Rugby League: Billy Boston* (The Who's Who Series of Publications, 1984), although it is well illustrated. There is an interesting and provocative essay on Boston by Phil Melling in *Heart and Soul: The Character of Welsh Rugby* (University of Wales Press, 1998), edited by Huw Richards, Peter Stead and Gareth Williams. A chapter on Boston appears in Robert Gate's *Gone North*, volume one (R.E. Gate, 1986).

Neil Fox – Two comprehensive testimonial brochures were produced in 1965 and 1979.

Vince Karalius – An autobiography, *Lucky 13* (Stanley Paul, 1963) is the only substantial work, although a small brochure, Patricia Bamber's *Vince: A Rugby Legend 1951-62* (Riley Publications, 1986) also covers his career at St Helens.

Roger Millward – Hull KR produced a testimonial brochure in 1977.

Alex Murphy – Two testimonial brochures were produced, by St Helens in 1966 and by Warrington in 1975. An autobiography, *Saints Hit Double Top* (Pelham, 1967) was followed by Brian Clarke's biography, *Murphy's Law* (Heinemann Kingswood, 1988). A second autobiography, with Peter Wilson, *Saint and Sinner* (Mainstream, 2000), has made Murphy the most written about rugby league player in the game's literature.

Jonty Parkin – There are no substantial sources but J.C. Lindley's and D.W. Armitage's *100 Years of Rugby: The History of Wakefield Trinity Football Club 1873-1973* (The Wakefield Centenary Committee, 1973) is a useful reference.

Gus Risman – An autobiography, *Rugby Renegade* (Stanley Paul, 1958), is the only substantial work. A chapter on Risman appears in Robert Gate's *Gone North*, volume two (R.E. Gate, 1988)

Albert Rosenfeld – none.

Jim Sullivan – Amazingly, there are no substantial works on Jim Sullivan. He did, however, contribute an instructive four-part account of his career to the *News of the World* in 1936. A chapter on Sullivan appears in Robert Gate's *Gone North*, volume one (R.E. Gate, 1986).

Tom van Vollenhoven – Alex Service's splendid *The Flying Springbok* (Author, 1993) is the only substantial source. The St Helens yearbook for 1967/68 incorporated a testimonial tribute to Vollenhoven, which carried a résumé of his career by club secretary Basil Lowe.

Harold Wagstaff – The best source on Wagstaff is the wonderful thirteen-part autobiographical series, which appeared weekly in the *Sports Post* (Leeds) beginning on 9 February 1935 and ending on 4 May 1935. This was followed by a fourteen-part series by Wagstaff on tactics entitled *Wagstaff Shows the Way*, which ran from 9 November 1935 to 8 February 1936. There is a very good essay on Wagstaff in V.A.S. Beanland's *Great Games and Great Players* (W.H. Allen, 1945).

Hunslet winger Alan Snowden arrives too late to stop Hall of Famer Billy Boston from scoring yet another try.

WILLIAM BATTEN

Billy Batten with the Yorkshire Cup in 1924

HUNSLET

Debut: 9 February 1907 v Barrow (h)
Last game: 1 March 1913 v Widnes (h)

	A	T	G	P
1906/07	2	-	-	-
1907/08	41	21	-	63
1908/09	27	13	2	43
1909/10	19	11	18	69
1910/11	17	8	3	30
1911/12	35	25	28	131
1912/13	28	18	14	82

HULL

Debut: 12 April 1913 v Keighley (h)
Last game: 5 April 1924 v Bramley (a)

	A	T	G	P
1912/13	3	4	-	12
1913/14	29	10	1	32
1914/15	24	5	-	15
1918/19	14	17	-	51
1919/20	35	21	-	63
1920/21	23	15	-	45
1921/22	35	8	-	24
1922/23	35	6	-	18
1923/24	28	3	-	9

WAKEFIELD TRINITY

Debut: 30 August 1924 v Halifax (h)
Last game: 27 December 1926 v
Featherstone Rovers (h)

	A	T	G	P
1924/25	37	4	1	14
1925/26	30	1	1	5
1926/27	13	1	-	3

CASTLEFORD

Debut: 5 February 1927 v York (h)
Last game: 9 April 1927 v Hull KR (a)

	A	T	G	P
1926/27	8	1	-	3

CAREER RECORD

	A	T	G	P
Hunslet	169	96	65	418
Hull	226	89	1	269
Wakefield	80	6	2	22
Castleford	8	1	-	3
Tests	10	3	-	9
England	15	3	1	11
Yorkshire	19	7	3	27
Represent	5	5	-	15
1910 Tour*	9	4	1	14
TOTALS	541	214	73	788

*Excluding tests

TESTS (10)

Great Britain	5	N Zealand	8	1908	Cheltenham
Great Britain	22	Australia	12	1908	London (2 tries)
Great Britain	15	Australia	5	1909	Newcastle
Great Britain	6	Australia	5	1909	Villa Park
Great Britain	27	Australia	20	1910	Sydney (1 try)
Great Britain	22	Australia	17	1910	Brisbane
Great Britain	52	N Zealand	20	1910	Wellington
Great Britain	11	Australasia	11	1911	Edinburgh
Great Britain	8	Australasia	33	1912	Villa Park
Great Britain	2	Australia	16	1921	Hull

INTERNATIONALS (15)

England	18	Wales	35	1908	Tonypandy
England	31	Wales	7	1908	Broughton
England	14	Australia	9	1909	Huddersfield (1 try)
England	17	Australia	17	1909	Glasgow
England	14	Australia	7	1909	Everton
England	19	Wales	13	1909	Wakefield (1try)
England	18	Wales	39	1910	Ebbw Vale
England	6	Australasia	11	1911	Fulham
England	5	Australasia	3	1911	Nottingham
England	31	Wales	5	1912	Oldham (1 try, 1 goal)
England	40	Wales	16	1913	Plymouth
England	35	Wales	9	1921	Leeds
England	33	Other Nat.	16	1921	Workington
England	12	Wales	7	1922	Herne Hill
England	2	Wales	13	1923	Wigan

COUNTY GAMES (19)

Yorkshire	30	Cumberland	0	1908	Huddersfield (1 try)
Yorkshire	0	Lancashire	13	1908	Salford
Yorkshire	11	Australians	24	1908	Hull
Yorkshire	5	Cumberland	3	1909	Maryport (1 try, 1 goal)
Yorkshire	11	Australasians	33	1911	Sheffield (1 try)
Yorkshire	13	Cumberland	16	1911	Millom (2 goals)
Yorkshire	12	Lancashire	13	1912	Halifax
Yorkshire	19	Cumberland	5	1912	Hull KR
Yorkshire	20	Lancashire	8	1912	Oldham (2 tries)
Yorkshire	5	Lancashire	15	1919	Broughton
Yorkshire	18	Lancashire	3	1920	Hull
Yorkshire	27	Cumberland	6	1920	Maryport (1 try)
Yorkshire	30	Cumberland	12	1921	Halifax (1 try)
Yorkshire	11	Lancashire	11	1922	Hull KR
Yorkshire	5	Lancashire	6	1923	Oldham
Yorkshire	0	Cumberland	20	1924	Whitehaven
Yorkshire	13	Cumberland	31	1925	Huddersfield
Yorkshire	5	Cumberland	17	1926	Whitehaven
Yorkshire	17	N Zealanders	16	1926	Huddersfield

WILLIAM BATTEN
Billy B – Lionheart

'A perfect blending of brawn and brain...'

Fred Marsh, *The Northern Union News*, 1911

Billy Batten was the most controversial player of his time and the biggest crowd-puller. For two decades his was the name on all lips when talk turned to Northern Union matters. If ever a player genuinely had charisma, it was Billy Batten. One of Batten's great rivals, Dinny Campbell, recalled Batten in 1938: 'Off the field Billy was a really good sport; on the field he became so obsessed with the game that he was the devil incarnate … wire and whipcord, resolute and relentless in all his actions. He must have been the strongest centre the game has known. If he was astounding in attack, his defence was cruel in its effectiveness. His tackle was a thing to remember. He was a great team-mate, but a stern and bitter opponent.'

Harold Wagstaff, who probably knew more about centre play than anyone on the planet and whom Batten revered more than anyone else, said: 'Billy Batten was a great footballer … I don't think I knew a man who was a harder tackler than Billy. When he set himself for the job, he went into it with every ounce he had got. He just put all his weight and power in the tackle, and when he hit you – well, you felt as though a cyclone had hit you'.

Billy Batten was born on 26 May 1889 at 9 Gorton Terrace, Kinsley – a mining village near Hemsworth in the West Riding of Yorkshire. His parents came from North Wales. His father, James Batten, was a miner from Denbigh, who had married Ann Hughes from Rhosllanerchrugog. They had migrated, along with hundreds of others, in the late 1870s to Atherton in Lancashire, where there was plenty of work in the pits and mills. However, they uprooted a final time and decamped to Yorkshire, where Billy found fame, fortune and, ultimately, tragedy.

Billy went down the mines at fourteen to earn a shilling a day. He already had an obsession with physical fitness, which would endure throughout his life, and he was a lifelong teetotaller and non-smoker. He took up rugby with Kinsley and later Ackworth United. He was quickly spotted by Hunslet and Hull. Hunslet struck first and their secretary James Goldthorpe signed seventeen-year-old Billy, who received a new suit (valued at £5) but no cash fee. The young Batten did not have a particularly happy start at Hunslet. He made his debut in the centre on 9 February 1907 in a 15-0 victory over Barrow at Parkside and a fortnight later was played at full-back at Huddersfield. Although Hunslet won 13-7, Billy had a stinker and he was transfer listed at £15. There were no takers, although Bramley could have had him had their secretary Walter Popplewell been able to persuade his committee to fork out the money. Billy went back to Ackworth and played a blinder in a cup-tie at Beverley, where Hull again saw him and contemplated approaching him once more. At that point Hunslet realized their error and made peace with the prodigy.

The following season was stupendously successful for both Hunslet and young Billy. For 1907/08 the Northern Union instituted Lancashire and Yorkshire League Championships, so it was now possible for a club to win four trophies – although most pundits considered such a feat highly unlikely. Within a year the sceptics had been confounded. Billy Batten had joined a team that was about to create history. Hunslet decided that Billy would serve them best as a winger. When the campaign began he was a few months past his eighteenth birthday and he stood 5ft 9ins and weighed 11st 4lbs. He would grow considerably in the next few years.

The Hunslet team was led by Albert Goldthorpe, a half-back who could dictate games and was the greatest drop-goal exponent the game has ever seen. By 1907 he was thirty-five years old and had been playing for the club since 1888. He and Fred Smith, his scrum-half partner, formed the side's fulcrum. They played behind a pack dubbed 'The Terrible Six', which comprised any half-dozen from Billy Jukes, Bill 'Tubby' Brookes, Jack Randall, Jack Smales, Harry Wilson, John Willie Higson, Tom Walsh, Harry Cappleman and Walter Wray. The power, defence and control exerted by those forwards constituted the team's greatest strength. The backs took a subsidiary role although Herbert Place (full-back), Bill Eagers, Charlie Ward and Walter Goldthorpe (centres) and Fred Farrar (wing) all attained representative honours. The style adopted by the team was conservative but deadly effective. It did not win many friends but it did win matches.

Billy thrived within this well-oiled machine. Indeed, he shone, despite the generally subservient role taken by the outside backs. He scored his first try in the opening game, an 11-0 home win against Dewsbury on 7 September, and his first hat-trick on 9 November when Hunslet crushed Bramley 50-0 in a Yorkshire Cup first round tie. Hunslet knocked out Leeds and Wakefield Trinity to earn a place in the final against Halifax at Headingley on 21 December. Hunslet's game plan worked perfectly, the forwards monopolized possession and Goldthorpe ran the show. Hunslet won 17-0 with Batten scoring the last try a few minutes from time in one of the few three-quarter line movements attempted by his side. Four days later, on Christmas Day, he scored both tries in an 8-6 home league victory over Halifax. The following afternoon, 19,000 crammed into Parkside to watch a gripping encounter with the first New Zealand touring team, which ended as an 11-11 draw. Hunslet remained undefeated in any type of football until 18 January 1908 – a run of 23 games. Then the wheels fell off briefly. Hull KR were the first to lower their colours, winning 23-11 before 13,000 at Craven Street, Batten scoring Hunslet's solitary try. Amazingly, they also lost their next four league fixtures before getting back on track with twelve straight victories.

In the meantime, Billy Batten's form had been so spectacular that he had won international honours. On 15 February he played right wing for the Northern Union in the third and deciding test against New Zealand at Cheltenham. A stormy, wet day and a rough match ensued from which the New Zealanders emerged victorious, 8-5. Billy, still only eighteen, acquitted himself well, however. One report said, 'He showed powers of initiative with which some critics… had not credited him. Batten was distinctly unlucky in not scoring at least one try in the first half … and in the second half his alertness saved two tries being recorded against his side. Perhaps his best feat was the holding up of the burly Trevarthen, when that player had only to ground the ball to score.' He was in the wars, however, damaging his leg 'though he pluckily remained to the finish'. He had done well enough to win selection for the England side that met Wales at Tonypandy on Easter Monday, 20 April – the first ever

Anglo-Welsh international. Again the result was a disappointment to Billy for, after leading 18-15 at the interval, England fell away disastrously to lose 18-35.

There would, however, be far more successes than failures in his international career, which would run for another fifteen years. Club rugby was, meanwhile, a triumphal march. The Challenge Cup took Hunslet across the river to Leeds, then floundering near the foot of the table, for a first round tie, which was won 14-5 before a crowd of 12,000. The second round pitted them against Oldham, who were carrying all before them in Lancashire. Hunslet lacked Albert Goldthorpe but a titanic performance by 'The Terrible Six' in front of 20,000 Parksiders ended in a 15-8 victory. Billy was a try-scorer in an 8-0 third round victory at Barrow, 700 of the 12,000 crowd having travelled from Hunslet on a special excursion. He scored another in a surprisingly comfortable 16-2 semi-final win against high-riding Broughton Rangers at Wigan on 11 April. By then Hunslet had won the Yorkshire League Championship and the possibility of winning all four cups came sharply into focus.

Two days after the semi-final Hunslet returned to Wigan for a league fixture with a virtual reserve side. Billy was at full-back and must have felt embarrassed as Wigan ran eight tries past him to win 36-0. Hunslet were fined £10 for fielding a weak team but they were playing for high stakes. On 18 April Broughton Rangers went to Parkside for the Championship semi-final and were clattered again, 28-3. It was reported that, 'Batten put in a lot of spirited work on his own account. This lad has fairly taken possession of the Hunslet crowd. They like him for his great fearlessness of heart. He does many things which a brainy player would not do, but his force and style is that of the player who "gets there".'

Billy and his colleagues now faced the challenges of Hull in the Cup final and Oldham in the Championship final. First up was the encounter with Hull on 25 April. A crowd of 18,000 gathered at Huddersfield for a game that was expected to go Hunslet's way. The bookies were clearly right. Hunslet led 7-0 by half-time and a second-half snowstorm was probably all that kept the final score down to 14-0. Tries by Fred Farrar and Fred Smith were augmented by a Bill Eagers drop goal, while Goldthorpe landed three goals, one from a mark.

Oldham provided sterner opposition in a gripping Championship final at Salford on 2 May. Oldham had won the Lancashire Cup and League double and had topped the league table with a percentage of 90.62, well ahead of Hunslet's 79.28. Hunslet were not favourites. Conditions were completely different from the previous week as The Willows was bathed in sweltering sunshine. Albert Goldthorpe scored all of Hunslet's points in a 7-7 draw, although Oldham would have won had half-back Tommy White been able to convert the only try of the second half or land a couple of late drop goal attempts. The replay took place at Wakefield on 9 May in perfect conditions. The game was not as stirring as at Salford but Billy Batten, his team-mates and the Hunslet supporters were not worrying too much about the level of spectacle as they won convincingly 12-2, Billy making a tremendous burst late on to provide the platform for Walter Goldthorpe to score his second try. This sealed the Parksiders' victory, the Championship and the team's immortality as the first team to win all four cups.

Billy Batten thus ended his first season as an international and test cap and having won all the major domestic medals. He had topped the try-scorers at Hunslet with 21 and finished seventh in the league's try-scoring list. He had still not passed his nineteenth birthday. Moreover, despite his tender years, he was already becoming a personality. There was something indefinable about Billy,

Portrait of Billy Batten.

which attracted admiration from players and fans. His appearance was striking: he was handsome and he was dark. Old moving film of Batten confirms his singularity of appearance. The eyes are immediately drawn to him and it is practically impossible to look at anyone else. Physical aura aside, Billy played the game in a spectacular fashion. He put everything he had into his game. As he grew – he was 5ft 10½ins and over 13st in his prime – and became ever more powerful through his addiction to exercise, his defence-destroying bursts and crunching tackling became the talk of the Northern Union.

Added to that, he was famous (or notorious) for his hurdling. Billy was one of many players who would resort to jumping over tacklers if there was no alternative. His own colleague Billy Eagers had long been known as a hurdler and Eagers's fellow Cumbrian Tom Fletcher, an England rugby union three-quarter, who made his name with Oldham, was renowned for jumping over opponents. There were plenty of others – before and after Billy – who practiced hurdling. None, however, seemed to be quite so spectacular. Hurdling was frowned upon as very dangerous, of course, and was eventually banned. It must have been alarming for anyone facing Batten when he flew through the air, at high velocity and with such strength. Casualties certainly occurred and Billy himself suffered grievously from his own impetuous leaps. Fear appeared to be missing from his vocabulary.

Although Billy got his share of tries, as his career tally of 204 testifies, he was more of a maker than a taker. His punishing, straight running demoralized defences and opened up countless chances for others, particularly for the wings outside him. He was a useful goal-kicker, often being called upon for that duty as a Hunslet player but infrequently once he left Parkside.

Billy remained with Hunslet for six years but after the heady triumph of 1907/08, decline set in at the club. Even so, the early part of 1908/09 promised well. The opening thirteen games brought only two defeats, at Wigan and at home, 11-12, to the Australians (Billy scoring a try in the latter). Moreover, the team again reached the Yorkshire Cup final only to lose 5-9 to Halifax at Wakefield. It would be Billy's last final for Hunslet. By the end of the season they had slipped to twelfth in the league and surrendered all their trophies.

Billy Batten prospered despite the club's fall from grace. On 17 October he made his county debut on the wing, scoring a try in Yorkshire's 30-0 victory over Cumberland at Huddersfield. For the first time he played in the same team as Harold Wagstaff, another debutant, who was his centre. The two would later pair up for Yorkshire to form one of the most brilliant centre partnerships in the annals of the game. Billy's county career lasted an extraordinary eighteen years.

During the 1908/09 campaign Billy Batten played eight times against the first Kangaroo touring team – for Hunslet, Yorkshire, three times for England and in three tests for the Northern Union, all as a wingman. Playing in the first test at Park Royal, London, on 12 December 1908, he had the distinction of being the first man to handle the ball in an Ashes test when he gathered Dally Messenger's kick-off. A thrilling 22-22 draw saw Billy rampaging over for two first half tries. His barnstorming running provided plenty of problems for the Australians in the following two tests, which were won 15-5 at Newcastle and 6-5 at Birmingham.

The 1909/10 season offered the prospect of a trip to Australia and New Zealand with the first Lions, if Billy Batten maintained form. Hunslet dropped to fifteenth in the league but Billy kept himself in the eyes of the selectors. He scored twice in the Yorkshire County trial at Bradford and won his first representative honour as a centre on 23 October when he scored

Yorkshire's try and goal against Cumberland at Maryport. Yorkshire were leading 5-3 when a blizzard caused the game to be abandoned after 47 minutes. He was chosen on the wing and scored a try in England's 19-13 defeat of Wales at Wakefield on 4 December and everything seemed to be going well. On 10 March 1910 he accepted the Northern Union's offer of a tour place. Two days later he played in Hunslet's first round Challenge Cup-tie with Wakefield Trinity at Parkside. A rough encounter ended in a 2-2 draw. Billy and Jack Randall were sent off along with Auton of Trinity and received two-match bans. Two days after the cup-tie Billy played in the tour trial at Headingley as one of 'The First Selected XIII', scoring twice but injuring his knee.

Billy did not play again until April 9 at Ebbw Vale, when he was in the England team which lost 18-39 to Wales. His knee injury recurred and was so bad that he was told by Leeds surgeon Dr Littlewood that he might never play again. The doctor's report caused the tour committee to withdraw Billy's invitation on 12 April. Remarkably, on 18 April Billy approached the committee and asked to be reinstated as a tourist, undertaking to test his knee by playing for Hemsworth against Normanton St John's on 23 April. The committee agreed and deputed W.H. Shaw and Joe Nicholl to watch the game. Billy duly turned out, scored a hat-trick and looked the fittest man on the field. Billy saw Dr Littlewood again and on 26 April he was drafted back into the touring team.

Twenty of the twenty-six players had already sailed for Australasia on the *Osterley* by then but one Oldham and four Wigan players, who had stayed behind to play in the

A group of 1910 Lions in Australia. From left to right, back row: Fred Webster, Billy Batten, Bert Jenkins. Front row: Jim Sharrock, Frank Young.

(Photo—"Athletic News," Manchester.

WILLIAM BATTEN,

Hunslet,

Left wing three-quarter back and the "hurdle jumper" of the team. Colonial full-backs, beware of Batten's jump! His style is in direct contrast to that of Leytham, but none the less effective. He suffered the usual ups and downs during his junior career, but went from Kingsley to Ackworth United, and ultimately arrived at Parkside. Is the most determined and dangerous (to defenders) three-quarter-back in the Northern Union. County honours for Yorkshire, International for England against "All Blacks," "Kangaroos" and Wales. A useful man in more than one position behind the scrummages, and has with success played throughout a game at full-back. Holds the Hunslet club record for tries scored in one season.

Born at Kinsley, 20 years ago ; is 5ft. 10½in. and 13st. 4lb.

The entry on Billy Batten from the Northern Union Official Handbook for the 1910 Australasian tour.

Championship final, left for the Antipodes on the *Malwa* on 27 April. Billy Batten packed his bags and joined them. A couple of newspaper comments would have whetted the Australian public's appetite. One declared him to be 'undoubtedly the most aggressive three-quarter back in the Union'. Another announced 'Batten's style should be most popular down-under'.

They were right. The tour was phenomenally successful. There were massive crowds, the Ashes were won and New Zealand were hammered 52-20 in the only test played there, when Batten again wrenched his knee. Billy played in all the tests and in twelve of the eighteen tour fixtures. His dashing play established him as a superstar. Unfortunately, circumstances were to deprive him from ever touring again.

On returning from the tour Billy endured a frustrating season with Hunslet. His injury and a dispute with the club meant that he did not turn out until 10 December. He was transfer listed and Oldham agreed to pay a record transfer fee of £400 for him, but at the last minute he backed out. Meanwhile, Hunslet denied that they had offered Batten plus £100 to Huddersfield for their promising wingman Stanley Moorhouse. Things eventually settled down and, on a happier note, Billy's brother Jim, a centre, joined Hunslet from Leeds. Jim would unfortunately die in 1914 while working as a miner. Another brother, Eddie, a half-back, played for Bramley, Hull and Hunslet.

Billy was back on song in 1911/12. He had moved from wing to centre, and although only twenty-two, he was made captain. Under his leadership Hunslet finished fourth but were beaten 27-3 in the Championship semi-final by Huddersfield, who also put Hunslet out in the Yorkshire Cup semi-final, 5-3. Billy enjoyed his most prolific campaign in 1911/12, topping Hunslet's try-scoring (25) and goal-kicking (28) lists. When he touched down for his second try in a 34-7 home win against St Helens on 13 April 1912, Billy equalled Fred Farrar's club record of 25 tries scored in 1908/09. After a barren representative season in 1910/11, Billy resumed his career at the top levels, playing three times for Yorkshire, three times for England and in two tests against Australia. Perversely, the selectors still preferred to play him on the wing in the majority of those games. Billy's hurdling technique let him down in Yorkshire's disastrous 13-33 loss to the Kangaroos at Bramall Lane, Sheffield. Yorkshire had already lost one winger, Sam Stacey, through a broken collar-bone after half an hour. They lost their other winger, Billy Batten, on the hour, when he tried to jump over Bert Gilbert only to land on his head and suffer concussion.

Billy again captained Hunslet in 1912/13, when they finished fifth in the league. Such was his form that he was made captain of Yorkshire, finally sharing the centre position with Harold Wagstaff, and leading them to the County Championship. He then won the ultimate accolade by captaining England in the only international of the season, when Wales were pasted 40-16 at Plymouth on 15 February 1913. There was no doubt that as a personality Billy Batten was a godsend to the Northern Union. He put bums on seats and now he was captain of Yorkshire and England. Suddenly, however, the sums did not add up. Hunslet paid Billy 50 shillings when they won, 45 shillings when they drew and 40 shillings when they lost. They did not pay him at all when the close season dawned. In reality they were very good terms for the period – and certainly better than at most clubs – and they were more than the majority of unskilled men earned for a week's work.

FOOTBALL SNAPSHOTS-CXXIV

BATTEN, Hunslet.

Nobody knows
How his body he throws
Past the foe with a flash and a buzz.
No one can tell
How he slips in so well
And collars a goal—but he does!

An Athletic News *caricature of Billy Batten in his days at Hunslet, 1911.*

After leading England at Plymouth, Billy Batten played only two more games for Hunslet, the last on 1 March in an 11-5 home defeat of Widnes. On 8 March, Hunslet lost 0-2 in the Challenge Cup at York. The *Yorkshire Post* tersely stated, 'The Parksiders were without the services of W. Batten, a circumstance which undoubtedly had something to do with their defeat'. There now began what the *Hull Daily Mail* coined 'The Affaire Batten'.

Hunslet were unhappy about Batten's absence, although they did acknowledge that they had received a doctor's certificate to the effect that Billy was unfit to play in the cup-tie. Billy was clearly intent on bettering his lot, while Hunslet were determined to hold fast. The upshot was his transfer-listing on 1 April. Hunslet wanted £600 for him. Coincidentally, his brother, Jim, was also listed at £40 and transferred to York. Hunslet circularized six clubs, Oldham, Huddersfield, Wigan, Leeds, Hull and Hull KR, about his availability.

Billy put his point of view to the press. On 5 April the *Yorkshire Post* reported that 'he felt that as a leading player he should be paid for his services on the same scale as other leading players – as some of the Colonials, for instance. He had heard (Huddersfield, Hull, Wigan) paid their Colonials as much for a season as the best soccer players'. The previous day he had told the *Yorkshire Evening Post*, 'I have agreed with Hull the wage they have offered me. It is equivalent to £4 a week all year round. That is what Manchester United offered me if I would go training as a soccer player two seasons ago… I am not grumbling at what Hunslet have paid me, but since I have had this bother with Hunslet I have been thinking things over and have come to the conclusion that, as I am getting my living out of football, I must make what I can out of it. Others make £4 a week in the Northern Union game, and why should not I? Anyway, according to the wages paid to other players, I reckon I have not been getting what I am worth at Hunslet.'

He was certainly correct about other players' terms. Just a few months earlier Huddersfield had given Australian Tommy Gleeson, who was not even an international, £200 as a signing-on fee and terms of £4 a win, £3 a draw and £2 a defeat.

Leeds heard that Batten was keen to sign for Hull and did not pursue their interest, while Wigan were too slow off the mark, despite reputedly sending over a deputation 'by motor car'. Hull Kingston Rovers agreed with Hunslet to pay the £600 asking fee and announced his capture on Saturday, 5 April. Rovers travelled to play Keighley that day and there were green posters throughout the town declaring Batten would be playing at Lawkholme Lane in the afternoon. Unfortunately for Rovers they did not have Billy's signature. By 3.30 pm the same day Hull did have his signature and Hunslet agreed to take their £600 rather than Hull KR's. The transfer fee was double the previous world record of £300 (which Oldham had paid to Salford for Jim Lomas in 1911).

Hull, under their President, J.A. Boynton, had embarked upon a high-risk policy of paying out large fees for the best players available. It was a gamble which could have misfired, for the club currently had a debt of £1,500. In the event Mr Boynton's policy paid off.

There remained only three more games for Hull that season, all at home. Billy made his debut on 12 April, ironically to Hull KR fans, against Keighley. Hull won 40-3 and the *Yorkshire Post* reported, 'Under normal conditions Hull would have had an easy task in disposing of Keighley, but with William Batten in the field to perform the hat-trick of tries, presenting his new colleagues with three more, and giving by his brilliant play a stimulus to the entire team, they had a triumphant procession, and the Boulevard crowd was in a hilarious mood'. One man who found the mood far from hilarious was the Keighley forward, Ike Cole, who was sent off just after half-time for a bad foul on Billy.

The crowd for the Keighley game was around 9,000 – far more than usual for a visit from that club. Two more home games, victories against Warrington (31-5) and Rochdale Hornets (42-5), provided virtuoso performances from Hull's new messiah and crowds in excess of 10,000. The club reckoned that Billy had paid off his fee in increased gate-takings by the close of the campaign.

When Billy Batten joined Hull they were a mid-table team. The club had a long pedigree going back to 1865 and considered itself one of the game's elite. However, Hull had won precisely nothing in almost half a century in either the amateur or professional code. They had lost in the Challenge Cup finals of 1908, 1909 and 1910 and they had been losing finalists in the Yorkshire Cup final (RU) in 1884 and 1912 (NU). Billy Batten changed all that and Hull won everything on offer in the eleven momentous years that he graced The Boulevard. It is doubtful if any player was ever such a hero to the Boulevard faithful as Batten. He brought excitement and success and he was worshipped. The crowds loved his never-say-die attitude, his defence-shattering straight running, his ability to send pinpoint passes to his winger, the ferocity of his tackling and his aerial antics. He was a sublime fusion of the spectacular and the unselfish. For all his dash, fire and ability to create controversy, Billy was a clean and sportsmanlike player.

Of course, there were other fine players at Hull. His centre partner and captain was Bert Gilbert, the Australian test player, who had cost Hull £450 in 1912. Gilbert was reckoned to be the hardest-tackling centre Australia had produced. With Batten and Gilbert to face, opposing centres must have had nightmares before playing Hull. Hull were at the forefront of importing Australians: Jimmy Devereux, another test man, and Steve Darmody, a 1911/12 Kangaroo, also being on the books. The three-quarter line of Welsh international Alf Francis, Gilbert, Batten and Jack Harrison was certainly as potent as any Hull ever fielded.

In 1913/14 injuries kept Billy out of a dozen of Hull's 41 fixtures and he did not play any representative rugby. Although he was a certainty for the 1914 Lions tour he declared his unavailability for domestic reasons. Hull improved sensationally in 1913/14 and Billy fulfilled the vast expectations of him. The team were runners-up in the Yorkshire League and finished fourth in the Championship but were well beaten at Huddersfield in the semi-final. The Challenge Cup began on 28 February with a tremendously difficult home tie against Salford, the eventual Champions. Hull squeezed through 8-6, courtesy of two Batten tries. Non-leaguers Featherstone Rovers fell 27-3 at The Boulevard before Halifax were ousted 13-0 in front of a crowd of 18,000 at Thrum Hall in the third round.

The semi-final at Headingley drew 30,000 for Hull's clash with the greatest team of the age, Huddersfield. This time Hull confounded the forecasts, winning convincingly 11-3 to reach the Challenge Cup final for the fourth time. Their opponents in the final at Halifax were Wakefield Trinity, who finished seventeenth in the league. Hull were expected to break their trophy hoodoo. For a long time, however, the 19,000 crowd doubted that Hull could throw off their albatross in major finals as Trinity fought like demons. Half-time arrived with no scoring and, even though their skipper Herbert Kershaw was sent off after 45 minutes, Hull had still failed to pierce Wakefield's armour with just seven minutes left. Cometh the hour, cometh the man, however. That man was Billy Batten, the hero of the match. With a replay looming, Billy managed to work a miracle, sending Jack Harrison over for the try which broke Trinity's hearts and won Hull's first trophy. A minute from time he was carried off having injured a knee, but there was still time for Alf Francis to gallop over for another unconverted try on the final whistle. 6-0 might as well have been 60-0 for the 40,000 delirious Hullites who gathered at City Hall that evening to welcome Billy and the Boulevard boys with that cherished and long-overdue Cup.

In 1914/15 Hull slipped to fifth in the league but reached the final of the Yorkshire Cup, only to be crushed 31-0 by Huddersfield at Headingley. Billy sustained a shoulder injury and concussion tackling Harold Wagstaff in the movement that led to Huddersfield taking their lead to 15-0. He missed the second half. Injuries caused him to miss eighteen of Hull's fixtures, but his absence appeared not to disturb his winger Jack Harrison, who scored a club record 52 tries which stands to this day.

As a miner, Billy Batten was not called up for war service and continued to play for Hull in 1915/16, scoring 18 tries in 28 games. On 26 February 1916 Billy played for a combined Hull-Hull KR team that beat an ANZAC Military XIII 12-10 at The Boulevard in a curtain-raiser. When the game was over he played for Hull against Batley in the main match.

Hull, Challenge Cup winners, 1914. From left to right, back row: Milner, Darmody, Hammill, Taylor, Herridge, Holder, Oldham, Melville (trainer). Seated: Devereux, Anderson, Gilbert, Batten, E. Rogers, Harrison. Front: Francis, G. Rogers.

In 1916/17 he was allowed to guest for Dewsbury. Controversy blew up on 20 October 1917 when Hull suddenly withdrew permission for him to play for Dewsbury at Leeds. He played anyway and on 27 October both Hull and Dewsbury named him in their teams against each other. Billy stuck with Dewsbury, scored a try and was the star of Dewsbury's 32–0 win. However, in November he returned to Hull.

After the war ended, Hull won an abbreviated Yorkshire League competition in 1918/19, Billy contributing 17 tries in 14 appearances. Billy was thirty when the first proper season of peace-time rugby began in 1919. He was the complete player but still ambitious and by then he had grown to 14st. He played in the Roses Match in September and was looking forward to touring with the Lions in 1920. However, after five players had been selected for the tour before any trials had been conducted, he felt his dignity affronted when told that he must play in a tour trial at Leeds. He refused point blank, quite reasonably stating that the selectors should know his qualities already. Neither side budged and Billy did not tour.

There were compensations. Billy had been granted a benefit, which he took with the game against York on 3 April. The benefit realized a record £1,079/13/5 – a small fortune and eloquent testimony to the esteem in which he was held. Perhaps even better, three weeks later he led Hull in the Championship final against Huddersfield at Leeds. Huddersfield lacked five tourists, Hull just Billy Stone. However, the odds were evened out when Hull forward Alf Grice was sent off and Huddersfield led 2–0 from the 25th to the 75th minute. It was then that Billy Batten confirmed his talismanic status by ripping through for the try that gave Hull a 3–2 victory and their first Championship.

To prove it was no fluke, Hull retained the Championship in 1920/21, beating Hull KR 16–14 in the final. Rovers had, however, beaten Hull 2–0 in the Yorkshire Cup final earlier in

A caricature from the The Football and Sports Favourite, *26 November 1921.*

the season. Batten's form was as good as ever. He won another County Championship medal with Yorkshire and earned England caps against Wales and Other Nationalities, both internationals ending in victories. However, more controversy arose in February 1921. Billy and Hull fell into a dispute resulting in Billy's absence for ten games. When the issue was settled in April, 'Full-back' wrote: 'Financially it must have been a most serious matter for Billy, who was in receipt of something like £14 per match'. For many years people have argued as to whether Billy Batten ever got £14 per match. The sceptics believed there must be confusion over his signing terms of £4 per week in 1913 but 'Full-back's' assertion came in 1921, when things were different. The man who signed Billy, Hull secretary Alfred Charlesworth, confirmed the story saying, 'It is correct that at the height of his career at Hull and up to his last game with Hull, Batten was paid £14 a match. I say he earned every penny of it. In fact, the interest in Batten was such that if the word got around that Batten was not playing, our gate decreased by at least three figures. There never was a Hull player in my time who complained that Batten got more than he deserved, although the next highest-paid man would get £6 less than Batten. All his colleagues recognized Batten's great match-winning powers. They were satisfied with their own money, and they were satisfied, too, that Billy got no more than he deserved in having special terms.'

In 1921/22 Hull relinquished their Championship after finishing third and losing in the semi-final at Wigan. They did, however, reach the Challenge Cup final, which was Billy's third and last. A record 34,700 crowd packed into Headingley, some of them apparently unemployed men who walked all the way from Hull. Hull lost an exciting game 9-10 to Rochdale Hornets. Billy scored a 30th-minute try with one of his famous leaps over the full-back and there were tries from skipper Jim Kennedy and Bob Taylor, but a failure to land any goals proved costly. Billy was recalled for his tenth and final test match when Australia beat Britain 16-2 at The Boulevard on 5 November 1921.

In 1922/23 Hull finished top of the table and Billy picked up a Yorkshire League Championship winners' medal. There was disappointment, however, when Hull KR dumped Hull 16-2 in the

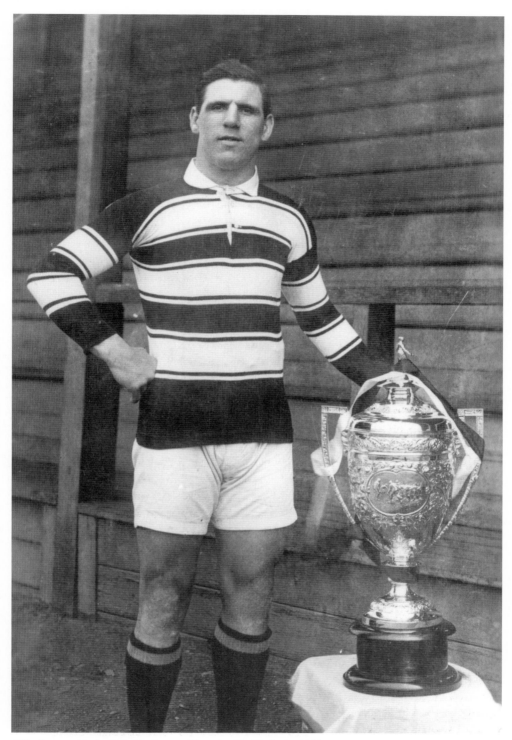

Billy Batten with the Yorkshire League Championship Trophy in 1923.

Billy Batten (right) with Harold Wagstaff. Batten is believed to have requested the photograph to be taken on the occasion of their last appearance together for Yorkshire, at Oldham in the Roses Match of 1923.

Championship semi-final and when Hull crashed 3-28 to Leeds in the Challenge Cup final, Billy missing the latter debacle. He also played his last two international matches against Wales.

The curtain on Billy's Boulevard career fell in 1924, but not before he helped the club to lift the Yorkshire Cup for the first time. Huddersfield were beaten 10-4 in the final at Leeds. Appropriately enough, Billy scored one of the two tries – his 89th and last for Hull. He made his final appearance for Hull exactly eleven years after his debut, Hull winning the match 31-18 at Bramley on 5 April 1924.

Billy was transferred for £350 to Wakefield Trinity on 6 May 1924 and, despite his teetotalism, became the licensee of the Old King's Arms, Kirkgate, Wakefield, a year later. His career with Trinity under Jonty Parkin lasted two and a half years, for he was still a force to be reckoned with. In 1924 he earned another Yorkshire Cup winners' medal when Wakefield beat Batley 9-8 in the final, and in 1926 he was in the team that lost to 3-10 to Huddersfield. Even in his last season he was good enough to play for Yorkshire against Cumberland and the New Zealanders. His professional career ended with a brief spell with the fledgling Castleford club (February-April 1927). He did, however, continue to turn out for Askern Welfare as an amateur and Castleford actually placed him on their transfer list at £75 in 1928.

A tremendously generous man, Billy was famous for helping other players with their benefits and personally raised many teams to play in testimonials, particularly in Hunslet and the West Riding. Billy gave at least £350 of his benefit money to suffering villagers in Kinsley and Fitzwilliam in 1921, when the mining community underwent acute hardship. His venture as a publican failed and in 1928 he was declared bankrupt, owing £175 and having no assets. He told Wakefield Bankruptcy Court that all his medals had been pawned and only one, a gold medal containing a diamond, had been redeemed by his sister-in-law. Billy also confirmed to the court that he had been paid 'about £14 a match at Hull'. He subsequently returned to pit work at Askern.

During the Second World War he was a member of the fire service but the last ten years of his life were blighted after an accident at his work in 1949. He was struck on the head by two heavy roof tiles, seriously debilitating him. He died on 26 January 1959. Billy's legacy to the game extended through his offspring. His eldest son, Billy junior, made his debut for Hull in January 1927, before his father's retirement, and later played for Hull KR. Two other sons, Eric and Bob, enjoyed long careers with a variety of clubs. Eric emulated his father by playing for Yorkshire, England and Great Britain and in his own right was a candidate for the Hall of Fame. Billy's nephew, Ray Batten, a great loose-forward with Leeds, was also capped by Yorkshire, England and Great Britain.

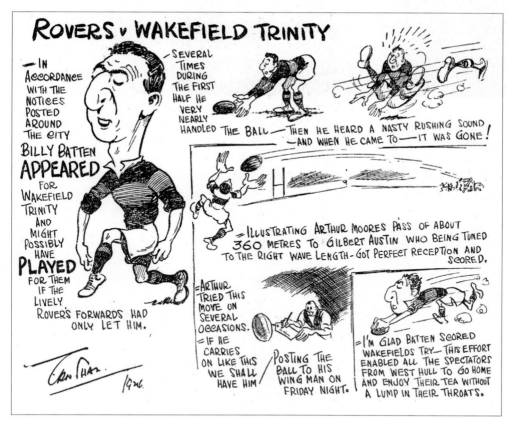

An Evening News *(Hull) cartoon depicting Billy Batten's first return trip to Hull following his transfer to Wakefield Trinity. On 6 September 1924, Trinity lost 3-22 to Hull KR.*

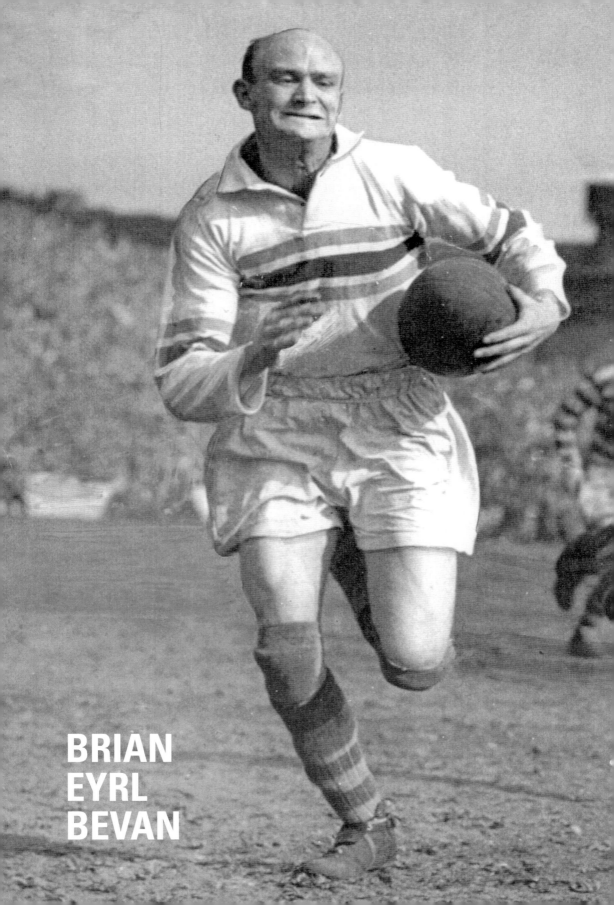

BRIAN
EYRL
BEVAN

WARRINGTON

Debut: 17 November 1945 v Oldham (h)
Last game: 23 April 1962 v Leigh (h)

	A	T	G	P
1945/46	1	-	-	-
1946/47	42	48	34	212
1947/48	43	57	-	171
1948/49	44	56	-	168
1949/50	39	30	-	90
1950/51	40	60	-	180
1951/52	39	46	-	138
1952/53	41	66	-	198
1953/54	45	62	-	186
1954/55	37	61	-	183
1955/56	41	53	-	159
1956/57	26	14	-	42
1957/58	40	45	-	135
1958/59	40	54	-	162
1959/60	40	40	-	120
1960/61	42	35	-	105
1961/62	20	13	-	39

BLACKPOOL BOROUGH

Debut: 22 August 1962 v Wigan (a)
Last game: 22 February 1964 v Oldham
(a), Western Division

	A	T	G	P
1962/63	22	10	-	30
1963/64	20	7	-	21

CAREER RECORD

	A	T	G	P
Warrington	620	740	34	2288
Blackpool	42	17	-	51
Other Nat.	16	26	-	78
Represent	10	13	-	39
TOTALS	541	214	73	788

Note – Bevan played eight first grade
games for Eastern Suburbs (1942-46),
scoring one goal.

INTERNATIONALS (16)

Other Nat.	13	England	7	1949	Workington (2 tries)
Other Nat.	6	Wales	5	1949	Abertillery (1 try)
Other Nat.	3	France	16	1950	Bordeaux (1 try)
Other Nat.	27	Wales	21	1951	Swansea (1 try)
Other Nat.	35	England	10	1951	Wigan (3 tries)
Other Nat.	17	France	14	1951	Hull
Other Nat.	22	Wales	11	1951	Abertillery (2 tries)
Other Nat.	18	England	31	1952	Wigan (2 tries)
Other Nat.	31	England	12	1952	Hudd'field (4 tries)
Other Nat.	29	France	10	1952	Marseilles (2 tries)
Other Nat.	16	Wales	18	1953	Warrington
Other Nat.	30	Wales	5	1953	Bradford (1 try)
Other Nat.	15	France	10	1953	Bordeaux (2 tries)
Other Nat.	22	England	30	1953	Wigan (2 tries)
Other Nat.	33	England	16	1955	Wigan (2 tries)
Other Nat.	32	France	19	1955	Leigh (1 try)

BRIAN EYRL BEVAN
The Great Bev

'Bald, droopy shoulders, no teeth, big pads on his knees. As soon as he got the ball he was gone like a whippet. I've never seen anything as good in my life. You'd never put a hand on him normally'

Billy Boston

There has never been a more prolific try-scorer than Brian Bevan. No one has ever scored tries quite as outlandish as many of those he claimed in nineteen glorious years after the Second World War. No rugby league follower who saw him in action can forget him. He was the bee's knees, king of the castle, top of the class, simply the best, better than all the rest – superman, really. He was also, among other things, 'The Bondi Streak', 'Old Knobbly Knees', 'The Skeleton in Braces', 'The Bony Ballerina', 'The Wizard of Aus', 'The Old Man' and 'The Great Bev'. One nickname is usually enough for a sportsman; Bevan was so uniquely eccentric in his play that contemporaries could not even agree on a sobriquet.

In Warrington they named the grandstand the Brian Bevan Stand. Near the ground a traffic island is named after him and on it stands a statue of him, ball in hand with his eyes fixed on some imaginary try-line. Statues to rugby league players are very thin on the ground – Wally Lewis at Brisbane's Lang Park and Puig Aubert at the Stade Albert Domec in Carcassonne are probably the only other examples. All three represent the embodiment of rugby league's truly legendary personalities, those who illuminated the periods in which they played, while also transcending them.

Brian Bevan was 5' 10" and 11st 8lbs of whipcord, muscle, elasticity, agility and athleticism. He could certainly run the hundred yards in 9.6 seconds, in rugby kit! He could have been an international sprinter but most of his running was not done in straight lines. Some of his tries were so extraordinary that the local papers produced diagrams of his meanderings as documentary proof that what they had described in match reports could somehow be corroborated. Half a century after Bevan mesmerized the rugby league world, people who saw his amazing feats can still scarcely credit what they saw.

Yet no man ever looked or acted so unlike the stereotypical rugby league player. He was quiet to the point of taciturnity, shy, self-effacing and, in later life, reclusive. Physically, he was pale, almost bald from his very early twenties, toothless and a smoker. He looked as if he was being held together by the many bandages and supports he applied to his knees, elbows and ankles and any other part of his anatomy that he felt was vulnerable. It may have presented a strange image but the padding and swathing boosted his confidence and was just another tool in the way he psyched himself up to excel in the most physically demanding team ball game on Earth.

On the pitch Brian Bevan may have looked like a geriatric who had been in a road accident but it was the opposition who left the field feeling the worse for wear. Catching shadows has never been a productive exercise. Rugby league wingers come in all shapes and sizes, or at least once upon a time they did. Some did their damage by sheer speed, some by brute force, some by trickery, some by persistence and bloody-mindedness. Some of the great wingmen exerted a combination of those traits. Bevan's armoury relied on speed, bewildering acceleration, swerve and a two-way sidestep, anticipation, determination, an instinct for self-preservation and total unpredictability. He was a master of the interception, had fly-paper hands and had an unerring capacity to judge the pace and bounce of a ball when chasing it to the goal-line. Smoking apart, he was a fitness fanatic, who put in many hours outside the usual club training sessions, perfecting the skills which looked so natural to the fans on the terraces. When one game finished he was focussing on the next – an attitude which would win the approval of modern coaches and sports psychologists. While he was not one of the sport's great defenders, he could tackle well enough when the chips were down. Anyway, no one went to a rugby league ground to watch Bevan tackle.

Brian was born on 24 June 1924 in Waverley, in the eastern suburbs of Sydney. His father Eric was a linotype operator with the *Sydney Sun* and had been a three-quarter and full-back in the lower grades with Newtown and Eastern Suburbs, while two of Brian's uncles had played with Newtown. Eric and his wife Veda had another son, Owen, who was also to make a fine rugby league player, and a daughter, Gwenda. Brian and his siblings grew up in a sporting environment with Bondi Beach almost on their back door. Brian grew strong and healthy, swimming, surfing, playing cricket and rugby and honing his competitive instincts. At Randwick Intermediate High School he shone in a variety of sports. At twelve he was sprint champion of New South Wales. He captained his school at cricket and in 1937 and 1938 he played rugby union for NSW against Queensland at fly-half. It was rugby league, not played by his school, which was his passion, however.

In 1941, two months short of his seventeenth birthday, he began playing for Eastern Suburbs reserves. Over the next four years he developed fairly slowly but found his true position on the wing after flirting with stand-off and centre. Easts were one of Australia's most famous and successful clubs and it would take some time to get into First Grade. At the season's end he scored a try in the 14-4 Third Grade Grand Final victory over Balmain at the Sydney Cricket Ground. On 2 May 1942 he made his First Grade debut in Easts' 14-18 loss to Souths at the Sydney Sports Ground.

Rugby began to take a back seat though as the Second World War rumbled on. Brian joined the Navy at eighteen and saw a good deal of action against the Japanese, being bombed north of New Guinea while serving on HMAS *Katoomba*. When the war ended fate decreed that Brian should be sent to England with the HMAS *Australia*, the Royal Australian Navy's flagship, which needed repairs after action in the Philippines.

While stationed on the south coast Brian played some rugby union for the ship's XV but could not wait to dash north in the hope of getting a trial with a professional rugby league club. He had an ally in Bill Shankland, his father's old friend, who had played in tests for Australia before joining Warrington before the war and was then the golf professional at Temple Newsam in Leeds. Bill failed to get Brian a run with Leeds or Hunslet. They never even offered to see him but Warrington agreed to give him a trial in the reserves. On 10 November 1945 he turned out for Warrington 'A' against Widnes 'A' at Wilderspool and after a quiet first half with little ball, he proceeded to astonish the crowd with a series of sizzling runs, culminating in a surge which carried him past four nonplussed opponents, none of whom laid a finger on him, as he sped over for a gobsmacker of a try. Warrington immediately offered to trial him in the first team against Oldham the following week and although he did not score in a 12-3 victory, they had seen enough to offer him a £300 signing-on fee and a three-year contract. Brian returned to Australia, played some final games for Easts and set sail again for England, where he disembarked on 4 September 1946. He arrived in England having played 37 games in all grades for Easts in which he had claimed 15 tries and a goal. He had played a mere eight games in First Grade, his only score being a goal against Souths in 1942. In theory Warrington were taking a colossal gamble but in reality they had recognized genius when they saw it.

In his first match, a Lancashire Cup-tie against Salford on 14 September, he scored the first of 796 tries he would plunder in British rugby league, neatly sidestepping two opponents before touching down. No one has ever come remotely near Bev's record, nor is it feasible that anyone ever will. His fellow Hall of Famer Billy Boston, like Bev a right wingman, is the next most prolific scorer in history with 571 tries – 225 behind. Bev also kicked a goal against Salford and by the end of the season had landed 34 to top the Warrington goal-kicking list. However, after 1947 he would never kick another. His mission in life, his passion, his *raison d'être* was to score tries. In his inaugural season he put down a marker – he broke the club try-scoring record. On 22 March 1947 Warrington beat St Helens 24-2 in a second round Challenge Cup tie. The 23,500 crowd were treated to a virtuoso performance from Bev, who scored three goals and three tries. His try hat-trick took him past Islwyn Davies's record of 34 set in 1938/39 and he finished the season with 48. Brian had also topped the league's try-scorers, his nearest challengers being Ernie Ashcroft (Wigan) and Emlyn Walters (Bradford Northern) on 34. It was a sensational beginning to his career in England but no one had seen anything yet.

The Warrington fans idolized him from the start. They implored the inside backs to get the ball to Brian at every opportunity for he invariably provided the thrills they craved. Whenever he got the ball the crowd were on tenterhooks. There was no telling what he might do or how he might do it. His impact was so deep that some critics felt that he would be burnt out within a few years, especially if he was given too much work. They need not have worried. Brian was so fit, so instinctive and so elusive that he usually avoided any mayhem and had a nineteen-year career in which he suffered very little serious injury. While he is rightly revered for his try-scoring ability and entertainment value, Brian Bevan was also durable enough to survive 688 matches in his English career, a figure bettered by only nine men in the game's history. If he had not been mentally and physically tough, that achievement would have been unthinkable.

Warrington finished fifth in Brian's first season and reached the Challenge Cup semi-final. In his second season, 1947/48, they gelled into a formidable team to launch a period of success hitherto undreamed of at Wilderspool. Brian regarded the 1947/48 Warrington team as the best he played with. Captain was the veteran loose-forward and goal-kicker, Harold Palin, who led a splendid pack. The front row of Bill Derbyshire, Dave Cotton and Bill Riley were also veterans but solid and wily. There was youth in the second-row, however, in Jimmy Featherstone and Bob Ryan, both future British Lions. Later in the season they would be joined by Australian Harry Bath, one of the greatest second-rowers the game has ever seen. On the opposite wing to Brian was 1946 Lion Albert Johnson, a bag of tricks with a side-step wider even than Bevan's (if somewhat slower). Full–back was the bandy–legged Les 'Cowboy' Jones and the halves were Jackie Fleming and Gerry Helme, the latter the best scrum–half of the era. In the centres were Bryn Knowelden, another 1946 Lion, and Albert Pimblett, just signed from Halifax. All seven of the regular backs were past, present or future internationals, and there were a couple more in Ossie Peake and Stan Powell, who usually had to make do with 'A' team rugby.

Albert Pimblett played 86 games as Brian's centre partner. There were those who thought that it did not matter who partnered Bev. He would create tries out of nothing, anyway. It was generally recognized, however, that Pimblett got the best out of his winger. Pimblett was big, fast and powerful and a good footballer, who made sure that his winger got good ball and also ensured that Bev had as little tackling to do as possible. The two would practice moves and sprint in spikes after normal training sessions – an arrangement appreciated by the painstaking and perfectionist wingman.

For Brian Bevan preparation and routine were paramount. He was fastidious about minor cuts and abrasions. His wife, Doreen, whom he married in April 1949, routinely attended to such injuries and had to accommodate into the family environment his obsessive preoccupation in the period leading up to the weekly game. His two daughters, Jeanette and Jennifer, learned how to steer discreetly clear of him on matchday mornings. Nothing had to disturb his pre-match ritual. It took yards of tape and bandage to protect his joints and it was reckoned that he got more attention on the strapping and massage tables than the rest of the team put together. No one complained, however, for they fully realized that the Australian wonder winger's contribution was often the difference between winning and losing pay. Although Brian's shyness was a barrier to close friendships with his playing colleagues, he did develop an extraordinary relationship with Jack Hamblett, the Warrington groundsman, kit-man and general factotum. Jack pandered to Brian's every whim, made sure he had the right kit in perfect order, and ensured that psychologically he was at ease with himself and the world.

Bev was certainly psychologically and physically well primed in 1947/48. He enjoyed his first trip to France at the start of November, Warrington beating Perpignan and Carcassonne, and on 15 November he played against a touring team for the first time when the New Zealanders were beaten 7-5 at Wilderspool. On 13 December Warrington crushed Salford 45-13, precipitating a run of 20 victorious league matches, only marred by a 5-5 draw at Leeds. During that spell, which ended at Castleford on 10 April 1948, Bev rattled up 28 tries, including a club record seven in a 28-8 home victory against Leigh on 29 March.

However, arguably the best and most important try he claimed in this period was at Workington Town on 14 February in a first round, second leg Challenge Cup tie, which Warrington won 7-0. The *Warrington Examiner* report described it thus: 'Workington were making one last all-out effort and when an attack developed just inside the Warrington "25" a try for the Cumbrians looked probable. As the pass reached Risman, who had come up to make the man over, he failed to hold the ball which fell to his left. Very quickly he bent and flipped it to his wingman but Bevan nipped in, stole the ball practically from Large's chest and was away in a flash. Carr pursued him for a few strides in desperation but Bevan sailed away with head thrown back and, as the Warrington enthusiasts roared themselves hoarse, was soon out on his own to cross the line near the corner and then go within a few yards of the posts for a magnificent try after a thrilling run of more than eighty yards. His colleagues hugged him, patted his face and shook his hand while cheer after cheer rolled out'. Throughout his career Bev made a habit of scoring wonderfully spectacular tries in games in Cumberland, where he appeared to be nearly as popular as in Warrington.

As the season climaxed Brian broke his own club record, when he scored a 40-yarder in a 15-8 home victory over Workington on 3 April and a fortnight later he grabbed five tries in a 45-3 win over Oldham at Wilderspool. They included his 100th try for the club. His first century had taken him 84 games. His final tally for the season was 57, making him the league's leading try-scorer again. The victory over Oldham had given Warrington the Lancashire League Championship and Brian had gained his first major medal. It was quickly augmented. Warrington beat Huddersfield 17-5 in the Championship semi-final, Bev scoring twice in his first confrontation with Lionel Cooper. Cooper and Bev had been colleagues at Easts but Cooper had stayed long enough to become a big star and had represented Australia in all three Ashes tests in 1946. Over the next eight years the clashes between these two great Aussies became the stuff of legends. The two could not have been more different. Cooper was a 14-stoner, powerful and capable of running through, over and round opponents, and he was quick. The Championship final, against Bradford Northern at Maine Road on 8 May, drew a crowd of 69,143. Warrington had never won the Championship but broke their duck with a comfortable 15-5 victory. Bev scored the first try from an overlap and the *Rugby League Review* declared him their man of the match, saying, 'This flying Australian, when in possession of the ball, is one of the most electrifying sights in the game. His will-o'-the-wisp side-stepping, allied to a fine turn of speed, leaves the opposition grasping thin air'.

On 14 August 1948 Warrington went to Wigan to play in the annual Wardonia Cup match, a friendly for charity. A crowd of 31,960 piled into Central Park to watch this clash between the Champions and the Cup-winners. Warrington won 18-8 and Bev claimed two

Warrington, winners of the Championship and Lancashire League, 1947/48. From left to right, back row: Riley, Davies, Cotton, Bath, Derbyshire, Ryan, Peake. Seated: Pimblett, Knowelden, Powell, Palin, Jones, Johnson, Bevan. Front: Fleming, Helme.

tries. The first went down in history as the 'Try of the Century' in many people's eyes. Down the years the legend has built up that every single player in Wigan's all-international side – although only eleven were actually internationals - were all beaten at some point in Bevan's labyrinthine run, some of them twice. It was not quite like that but it was so thrilling and audacious that the *Warrington Guardian* published a diagram of the effort, the first of several such illustrations down the years. To summarize the try: a scrum was formed five yards from the Warrington line to the right of the posts. Warrington won the ball, Helme passed to Palin, who had stood out of the pack. Palin shipped it to Pimblett, who drew in Wigan winger Hilton, and gave it to Bevan. Most wingers would have shot down the wing but not Bev. He careered infield, aiming for the centre spot. Ces Mountford, an exceedingly quick half-back, chased him seemingly into the arms of test full-back Martin Ryan. Somehow when Ryan came to envelop Bevan, there was nothing to envelop! Bev did that a lot – just disappeared! At least that was the experience of many great players who thought they had him. A bit more swerving and acceleration had him flying over halfway and streaking diagonally for the left corner. Ashcroft and Hilton had given up the chase and only Mountford was still in the race but he had no hope. Bev scorched to the line and collapsed in a heap, worn out after his breathtaking 120-yard dash.

One writer reckoned the try took 14 seconds to score. 'Criticus', of the *Warrington Examiner*, wrote of the try that it was, 'one of the most amazing I have seen … [Bevan] must have beaten five or six opponents and the great crowd rose to him and cheered him for several minutes'. Jack Steel (*Warrington Guardian*), who had followed the game for thirty years, was more emphatic, saying, 'After that Bevan effort I feel I have seen practically everything the code can offer'. Ironically, Bev's super-try did not even count in his official record, as the game was classed as a friendly. Never mind, there were actually many more like that to come.

The 1948/49 season saw Warrington finish top of the league. They won a second successive Lancashire League Championship but were beaten 14-8 in the Lancashire Cup final by Wigan. On 30 October Bev had the pleasure of playing against the Kangaroos, when 26,879 saw a 16-7 Warrington victory. Crowds in excess of 20,000 were commonplace in those days at Wilderspool and there was no doubt that Brian Bevan was a major contributory factor. Warrington's average home league crowd was 20,199. On 22 January 1949 a ground record crowd of 34,304 assembled at Wilderspool for the visit of Wigan, who won 8-4 in one of the most thrilling games ever staged at the stadium. Three weeks later Brian's brother, Owen, made his debut for Warrington against Liverpool Stanley. Owen's contract was for £2,000, which made Brian's signing on fee of £300 look a bit sick. Owen played centre to Bev on his debut but it was Bev who stole the show with a hat-trick, which included a try from his own goal-line. Reports indicated that it was even better than the try against Wigan in the Wardonia Cup, with Brian outrunning the entire Stanley team and side-stepping at least six of them.

By the end of the season Brian had piled up another 56 tries but had to settle for second place in the try-scoring chart as Lionel Cooper had bagged 60. He also had to accept second best on 14 May when Warrington met Huddersfield in the Championship final before 75,194 animated fans at Maine Road. A marvellous encounter ended in victory for the Fartowners 13-12. Bev was thwarted of tries in controversial circumstances on a couple of occasions and was unable to stop Cooper from scoring when Lionel flattened him with a pulverizing hand-off.

Warrington relapsed in 1949/50, finishing eleventh in the table. Bev only scored 30 tries for them – a fine total for almost anyone else but not for the try-hungry Australian. He was out with a rare injury problem between October and December, missing half a dozen games. There were a couple of compensations, however. The RFL had introduced a new team to the international scene – the Other Nationalities – who competed with England, France and Wales in the European Championship. With the high quality of Australians and New Zealanders who were available, plus a few South Africans, Scots and Irishmen, the Other Nationalities became a formidable and popular force and caps were highly prized. Bev's inclusion in the Other Nationalities XIII gave him the opportunity to play international rugby, which he had forfeited in coming to England, although it was always a source of regret to him that he was never able to represent Australia.

He made his debut in the green jersey of the Other Nationalities against England on 19 September 1949, when 17,000 shoehorned themselves into Workington's Borough Park. Typically, he scored twice in a 13-7 victory. A month later, in vile conditions at Abertillery, he scored another in a 6-5 victory over Wales. Between 1949 and 1955 Brian played in 16 internationals in which he claimed a remarkable 26 tries for the Other Nationalities – a rate unparalleled at that level.

A second consolation came in the form of a Challenge Cup-winners' medal and an appearance at Wembley. Widnes beat Hull KR, Swinton, Hunslet and Leeds on the way to the final. Bev's most important contribution came in the 21-7 third round victory over Hunslet, two classic tries effectively killing off the Parksiders in the last quarter.

On 6 May 1950, Warrington met deadly local rivals Widnes at Wembley before a sell-out 94,249 crowd. Warrington were hot favourites and justified the bookies' faith in them. An open, entertaining game ended 19-0 in Warrington's favour. Bev, now playing with Ron Ryder as his centre, surprisingly failed to score, although he did provide many thrills with his bewildering running, and had a try disallowed after a forward pass. He was, however, delighted with his winners' medal, presented by the Prime Minister, Clement Attlee, and his biggest pay packet yet – £40.

Warrington bounced back to the top of the league in 1950/51 and Brian received a third Lancashire League Championship-winners' medal. Although that was all that Warrington won during the season – they lost to Wigan 5-28 in the Lancashire Cup final and 2-3 to them in the Challenge Cup semi-final – Brian returned to his most scintillating form. By the end of January he had scored 48 tries in a mere 27 games and he had Albert Rosenfeld's record of 80 tries in a season in his sights. In four consecutive matches in September he had scored hat-tricks against Swinton and Liverpool Stanley (twice) and, finally, six tries against York – probably another unique occurrence. In the event he failed to oust Rosenfeld from the record books but he did rack up 68 tries, including eight in five international and representative fixtures. On 28 March he scored both tries in a 10-0 home win against Bradford to break his own club record for a third time. His 68 tries enabled him to top the leading try-scorers, nine ahead of Lionel Cooper, and his total was the third highest in history. The season ended disappointingly at Maine Road on 12 May 1951, when Warrington went down 11-26 to Workington Town in Bev's third Championship final. Bev's co-winger, Albert Johnson, broke his leg in the third minute and never played again.

In 1951/52, for the first time since his inaugural season, Brian failed to pick up a winners' medal in at least one competition. Warrington dropped to sixth in the league but their winger continued to amaze massive crowds with his eccentricities and dazzling tries. One, another masterpiece at Workington on 15 September, almost beggared description and was christened the 'Waltzing Matilda Try' – it required another diagram in the *Warrington Guardian*. Basically, Bev intercepted and danced and darted through a bemused defence to leave 'onlookers breathless for several seconds and then the roar of applause almost awoke the beloved patron saint John Peel from his resting place'.

On 17 November he roared over for six tries in a 30-10 beating of Rochdale Hornets at Wilderspool and followed with four in the away fixture at Rochdale on 8 December and another four the following week at home against Liverpool City. However, his most memorable game of the season was undoubtedly one in which he hardly had any possession and no chance to shine. On 3 November he played for Other Nationalities against France at Hull. It was probably the most spiteful match in which he ever participated and became notorious as 'The Battle of The Boulevard'. When the mayhem and skulduggery had ended France had been beaten 17-14, thanks largely to a brave and brilliant hat-trick from Lionel Cooper and four goals by fellow Australian Pat Devery. Bev had plenty of running chances in games against Wales (won 22-11) and England (lost 18-31), scoring twice in each, while he also claimed a spectacular try for a British Empire XIII that beat New Zealand at Chelsea on 23 January 1952. This was the first televised game in which Bev appeared. On 2 February he recorded his 300th career try in a 14-4 home success against Oldham and three weeks later his astonishing 85-yarder at Whitehaven was acknowledged as the best try ever seen on the ground. When the season finished, Bev had scored 51 tries, a fine achievement, but this time he had finished fourth in the try-scoring lists way behind Cooper, who had amassed 71.

Not to be outdone, Bev proceeded to claim 72 in 1952/53 – his best ever total. His feat was all the more remarkable, for Warrington had a comparatively barren season, finishing ninth and losing to St Helens in the semi-finals of both the Lancashire and Challenge Cups. On 18 October he equalled the record for international/test matches when he mesmerized England at Huddersfield, running in four tries in Other Nationalities' 31-12 victory. Later in the season he picked up his first European Championship-winners' medal, as the Other Nationalities demolished France 29-10 in Marseilles but lost to Wales 16-18 at Wilderspool, points averages giving them the title. On 22 April Bev equalled his own club record by scoring seven tries in a 71-10 home butchering of Bramley. His second try took him past his record of 60 tries in a season for the club and the 66 with which he finally finished remains a Warrington record to this day. His 72 tries in all matches during the season has only ever been bettered by Rosenfeld's seemingly unbeatable 80 recorded in 1913/14 and his 78 in 1911/12.

Brian was scarcely less devastating in 1953/54. He scored 62 tries for Warrington and another five in three games for Other Nationalities, to finish as the leading try-scorer for the fifth time in eight seasons. Along the way he claimed his 400th try for Warrington at Rochdale, on 23 January, and on Easter Saturday, 17 April, he became the most prolific try-scorer in history when he broke Alf Ellaby's record of 446 (1926-39). That afternoon he ran Whitehaven ragged with four brilliant tries in a 43-7 victory to take his total to 448. Among his finest performances during the season was the international at Bordeaux on 18 October

Above: *Brian Bevan prepares to take evasive action against Halifax's Johnny Freeman.*

Below: *Brian Bevan and Warrington scrum-half Gerry Helme work a scissors move as Oldham's Johnny Noon attempts to tackle Helme.*

Jumping to it – Brian Bevan boots the ball forward against Blackpool Borough.

1953, when Other Nationalities beat France 15–10. Bev was the match-winner with two fabulous tries. Bill Fallowfield, Secretary of the RFL, described them thus: 'For twenty minutes every movement of the visitors was nipped in the bud. Then Bevan got the ball! A rapid succession of side-steps left three would-be tacklers trailing on the ground and then Brian, having perfectly demonstrated his elusiveness, gave us an equally effective demonstration of his speed with a diagonal run of forty yards in which he outpaced all opposition to score in the opposite corner … Twenty minutes after half-time Bevan again had the ball. There was no possible chance to score – or so we thought. From a standing start near the touch-line Brian side-stepped again and again into the thick of the French players and then with a prodigious spurt he bounded clear to gain what must have been the best individualist's try ever scored on the ground.'

Personal form apart, Brian enjoyed a hugely successful season with Warrington, who finished second to Halifax in the league, won the Lancashire League Championship and ended the season with three epic games against Halifax in the two major finals. He had made a monumental contribution to getting Warrington to the Challenge Cup final, scoring in every round up to the final: two in a 17–0 first round, first leg victory over Bramley and six in the 30–5 second leg win; one (possibly the most crucial he ever scored in a cup-tie) in a 7–4 second round success at Oldham; one in a home 26–5 beating of York and another in the 8–4 semi-final triumph over Leeds at Swinton.

Warrington met Halifax at Wembley on 24 April and ground out a 4–4 draw, the first at the Empire Stadium. It was not a game for three-quarters and Bev only had a couple of chances to run. Halifax full-back Griffiths failed with a penalty two minutes from time so Warrington could

Above: *The 1954 Championship Final at Maine Road. Brian Bevan attempts to evade Halifax winger Dai Bevan — one of the few men who seemed to have the knack of keeping the great Australian off the score sheet with any regularity.*

Left: *Not this time! Bevan's run has been in vain as he has crossed the touch-line.*

probably be thankful for small mercies. Before the replay Warrington beat St Helens 11-0 in the Championship semi-final, Bev scoring the only try of the match. The Challenge Cup replay took place at Odsal on Wednesday, 5 May and produced a much better game and a world record crowd of 102,569 – although that was only the official attendance, many more thousands, perhaps upwards of 120,000 in reality, gatecrashing what was, arguably, the most momentous event in the game's history. Bev was much more involved than at Wembley but still could not score. He was happy enough with the result, however, as Warrington won 8-4. Three days later, at Maine Road in the Championship final, Halifax scored the only try of the match and Bev had what appeared a perfectly good try disallowed for offside. Even so, Warrington sneaked home 8-7 with four Harry Bath penalty goals and Warrington added the Championship to the Challenge Cup and the Lancashire League Championship.

When the 1954/55 season kicked off Brian was thirty years old, but his unfathomable powers showed little sign of deterioration. Equally, Warrington carried on as a premier power in the game, finishing top of the league and retaining the Lancashire League title. Bev terrorized opposition defences for 63 tries but finished three behind Lionel Cooper, who was in his last season. By this time Bev had acquired a regular centre partner in classy, lanky Jim Challinor, who was to partner him in 181 games. Challinor, like Bev's three other major centre partners, Albert Pimblett, Ron Ryder and Ally Naughton, won test honours. However, it did not really matter who partnered him as he simply scored tries – in torrents – for years.

The fans showed their respect for Bev by contributing £1,528 to his joint benefit with second-rower Bob Ryan, but if anybody thought his career was nearing its end they were under a grave misapprehension. On 17 November 1954, Bev and Lionel Cooper appeared together for the last time. They were on the wings in the Rugby League XIII which lost 13-25 at Odsal to Australasia, a team composed of Australian and New Zealand players over for the World Cup in France. Bev stole the show, Leslie Temlett (*Yorkshire Evening Post*) writing, 'It was from Brian Bevan that the two greatest thrills and the two best tries of the match came. What gems they were! Bevan at his best. The men from Australia and New Zealand, to whom Bevan, despite his Australian birth, is but a name and a legend, will go home with something to talk about.'

On 22 January 1955 Bev scored a hat-trick in a 30-3 home win against Whitehaven, all three tries resulting from sheer, blinding pace. The third was his 500th in first-class rugby league. A few months later, on 14 May, Bev figured in his fifth Championship final, when Warrington met Oldham before a crowd of 49,434 at Maine Road. The conditions were truly appalling, many parts of the pitch appearing more like lakes. Warrington managed just one try but won a tremendous game 7-3. Bath and Challinor carved it out for Bev, who merely had to beat the full-back, Frank Stirrup. By Bev's standards it was a doddle but it was one of his most important scores and helped Warrington take their third Championship in seven years.

In 1955/56 Warrington topped the league but failed to win any trophies, except the one-off ITV Trophy, beating Leigh 43-18 in the final at Loftus Road, London, Bev scoring twice. He did, however, win a European International Championship medal when, for the last time, Other Nationalities competed. They completed their life cycle in style, beating England 33-16 at Wigan (Bev grabbed two tries) and France 32-19 at Leigh (one try). Apart from a few appearances with Rugby League XIIIs against the French, Australians and New Zealanders over the next few years, his international career had ended.

Above: *The Lancashire Cup final, 1959.* Above: *Fellow Hall of Famer Alex Murphy crashes Bevan into touch at the corner flag.*

Left: *Bevan leaps for joy after scoring the winning try.*

Cartoonist Frank Barton's tribute to Brian Bevan's wonderful performance against Swinton in Warrington's 13-5 Championship semi-final victory over Swinton in 1961.

Bev scored 57 tries in 1955/56 but finished second to Bradford's powerful former All Black, Jack McLean, who claimed 61. The following season Warrington fell heavily from grace, finishing tenth in the league, while Brian had a veritable *annus horribilis*. Toe and knee injuries ruined his season, which yielded only 17 tries. In truth Warrington had begun a steady decline, but once Bev had overcome his injuries he bounced back almost as good as ever. Warrington were no longer challenging for honours but Bev continued to pile up the tries – 46 in 1957/58, 54 in 1958/59, 40 in 1959/60 and 35 in 1960/61. He was simply phenomenal, matching the new generation of wingers such as Billy Boston, Mick Sullivan, Tom van Vollenhoven and Ike Southward try for try.

The one honour Brian had not won by 1959 was a Lancashire Cup winners' medal. He had played in losing finals twice, so when Warrington reached the final against St Helens on 31 October 1959, it seemed as if the entire rugby league fraternity, outside St Helens, was willing Warrington to win – thereby completing Brian's medal collection. A crowd of 39,237 crammed into Central Park on a damp, drizzly afternoon. A gripping game had the onlookers on tenterhooks throughout and there was a fairytale result. Warrington won 5-4 and Bev scored the only try, probably the most controversial of his life, when he plunged between Vollenhoven and Prinsloo to touch down a kick through just as Vollenhoven booted the ball away. Some still say it was no try. The record books say it was.

There was just one more major final for Bev but no more fairytale endings. Warrington contested the 1961 Championship final with Leeds at Odsal, his sixth. Leeds emerged easy winners, however – 25-10. Bev finished his stupendous career with Warrington in 1962 and spent a further two years playing for Blackpool Borough in the Second Division, scoring his 796th and last try on 7 December 1963, when Borough lost 11-12 at home to Doncaster.

In his private life Bev had a number of occupations, working as a compositor, an insurance agent, a barber, a shopkeeper and security officer. When he died, aged 66, on 3 June 1991, twenty Members of Parliament signed a House of Commons motion lauding his tremendous contribution to rugby league. It stated, 'This House very much regrets the death of Brian Bevan, a legendary figure in rugby league. In the opinion of many he was the greatest winger to have graced the game and all of sport will be poorer for his passing'.

WILLIAM JOHN BOSTON

WIGAN

Debut: 21 November 1953 v Barrow (h)
Last game: 27 April 1968 v Wakefield
Trinity (a), Championship semi-final

	A	T	G	P
1953-54	10	14	-	42
1954-55	31	31	3	99
1955-56	29	43	-	129
1956-57	35	50	-	150
1957-58	37	41	-	123
1958-59	45	54	-	162
1959-60	38	46	-	138
1960-61	38	35	-	105
1961-62	40	49	-	147
1962-63	18	12	1	38
1963-64	36	26	-	78
1964-65	39	24	-	72
1965-66	34+2	19	-	57
1966-67	29	18	1	56
1967-68	27	16	2	52

BLACKPOOL BOROUGH

Debut 26 December, 1969 v Rochdale
Hornets (h)
Last game: 25 August 1970 v Huyton (h)

	A	T	G	P
1969-70	9	5	-	15
1970-71	2	-	-	-

CAREER RECORD

	A	T	G	P
Wigan	486+2	478	7	1448
Blackpool	11	5	-	15
Tests	31	24	-	72
Internation	3	6	-	18
Represent	4	5	-	15
1954 Tour*	13	30	-	90
1957 Tour*	1	4	-	12
1962 Tour*	13	19	-	57
TOTALS	562+2	571	7	1727

*Excluding tests

TESTS (31)

Great Britain	38	Australia	21	1954	Brisbane (2 tries)
Great Britain	16	Australia	20	1954	Sydney
Great Britain	27	N Zealand	7	1954	Auckland (4 tries)
Great Britain	14	N Zealand	20	1954	Greymouth
Great Britain	12	N Zealand	6	1954	Auckland
Great Britain	25	N Zealand	6	1955	Swinton (1 try)
Great Britain	21	Australia	10	1956	Wigan (2 tries)
Great Britain	9	Australia	22	1956	Bradford
Great Britain	19	Australia	0	1956	Swinton (1 try)
Great Britain	45	France	12	1957	Leeds (1 try)
Great Britain	19	France	19	1957	Toulouse (1 try)
Great Britain	29	France	14	1957	St Helens
Great Britain	23	France	5	1957	Sydney* (1 try)
Great Britain	6	Australia	31	1957	Sydney*
Great Britain	25	France	14	1957	Toulouse
Great Britain	44	France	15	1957	Wigan (1 try)
Great Britain	23	France	9	1958	Grenoble (1 try)
Great Britain	14	Australia	22	1959	Swinton (1 try)
Great Britain	10	Australia	3	1960	Bradford* (1 try)
Great Britain	21	France	10	1960	Bordeaux
Great Britain	27	France	8	1961	St Helens (1 try)
Great Britain	11	N Zealand	29	1961	Leeds (2 tries)
Great Britain	23	N Zealand	10	1961	Bradford
Great Britain	35	N Zealand	19	1961	Swinton
Great Britain	15	France	20	1962	Wigan
Great Britain	13	France	23	1962	Perpignan
Great Britain	31	Australia	12	1962	Sydney (1 try)
Great Britain	17	Australia	10	1962	Brisbane (2 tries)
Great Britain	17	Australia	18	1962	Sydney
Great Britain	8	N Zealand	27	1962	Auckland
Great Britain	42	France	4	1963	Wigan (1 try)

* World Cup

INTERNATIONALS (3)

Great Britain	17	France	8	1954	Bradford (1 try)
Other Nat.	33	England	16	1955	Wigan (3 tries)
Other Nat.	32	France	9	1955	Leigh (2 tries)

WILLIAM JOHN BOSTON
Bouncing Billy

'Billy Boston was a lyrical and charismatic genius. As a running-back Boston had the timing of a Gary Sobers, a Muhammad Ali, a Pele, a Tiger Woods. As a rugby player he was beyond comparison in the post-war era, and in any World XIII of the last fifty years his would be one of the first names on the team sheet. He was one of the few players from rugby union to make the game look easy'

Phil Melling, 1998

Billy Boston was born in Butetown in Cardiff's Tiger Bay area on 6 August 1934. He came from a big family, having five sisters and five brothers. His mother, Nellie, was Irish and his father, John, was a seaman from Sierra Leone but in reality Billy was half battering-ram and half ballet dancer. Certainly no one who saw Billy Boston play in the 1950s and 1960s will forget him and they would be extremely hard pushed to describe the frisson which convulsed spectators when he received the ball or set himself to crash tackle some unfortunate centre, whose eyes had not focussed on what was approaching doom-laden at 45 degrees from the opposing wing. Imagine a cross between Jonah Lomu and Jason Robinson but faster, stronger, more aggressive and more charismatic. Boston was power and poetry, agony for opponents and ecstasy for onlookers.

As a youngster Billy wanted to play for Cardiff at rugby and Glamorgan at cricket. He had to settle for immortality in rugby league. It was more than a fair swap, certainly as far as rugby league was concerned. Billy made rapid progress as a centre in Cardiff schools rugby and when he left school he played internationals at Boys Clubs level, captaining them, and for Wales Youth. He turned out once for Neath at senior level but played his post-school club rugby for the Cardiff International Athletics Club, which embraced the full racial diversity of the Tiger Bay community and was popularly known as the Kyaks. He never did play for Cardiff but he had the honour of captaining Cardiff & District against Cardiff at the Arms Park on 3 September 1952, in the annual pre-season fixture. At eighteen Billy was probably the youngest man to have captained the District XV, which lost 0-22.

From the age of sixteen, Billy was being tracked by rugby league scouts but he knew little about the game, nor did he want to leave home. Persistence was something rugby league scouts have in abundance, however. Hunslet and Workington Town led the chase with Town's player-manager Gus Risman expending much time and energy in the pursuit of a young man, of whom he wrote in 1957, 'He has speed and handling ability right out of the ordinary and I have yet to see any player with the same ability as Boston for bursting out of a half-tackle … Somehow or other he can throw tacklers off and not lose a split second. He is incredible and will most assuredly develop into one of the greatest players of all time.'

It was probably something of a relief for the retiring and diffident Billy Boston when he was called up for National Service in 1952. At least he might escape from the attentions of the men from the north waving chequebooks and wanting to take him away from home, hearth and Cardiff. Wrong, of course. He was stationed near rugby league land, at Catterick in Yorkshire with the Royal Signals. The Signals were the best rugby-playing unit in the British forces. They lifted the Army Cup in five out of six years from 1948 to 1954, and were then discreetly removed from the competition for a while to give others a chance. Billy scored 37 points on his debut and was reported to have scored 126 tries in 30 games in his first season. Services rugby was well reported in those times and there was little chance that Billy's exploits would go unnoticed.

Among the players in the Royal Signals were Phil Jackson, who had played for Barrow at Wembley in 1951 and would become one of the game's greatest centres, Brian Gabbitas, a classy stand-off with Hunslet and a future test player, and Jimmy Dunn, a goal-kicking full-back for Leeds, as well as Norman Mackie, a hooker who signed for Bradford Northern. There were some good union men, too, such as flanker Reg Higgins, who was to win 13 England caps and go on a Lions tour, and who was a member of a famous Widnes rugby league-playing family. Russell Robins, a back-rower, who later joined Leeds, won 13 caps for Wales and was another Lion. Phil Horrocks-Taylor, a future Yorkshire captain and England cap, was available at fly-half. Billy and Phil Jackson made up an unimaginably potent centre pairing in a side that became practically unbeatable.

On 11 March 1953 the Signals met the Welsh Guards in the Army Cup final at Aldershot. Billy produced a *tour de force* in running in six tries in a 35-0 victory, Jimmy Dunn adding four conversions and a penalty. A couple of days later Billy finally succumbed to the lure of rugby league and signed for Wigan for £3,000. The signing was not made public, however, for some months.

When he made his debut for Wigan 'A' against Barrow 'A' on 31 October 1953, a crowd of 8,500 turned up to see 'the second Jim Sullivan'. Billy did not disappoint, scoring twice in a 21-12 success. The crowd were soon shouting, 'Give it to Boston', a refrain which would echo down the years. His first-team debut, also against Barrow, followed on 21 November when 18,247 saw him score a try from the left wing in a 27-15 victory. Phil Jackson played for Barrow at right centre. His first five games in the cherry and white hoops of Wigan brought him a dozen tries and the first time he failed to score was in a third round Challenge Cup tie at Central Park, when Halifax won 2-0 before 43,953 enthralled spectators on 20 March 1954.

The Wigan management had decided to play Billy on the right wing by then and his performances were so stunning that the Great Britain selectors chose Billy for the 1954 Lions tour after only six first-team appearances. However, Billy was still in the Army, as a PTI, and had to fulfil his duties as a union player for them. On 11 February he had rattled up four tries, out of five, for the Army, who beat the Territorial Army 23-8 at Aldershot. Three of his tries had been almost length-of-the-field efforts. His fellow centre that afternoon was Syd Lowdon, another exceptionally talented league man from Cumberland. The famous union writer Pat Marshall declared, 'If he had not signed professional forms he must have been in the current Welsh Rugby Union side. Quite simply, he is one of the greatest running backs I have ever seen'.

A month later Billy was in Germany scoring the Royal Signals' first try as they beat the South Wales Borderers 11-6 at Hanover in the Army Cup final. Lance-Corporal Boston finally won his full Army cap on 27 March, along with five other Royal Signalmen, when the RAF were beaten 16-3 at Twickenham. He scored a try. Both he and Phil Jackson had been injured when the Army

Billy Boston.

met the Royal Navy but he was in the Army XV that hammered the French Army 27-0 at Twickenham. Billy's last big occasion as a rugby unionist came on 10 April 1954 when the Royal Signals won the Yorkshire Cup ('T'owd Tin Pot') beating Roundhay 17-0 at Otley.

On 27 April Billy was given some experience of rugby league at international level, appearing, along with ten other tourists, in Great Britain's 17-8 victory over France at Odsal. Billy scored a try, engineered for him by the game's star, Phil Jackson. His rugby league experience at first-class level now amounted to 10 games (14 tries) for Wigan and an international. His selection for the tour made him the youngest Lion on record, the previous youngest being fellow Welsh winger Alan Edwards in 1936. The tour would be almost over by the time he passed twenty. There was more pressure on Billy, however. He was the first black Briton to tour Australia, although he was not the first to represent Great Britain. Roy Francis had been the first in 1947 and there had been ructions when he had been denied a place on the 1946 Lions tour. Wigan's elusive stand-off George Bennett probably deserved to have toured in 1936 and Alex Givvons (Oldham) may have been a 1940 tourist. Francis, Bennett and Givvons were all black Welshmen and British rugby league, to its credit, just picked the best men, irrespective of colour – in Britain, at least. Politics – the RFL's reluctance to challenge the Australian colour bar – had possibly prevented one if not all of them from touring.

The 1954 tour was arguably the most controversial of all Lions tours. The Ashes tests were played in a good spirit but there were many ugly scenes in other games. The most notorious affair was on 10 July at Sydney, when the game against New South Wales was abandoned after 56 minutes following a number of brawls. Billy did not play in that game. The tour was bedevilled by charges of rough play, substandard refereeing and hostile, unsporting crowds and when the tourists returned home the RFL compiled a blacklist, never published, of players whose international careers were jeopardized.

Away from the controversy, Billy had a wonderful tour and more than fulfilled all expectations. His fellow tourist, Charlie Pawsey, wrote in the *Manchester Evening News*, 'It is the tendency for the young and innocent, who have been honoured with tour selection to become blasé and to take their future into their own hands. On this trip there were no "know-alls", and I could not help but admire the modesty, almost nonchalance, of record-scorer Billy Boston … Billy, always a favourite with the crowd, particularly the children, took the blaze of honour in the same easy stride with which he took his tries'.

Billy captivated the Australian crowds. He was perfectly built at 5ft 10½ins and 12st 8lbs, athletic, instinctive, with a good side-step, particularly off the right foot, a lovely swerve and a hand-off like Thor's hammer. He specialized in spectacular tries and he scored plenty of them. His workload on tour was heavy. He and Oldham's Terry O'Grady, who was just four months older than Billy, were the only wingers available after just a few matches, Drew Turnbull (Leeds) and Frank Castle (Barrow) being injured and playing only seven games between them.

The record try-scorer on a Lions tour had been Salford's Tom Danby, who had claimed 34 in 1950. Billy shattered Danby's record in New Zealand on 7 August, the day after his twentieth birthday. Against Canterbury, in a 60-14 romp, Billy powered over for four tries taking his tally to 36 in only 15 games. Oddly enough, he failed to score in the remaining three games in which he figured.

Billy was not selected for the first Ashes test at Sydney, when the wings were Castle and Lewis Jones, another fantastically successful tourist, who created records of his own by scoring 278 points (127 goals, 8 tries). Britain were routed 37-12. Both Billy and O'Grady were drafted in for their test debuts for the second test at Brisbane, where Britain, superbly led by stand-off Dickie Williams, paralysed the cock-a-hoop Australians to win 38-21 before a ground record crowd of 46,355. Lewis Jones landed a record ten goals and Billy played his part with two tries and a third disallowed. Tom Goodman wrote, 'Britain played a lot to Boston's right wing. The bouncing six-footer, weaving and side-stepping, was a constant menace and Pidding could not handle him'. For his first try Billy took a reverse pass from Phil Jackson in his own half and raced 45 yards as Clive Churchill slipped in trying to cut him off. His second followed a classic three-quarter line movement from a scrum on the Australian '25'.

The third test at the SCG took place on 17 July, a week after the infamous abandoned game against NSW, and drew a crowd of 67,577. There were, however, no reverberations, simply an excellent Ashes decider, which went Australia's way 20-16. On a greasy surface Billy had few chances but thought he was through on three occasions in the second half only to slip when turning infield.

Two weeks later he created history at Carlaw Park, Auckland in the first test against New Zealand. On another awful pitch Britain led 13-2 at the interval, Billy having scored a hat-trick. One New Zealand critic described Billy's play as 'an almost faultless performance'. Another said, 'His powerful thrusts and clever changes of direction did much to unsettle the New Zealand backs'. As the game entered its final minute, forwards Jack Wilkinson and Dave Valentine opened up the way for Billy to crash through for his fourth try. He thus equalled the record for tries in a test set by fellow Wiganer Jim Leytham against Australia in 1910. Billy played in the remaining two tests against the Kiwis at Greymouth, which was lost 14-20, and at Carlaw Park, where a 12-6 victory brought a 2-1 series triumph.

In his first full season of rugby league, 1954/55, Billy scored 31 tries and kicked 3 goals in 31 games for Wigan, who finished fifth in the league. He was one of only five of the 1954 Lions who were selected for Britain in the inaugural World Cup in France in October and November 1954. However, on 23 October after scoring a hat-trick against Blackpool Borough, he was crocked and had to withdraw from the World Cup party, thereby missing out on one of the game's major historic events. There was no representative rugby for him again until 19 May 1955, when as a centre he represented a Welsh XIII which lost 11-24 to France 'B' at Nantes. The Wales international team had been disbanded the previous season and would not reappear until 1968. Consequently Billy Boston never played in a full international for Wales.

He was, however, lucky enough to catch the final season of the Other Nationalities' existence in 1955/56. He appeared in both their games as they won the European Championship, sweeping away England 33-16 at Wigan, on 12 September and France 32-19 at Leigh, on 19 October. On both occasions he played left wing outside Lewis Jones. In the game at Central Park Billy ran in three tries between the 17th and 35th minutes, the second of which was his 100th in first-class rugby league. It had taken him only 68 games to achieve his century, the fastest hundred ever. He scored another two against France.

Billy opened the 1955/56 season with a bang. In the opening league fixture, a 52-5 walloping of Dewsbury, he crossed for seven tries to equal the Wigan club record jointly held by Johnny Ring and Gordon Ratcliffe. Three days later he scored four at Blackpool Borough. On 24 September in a thrilling 17-15 victory, he scored a 50-yarder against the New Zealanders, which was regarded as one of the best tries ever scored at Central Park. He played against New Zealand again on 8 October for Britain in the first test at Swinton, scoring a try in a 25-6 victory but he picked up a bad foot injury, which kept him out of the following tests. Things were going really well and for some time he led the league's try-scoring lists, having rattled up 35 by Christmas.

Wigan too were thriving. It seemed a real possibility that they would reach Wembley for the first time since 1951. Featherstone Rovers, Keighley and Huddersfield were dismissed in the first three rounds of the Challenge Cup and then Wigan came up against Halifax in the semi-final at Odsal on 7 April 1956. Over 52,000 saw a cliff-hanger, in which Billy gave Wigan the lead with a stupendous run, beating two tacklers and taking two more over the line with him. Billy had been troubled with an ankle injury prior to the semi-final and felt that he was not really fit but Wigan had persuaded him to play. As he scored, the ankle went again. Billy stayed on and was regarded by many pressmen as Wigan's player of the match. However, in the second half centre Jack Broome and he had to swap positions when Broome was injured.

Geoff Palmer, a gargantuan and very quick centre, playing opposite Billy, crashed through for two tries which won the game for Halifax 11-10. Billy appeared to be the scapegoat, for soon afterwards the Wigan board met and announced to the press that, 'It was unanimously decided to suspend Boston. We have done it because of events before, during and after the semi-final'. This was a real bombshell for Billy, the fans and the game at large. Billy missed Wigan's four remaining league matches but the matter was soon resolved and, whatever the rights and wrongs of the affair, the unthinkable prospect of losing one of the game's most coruscating stars receded into the distance.

Billy had scored 49 tries in 1955/56 to finish third in the try-scoring lists behind Bradford Northern's Kiwi Jack McLean (61 tries) and Warrington's Brian Bevan (57).

Season 1956/57 was one of Billy Boston's most successful campaigns. New coach Joe Egan seemed to be able to get the best out of him and there was the small matter of the transferring of Eric Ashton from left wing to right centre. Billy now had a partner, who was to be his perfect foil for the remainder of his career. The two first played as a wing-centre partnership on 13 October 1956, when both scored tries in a 17-11 win at Leigh. They would form Britain's right flank in a dozen test matches between 1957 and 1963. Their partnership at club level was regarded as one of the finest anywhere in any era. With Ashton as captain and Billy as the main attraction, Wigan would enjoy a decade of glorious rugby league.

Billy scored 50 tries for Wigan that season and 60 in all games to finish as the league's leading try-scorer for the first time, 9 ahead of Jim Lewthwaite of Barrow and 12 ahead of his old friend and playing colleague from Tiger Bay, Halifax's Johnny Freeman. Ashton did his share, too, with 18 tries and 95 goals for Wigan. Billy enjoyed a profitable season at representative level. He played in all three tests against Australia, scoring twice in the first test, a 21-10 victory at Wigan, and one try in the third test, a 19-0 win at Swinton. He played in three tests against France at Headingley (won 45-12, one try), at Toulouse (19-19, one try) and at St Helens (29-14). He grabbed four tries in Great Britain's 26-23 victory over the Rest of the League in a pre-Ashes test trial at Odsal and another in a particularly brutal game at Marseilles, where a Rugby League XIII survived an almost murderous mauling by a French XIII to win 18-17.

It was no surprise that Billy won the *Manchester Evening Chronicle* Player of the Year award for 1956/57, polling 25,545 votes – 165 more than runner-up Alan Prescott. Equally, it was no surprise that Billy was selected for the 1957 Great Britain World Cup squad, led by Prescott. Britain were favourites to win the tournament, which took place in Australia, but things did not go according to plan. There was an added complication for Billy. The tourists were scheduled to visit South Africa to play a series of propaganda games with the French after the tournament. South Africa's apartheid laws would have meant that Billy would have to be accommodated separately from his team-mates. Why the RFL should even consider such a possibility beggars belief now. Billy decided that he would not go to South Africa, anyway.

The expedition began well enough for Billy. On 9 June Britain met Western Australia at Perth in a warm-up game and won 66-5. Billy scored four tries and Mick Sullivan, on the left wing, bagged seven. Stand-off Ray Price, however, received an injury which put him out of the rest of the tour. The first World Cup game was played on 15 June before over 50,000 fans at the SCG, where Britain played excellent football to beat France 23-5. Billy scored a try from a kick-through by Sullivan. Two days later at the same venue before a crowd of 57,955 Britain were swamped by

Australia 31-6. There were mitigating factors: centre Alan Davies was hospitalized after 15 minutes with a severe leg injury. Billy was also in the wars. He spent the last 20 minutes hobbling, having badly strained ligaments in his left knee. Even so, he bravely remained on the pitch, stopping at least three Australian tries.

The injuries finished the tour for both Billy and Davies and, with Price already *hors de combat,* Britain were left with only fifteen players to complete the World Cup series and a further six games in New Zealand and South Africa. Billy's early return home meant that any furore over entry to South Africa would have been academic, anyway.

Billy's weight in the 1957 World Cup press releases was 14st 8lbs, two stones more than for the 1954 tour. He had become a hell of a problem for opposing back lines, for he had hardly lost any pace despite the increase in poundage and he had four years' experience of the game to draw on. He was now the complete player and Wigan were on the verge of breaking back into the sport's elite. During the 1957/58 season Wigan's pack developed into one of the best in the game, at its strongest consisting of John Barton, Bill Sayer, Brian McTigue, Norman Cherrington, Frank Collier and Roy Evans. All were destined for the test arena. The three-quarter line of Boston, Ashton, Ernie Ashcroft and Terry O'Grady was bolstered in October when Wigan paid a world record £9,500 for Huddersfield winger Mick Sullivan. Full-back was adequately covered by Don Platt and the ageless Jackie Cunliffe, while quicksilver Dave Bolton and Welshman Rees Thomas were the regular half-backs.

This was a team good enough to win trophies. So when they proceeded to reach the Lancashire Cup final on 19 October against Oldham, the current League Champions, there was great disappointment when an 8-13 defeat at Swinton was the outcome before a massive crowd of 42,497. Billy played in his first final at stand-off. He had played in the previous five games in that position, scoring a dozen tries and reinvigorating Wigan's back play in partnership with Dave Bolton. On the day, however, Oldham were too good for Wigan and the experiment of playing Billy at half-back was soon ended.

Britain fielded him in his usual wing spot a fortnight after the county final, when they beat France 25-14 in Toulouse. Billy tackled well but bombed several try-scoring chances. Three weeks later, on 23 November, Billy scored a last-minute try in Britain's 44-15 victory over the French but had a nightmare of a match generally. He complained after the game that he was lacking confidence and was down to 13st 3lbs. A shoulder injury then kept him out of six games. When he returned, on New Year's Day 1958, he put the skids under Warrington with a couple of typical tries and was a try-scorer in eight of the next nine games. His form was good enough to warrant selection for Great Britain's third test against France in Grenoble on 2 March. Britain won 23-9 and Billy obliged with a try. He seemed assured of selection for the 1958 Lions tour but was surprisingly asked to appear in the second tour trial at Leeds on 19 March. There was widespread disbelief when he was subsequently left out of the touring team, ostensibly because of injury doubts.

There was a consolation, however. Wigan made good progress in the Challenge Cup. Billy scored twice in a 39-10 first round rout of Whitehaven and further tries in epic encounters at Wakefield (won 11-5) and Oldham (won 8-0). The semi-final, against Rochdale Hornets at Swinton, was considered a formality. On 1 October Billy had recorded a hat-trick against them at Rochdale, when Wigan had thrashed the Hornets 52-0 in the semi-final of the Lancashire Cup. A gluepot pitch and lashings of rain, however, proved a great leveller and Wigan were happy to scrape through 5-3, thanks to a try from Sullivan and a goal from Cunliffe.

On a lovely sunny afternoon Billy walked out behind his skipper Eric Ashton for the first time at Wembley on 10 May 1958. The pair would repeat the exercise another five times in the following eight years. Wigan's opponents were Workington Town, tough nuts who had been to Wembley in 1952 and 1955. It was anybody's game – Town had finished third in the league, Wigan fifth. Billy needed a cartilage operation but was so vital to Wigan's hopes that he was persuaded to put it off. He took the field with his knee heavily bandaged, having received a pain-killing injection. He was again displaying his versatility by turning out at left centre in place of Ernie Ashcroft, who had broken ribs. Neither Billy nor Eric Ashton had much chance to shine on attack but they defended mercilessly in a game which Town could easily have won. Wigan just about deserved their 13-9 victory. They had been 0-5 down when, in the seventeenth minute, O'Grady began a back-line movement. Cunliffe linked up from full-back and served Billy, who drew in two defenders before sending out a pass to Sullivan, who sailed over for an equalizing try. Props Barton and McTigue added later tries for Wigan, Cunliffe adding a couple of goals. The man who temporarily replaced Billy as Great Britain's right winger, the redoubtable Ike Southward, scored all nine of Workington's points.

During 1958/59 Billy was not selected in any representative sides despite scoring 54 tries for Wigan, his best ever haul for the club. Wigan had a marvellous season, finishing second to St Helens in the league but pipping Saints for the Lancashire League Championship. There was a shock home defeat by Hunslet in the Championship semi-final but Wigan returned to Wembley. They went via Leeds 12-5, Hunslet 22-4 (Billy two tries), Halifax 26-0 (Billy three tries) and Leigh 5-0 in the semi-final, when Mick Sullivan was again the match-winning try-scorer. There

There is little hope for the Oldham chasers as Billy Boston surges away at Central Park in 1958.

Wigan after their Challenge Cup final victory over Workington Town at Wembley in 1958. From left to right: McTigue. Cunliffe, O'Grady, Thomas, Collier, Ashton, McGurrin, Sullivan, Cherrington (obscured), Bolton, Boston, Barton. Front: Sayer.

were almost 80,000 at Wembley on 9 May 1959, another gloriously sunny day, for Wigan's clash with Wembley first-timers Hull.

The expected close struggle never materialized as Wigan outplayed Hull, whose much feared pack simply failed to rise to the challenge. Brian McTigue won the Lance Todd Trophy with a towering performance and Wigan broke all sorts of records in a 30-13 canter, becoming the first club to win consecutive Wembley finals. Among their six tries were two from Billy Boston, the only tries he would score at the stadium. His first, after 35 minutes, followed a delightful run by Dave Bolton, who created a massive overlap for Billy to run the last ten yards and through Arthur Keegan's forlorn tackle for an easy score. The second, on 70 minutes, was again attributable to Bolton, who kicked from around halfway down the right flank. Billy followed at a rare lick and touched down inches before the ball went over the dead-ball line.

The 1959/60 season opened well for Billy, if not for his team, who lost four and drew one of their first nine league games and lost to Warrington in the Lancashire Cup semi-final. He scored 13 tries in the 9 games he played in that period and was rewarded with selection for the first test against Australia at Swinton, along with four other Wigan players. It turned out to be a poisoned chalice. The Kangaroos, inspired by Reg Gasnier and Brian Clay, were easier winners than the 22-14 score-line suggested. It was already 22-4 with ten minutes remaining, when Billy chased a Dave Bolton kick and dribbled to the posts to touch down. The side was heavily changed for the next test and Billy was one of the victims. Ironically, the week before the second test Wigan beat the Aussies 16-9. A crowd of 24,466 saw a tough, try-less first 65 minutes before Ashton kicked forward for Billy to gather on the first bounce at breakneck pace to shatter the deadlock. Ashton scored a brilliant try five minutes later to seal a terrific victory.

Billy ended the season in prime form. On 2 and 9 April he scored six tries in consecutive games, a 42-9 win at Widnes and a 58-6 battering of Dewsbury at Central Park, an unparalleled feat for the club. Wigan won 13 of their last 14 league fixtures to scrape into fourth position. The Championship semi-final, on 7 May took them to all-conquering St Helens, who had finished 13 points clear of Wigan. A crowd of 32,094 were treated to a rumbustuous affair and a shock result. Mick Sullivan and Alex Murphy were sent off just before half-time. One critic wrote, 'In Billy Boston Wigan had a shock trooper St Helens couldn't contain. Only twice did Billy get the attack signal, once in each half. Twice he stormed through the Saints' defensive line, leaving opponents

Workington Town scrum-half Sol Roper attempts to cut off Boston at Derwent Park in 1959.

straggling, for decisive tries.' A 19-9 victory took them through to a final against Wakefield Trinity, who had won the Challenge Cup the previous Saturday.

Odsal was heaving with a record Championship final crowd of 83,190. Mick Sullivan's suspension meant Wigan reshuffled their backs with play-anywhere Billy at right centre, Ashton at stand-off and Bolton at scrum-half. Jack Bentley (*Daily Express*) saw 'Boston give one of the most devastating right-centre displays of the season and Ashton use his classy football ability superbly at stand-off'. Billy was directly opposed to Neil Fox, who unfortunately suffered a severe thigh injury after 13 minutes and spent the rest of the game limping on the wing. Even so, Wigan played exquisitely and Billy had one of the games of his life. Wigan led only 4-3 as half-time loomed when Bolton gave a cute reverse pass to set Billy free. He was faced by full-back Round, who had stopped him twice before as he tried to come inside. This time Billy feinted to come inside but thundered past a stationary Round on the outside to extend the lead to 9-3. Wigan pulled away to win 27-3, with Billy pounding 50 yards for a 68th-minute interception try – his 47th of the season. Amazingly, 1960 was the only time Wigan would lift the Championship in Billy's career.

Billy began the 1960/61 season with a bang with 15 tries, including four hat-tricks, in nine games, shooting to the top of the try-scoring lists. He was selected for the Great Britain World Cup squad for a third time but his jinx on such occasions struck again. In a 2-14 defeat at Whitehaven on 17 September he strained his thigh. Despite the first World Cup game against New Zealand being only a week away, the selectors decided not to replace him. New Zealand were beaten 23-8 and France 33-7, with Billy on the sidelines. He was declared fit for the game which would decide the World Champions, Britain *v.* Australia at Odsal on 8 October.

Billy picked a truly foul day to make his return. Teeming rain kept the crowd down to 32,773, the pitch was a quagmire and the game a running battle. The press, the administrators and many of the fans were outraged by the kicking, punching, high and late tackles. The great mystery was how no one was sent off or maimed. Billy's Wigan team-mates, Ashton, the captain, Sullivan and McTigue were also in the British team. The Australians decided to move their star winger, big Brian Carlson, from the right to the left wing to counter Billy. It did not work. Every time Billy got the ball Australia were at panic stations for he made plenty of ground and broke numerous tackles. Britain had led 2-0 after six minutes and on the half-hour Billy pushed his team into an unassailable lead in the conditions. Vince Karalius and Ashton moved the ball sweetly out to the winger, who brushed aside an unavailing tackle and romped over for a vital converted try. Just before the break Sullivan crossed on the other flank and Britain led 10-0. The only score in the second half mayhem was a late try from Billy's shadow Carlson. Billy's World Cup, beginning in frustration, ended in triumph.

Billy held his place in the test team's two victories over France later in the season. He went back to Wembley for the third time in four seasons but Wigan lost 6-12 to St Helens in a game played in almost tropical conditions.

Another highly successful season followed in 1961/62. Wigan topped the league and Billy gained his second Lancashire League Championship winners' medal. Throughout the season he was involved in a rare tussle with Tom van Vollenhoven to finish as leading try-scorer. Vollenhoven looked to have won the race when he scored six against Blackpool on 23 April 1962, but a week

Billy Boston leaves the field after Wigan's stunning Championship Final victory over Wakefield Trinity at Odsal in 1960.

Billy Boston powers away from a tackle by Brian Carlson at Odsal in 1960, when Great Britain clinched the World Cup with a fine 10-3 victory.

later Billy plundered seven at Salford. Billy ended up with 51 tries to Tom's 46. It was the last time anyone would score a half century until Ellery Hanley in 1984/85.

Boston figured in all three tests against the 1961 Kiwis and both tests against France. He could not be left out of the 1962 Lions party, being one of seven Wigan tourists. Billy now topped 15st and the Australians could not cope with his brand of wing play in one of the greatest of all Lions teams. Billy played in 17 fixtures and was the leading try-scorer with 22, skipper Ashton claiming 21. In the Ashes tests Billy was magnificent, scoring once in a 31-12 victory at Sydney and twice at Brisbane when a 17-10 win secured the Ashes. Billy would not play any more tests against Australia but his mark was indelible – his nine Ashes tries remaining a record for a Briton. One distinction he would have liked to have avoided on tour was his dismissal, with five others, in a game against New South Wales. He had never been sent off before, a remarkable testimony to his demeanour on the pitch, for Billy was often heavily targeted and subject to provocation.

After the 1962 tour Billy still had six years as a Wigan player ahead of him. He played his 31st and last test in a 42-4 drubbing of France at Central Park on 3 April 1963, scoring his 24th test try. Season 1962/63 saw him pass Johnny Ring's record aggregate 368 tries for Wigan and by the time he retired he had piled up 478 tries for the club.

There were still Cup finals to relish too. Wigan lost at Wembley to Wakefield Trinity in 1963 and to St Helens in 1966 but won the final of 1965, when Hunslet were beaten 20-16 in one of the most splendid games ever staged at Wembley. Oddly enough, by 1966 Billy had still not gained a Lancashire Cup winners' medal, nor had Eric Ashton. There was delight everywhere in rugby league land (apart from opponents Oldham) when their collections were completed on

Billy Boston flies up in support of his Wigan captain and long-time centre partner Eric Ashton at Halifax in 1961. Stand-off Dave Bolton is on the right.

29 October 1966 at Swinton. Most of the Wigan old brigade had departed but Billy and Eric both claimed tries as the Roughyeds were beaten 16-13. Billy made his last appearance for Wigan on 27 April 1968 in a 9-26 Championship semi-final defeat at Wakefield. On Boxing Day 1969, Billy made a comeback with Blackpool Borough, scoring a try in a 6-20 home defeat by Rochdale. He played his last game against Huyton as a second-rower on 25 August 1970. The next generation of rugby league wingmen could breathe more easily!

There will certainly never be another Billy Boston. Only Brian Bevan stands above Billy in the all-time top try-scorers and despite the myriad of wonderful players who graced Central Park, it is doubtful if any of them were ever as popular as Bouncing Billy. Billy never left Wigan, where he became licensee of The Griffin, within easy shouting distance of the ground. His pub became a Mecca for rugby league fans of all persuasions visiting Central Park. In 1990 Billy was among the ten inaugural inductees to the Welsh Sports Hall of Fame, along with national icons such as Lynn Davies, Billy Meredith and Ken Jones. In 1996 he was awarded the MBE 'for services to the community in Wigan' and in 1999 he was awarded the Tom Mitchell British Lion of the Year Trophy. In 2003 a programme of events celebrating his fifty years with and in Wigan was launched at Wigan Pier.

NEIL FOX

WAKEFIELD TRINITY

Debut: 10 April 1956 v Keighley (a)
Last game: 10 March, 1974 v Hull KR (h)

	A	T	G	P
1955/56	2	-	6	12
1956/57	23	10	54	138
1957/58	37	32	124	344
1958/59	40	26	146	370
1959/60	40	30	140	370
1960/61	32	18	81	216
1961/62	42	27	163	407
1962/63	30	10	100	230
1963/64	34	20	108	276
1964/65	35	12	113	262
1965/66	29	11	94	221
1966/67	37	15	132	309
1967/68	29	17	88	227
1968/69	29	9	87	201
1969/70	2	1	6	15
1970/71	28+2	12	110	256
1971/72	36+5	6	84	186
1972/73	38+4	8	138	300
1973/74	19+1	8	62	148

BRADFORD NORTHERN

Debut: 23 August 1969 v Dewsbury (h)
Second debut: 5 February, 1978 v Hull (h)
Last game: 19 August 1979 v Huddersfield (a), Yorkshire Cup

	A	T	G	P
1969/70	26+1	4	11	34
1977/78	9+4	4	22(1)	55
1978/79	21+8	4	50	112
1979/80	1	-	2	4

HULL KINGSTON ROVERS

Debut 25 August 1974 v Doncaster (a)
Last game: 14 December 1975 v Warrington (a)

	A	T	G	P
1974/75	44	14	146(1)	333
1975/76	15	2	66(1)	137

Figures in brackets represent one-point drop goals, which are included in the total of goals preceding them.

YORK

Debut: 11 January 1976 v Bramley (h)
Last game: 26 September 1976 v New Hunslet (a)

	A	T	G	P
1975/76	10	2	36	78
1976/77	2+1	-	6	12

BRAMLEY

Debut: 3 October 1976 v Hull (home)
Last game: 24 April 1977 v Doncaster (a)

	A	T	G	P
1976/77	23	6	73	164

HUDDERSFIELD

Debut: 21 August, 1977 v York (h), Yorkshire Cup
Last game: 29 January 1978 v Batley (a)

	A	T	G	P
1977/78	21	5	73+1	160

CAREER RECORD

	A	T	G	P
Wakefield	562+12	272	1836	4488
Bradford	57+13	12	85(1)	205
Hull KR	59	16	212(2)	470
York	12+1	2	42	90
Bramley	23	6	73	164
Huddersfield	21	5	73(1)	160
Tests	29	14	93	228
England	1	1	3	9
Yorkshire	17	9	60	147
Represent	2	-	6	12
1962 Tour*	14+2	17	73	197
1962 GB in SA	3	4	19	50
TOTALS	800+28	358	2575(4)	6220

*Excluding tests

Fox scored 5 tries, 45 goals (3 drop goals), 102 points as player-coach to Wellington (New Zealand) in 1975 (not included above).

TESTS (29)

Great Britain	15	France	24	1959	Grenoble (2 tries)
Great Britain	11	Australia	10	1959	Leeds (1 try, 1 goal)
Great Britain	18	Australia	12	1959	Wigan (1 try, 6 goals)
Great Britain	18	France	20	1960	Toulouse (2 tries, 3 goals)
Great Britain	17	France	17	1960	St Helens (1 try, 4 goals)
Great Britain	21	France	10	1960	Bordeaux (2 tries, 2 goals)
Great Britain	23	N Zealand	10	1961	Bradford (4 goals)
Great Britain	35	N Zealand	19	1961	Swinton (7 goals)
Great Britain	15	France	20	1962	Wigan (3 goals)
Great Britain	13	France	23	1962	Perpignan (2 goals)
Great Britain	31	Australia	12	1962	Sydney (5 goals)
Great Britain	17	Australia	10	1962	Brisbane (3 goals)
Great Britain	17	Australia	18	1962	Sydney (1 try, 4 goals)
Great Britain	0	N Zealand	19	1962	Auckland
Great Britain	8	N Zealand	27	1962	Auckland (1 try)
Great Britain	12	France	17	1962	Perpignan (1 try, 3 goals)
Great Britain	42	France	4	1963	Wigan (1 try, 9 goals)
Great Britain	2	Australia	28	1963	Wembley (1 goal)
Great Britain	12	Australia	50	1963	Swinton (3 goals)
Great Britain	39	France	0	1964	Leigh (1 try, 9 goals)
Great Britain	17	France	7	1965	Swinton (7 goals)
Great Britain	13	France	18	1966	Perpignan (2 goals)
Great Britain	16	France	13	1967	Carcassonne (2 goals)
Great Britain	13	France	23	1967	Wigan (2 goals)
Great Britain	11	Australia	17	1967	White City (3 goals)
Great Britain	22	France	13	1968	Paris
Great Britain	19	France	8	1968	Bradford
Great Britain	34	France	10	1968	St Helens (5 goals)
Great Britain	9	France	13	1969	Toulouse (3 goals)

ENGLAND (1)

England	18	France	6	1962	Leeds (1 try, 3 goals)

COUNTY GAMES (17)

Yorkshire	7	Cumberland	29	1958	Whitehaven (2 goals)
Yorkshire	47	Australians	15	1959	York (1 try, 10 goals)
Yorkshire	38	Lancashire	28	1959	Leigh (1 try, 7 goals)
Yorkshire	20	Lancashire	21	1960	Wakefield (4 goals)
Yorkshire	19	Cumberland	43	1960	Whitehaven (5 goals)
Yorkshire	21	N Zealand	11	1961	Hull KR (1 try)
Yorkshire	8	Cumberland	23	1961	Wakefield (1 try, 1 goal)
Yorkshire	12	Lancashire	14	1961	Leigh (1 try, 3 goals)
Yorkshire	11	Cumberland	2	1962	Workington (1 try, 1 goal)
Yorkshire	22	Lancashire	8	1962	Wakefield (5 goals)
Yorkshire	11	Australians	5	1963	Hull KR (4 goals)
Yorkshire	14	Cumberland	6	1964	Whitehaven (1 try, 1 goal)
Yorkshire	16	Lancashire	13	1965	Swinton (2 goals)
Yorkshire	17	Cumberland	17	1966	Workington (4 goals)
Yorkshire	17	Lancashire	22	1966	Leeds (1 try, 4 goals)
Yorkshire	15	Australians	14	1967	Wakefield (1 try, 3 goals)
Yorkshire	17	Lancashire	23	1968	Widnes (4 goals)

NEIL FOX
The Points Machine

'With brute strength, Fox was able to break the line and was always a dangerous player close to the try-line. On the soft English grounds, Fox was in his element and we always knew we were in for a tough afternoon against him'

Reg Gasnier, *Big League*, 1990

A recital of Neil Fox's achievements is sufficient to illustrate his immense stature in rugby league. His 29 caps for Great Britain remain a record for a centre. He is the world's greatest scorer with 6,220 points and stands second only to Jim Sullivan in the all-time goal-kicking lists with 2,575. His first-class career record of 828 appearances has been bettered only by Jim Sullivan and Gus Risman and his 358 tries places him seventeenth in the all-time lists. He was a 1962 Lion, scoring 277 points on tour, amassed 61 points in eight Ashes tests, was a member of Ashes-winning teams in 1959 and 1962, skippered Great Britain three times and was captain-elect of the 1968 World Cup squad. He held or broke virtually all goal-kicking and points-scoring records for Wakefield Trinity at one time or another, won the Lance Todd Trophy in 1962, and scored 38 points for Trinity in three Wembley finals. He was three times rugby league's leading goal-kicker and four times its leading points-scorer, and he kicked 100 goals in a season 12 times.

However, when all the records, caps and cups have been catalogued there remains Neil Fox the player. Some would say that the facts and figures speak for themselves. Of course, in a way they do. In another way they cannot. Only those who saw Fox in his pomp can really appreciate his gifts and the pleasure they brought to the fans on the terraces and in the stands. In simple terms he won matches. One way or another he won matches – by kicking shoals of goals with his lethal left foot, toe-ending the ball in the old-fashioned style, by scoring crucial tries, by creating scoring chances for his colleagues or by inspiring his teams through his own genius, drive and creativity.

With the current dependence on imported rugby league players creating a dearth of top quality British centres, it is a little galling to recall that when Neil Fox bestrode the game from the late 1950s through the 1960s, he was vying with high-class rivals, who included Eric Ashton, Ian Brooke, Alan Buckley, Jim Challinor, Alan Davies, Dick Gemmell, Phil Jackson, Lewis Jones, Frank Myler and Geoff Shelton, to name but a few. With such opposition for the centre spots his record tally of 29 test caps assumes remarkable proportions.

All the hype and bluster which currently bombards us about modern players being bigger, better and stronger doubtlessly provokes a few guffaws among those who remember Neil Fox. At 6ft and 15st, Neil was arguably more powerful than any present-day British centre and as a footballer he had all the gifts, except sheer speed – although he got faster the further he ran. While recent generations of British fans and players have rightly revered Mal Meninga, it is comforting to know that previous generations of Australians felt the same about Neil Fox.

Neil was born on 4 May 1939 into a rugby league family in the rugby league stronghold of Sharlston, between Wakefield and Pontefract. His father, Tom, had played in the Featherstone

Rovers pack in the early 1930s. He and his wife Stella produced three sons, who all made a huge impact on the game. The eldest, Peter, won county honours as a schoolboy and played in the forwards for Featherstone, Batley, Hull KR and Wakefield Trinity. His biggest contribution, however, was as a highly successful and perceptive coach with a variety of clubs, Yorkshire, England and Great Britain. Don Fox, three and a half years older than Neil, also played for Featherstone Rovers for twelve years (1953-65) before joining Neil at Wakefield and ending his career at Batley in 1971. As a footballer and tactician, Don was outstanding, having a long career at scrum-half, where he won county and international honours, before gravitating to the pack and winning a test cap at loose-forward. Like Neil, Don was a tremendous goal-kicker, who set and broke his own share of records at Featherstone.

Neil's earliest rugby was at school in Sharlston and he ultimately captained Yorkshire Schools, before going into junior rugby with Featherstone Rovers Under-18s. To most people's surprise, in October 1955 Neil broke with family tradition and joined Wakefield Trinity rather than Rovers. Theoretically there was much more potential at the club in 'The Merrie City' than at the colliery village club just down the road. Yet in 1955/56 Rovers were to finish sixth in the league and Trinity seventeenth.

Neil was quickly promoted to the 'A' Team (Reserves), which performed the double, beating Halifax 'A' 17-4 in the final of the Yorkshire Senior Competition Shield and York 'A' 31-0 in the Yorkshire Senior Competition Challenge Cup final. Two medals as a professional in his first season was a portent of many to follow. His first-team debut at Keighley on 10 April 1956 saw him paired at left-centre with the experienced Don Froggett. Trinity lost 5-9 and Neil did not score, one of only 39 such occasions in his 574 appearances for them. Trinity lost too in his second game, 15-19 at Huddersfield where he played full-back, but Neil landed 6 goals, with another 1,830 to follow.

By the time Neil next appeared in the first team on 10 November Trinity had won the Yorkshire Cup, beating Hunslet 23-5 in the final at Headingley. He scored his first try in a 16-14 home win against Swinton and the following week played against brother Don in a thrilling 20-21 defeat at Featherstone, kicking four goals. On 10 December Neil found himself in opposition to the touring Australians, a saga which would run until 1978. Trinity gained a 17-12 victory over the Australian second-stringers and Neil kicked four goals and had a try disallowed. Clive Churchill, the legendary Australian full-back, made his last appearance in England in this game. In his first full season, still aged only seventeen, Neil gathered 138 points in 23 games. He also scored 163 for the reserves, who had finished top of the league.

In 1957/58 Fox set about breaking records in earnest. He took over from Frank Mortimer, Britain's full-back against Australia the previous season, as first choice goal-kicker. He did it to such good effect that by the close of the season he had swept away Sam Lee's club record of 111 goals set in 1938/39. Neil passed the mark by kicking eight goals in a 40-5 victory at Dewsbury on 12 April 1958. His final total was 124. The following week Neil scored his 32nd try in an 8-20 home defeat by Hunslet, thereby equalling Dinny Boocker's club record established in 1953/54. His total of 344 points created another club record and gave him second place in the league's points scoring lists. The leader, Oldham's Bernard Ganley, had amassed 453, including a world record 219 goals. Individual match records fell like ninepins too. On 29 March Trinity beat Doncaster 48-13 at Belle Vue. Neil was unstoppable, pillaging six tries and six goals. No Trinity player had ever scored six tries, nor had anyone claimed 30 points. The latter record lasted just six days. On 4 April Neil extended it to 31 points, when Batley were thrashed 61-12. He bagged a hat-trick and landed 11 goals, which equalled another club record jointly held by Jimmy Metcalfe, Charlie Pollard and Harry Murphy. In a riot of scoring over five games in March and April, Neil went over for 14 tries and kicked 32 goals (106 points). It was, however, just a little late to get him into the 1958 Lions touring squad. He was probably considered too young and, anyway, Eric Ashton, Jim Challinor, Alan Davies and Phil Jackson proved quite capable of doing the business in Australia.

Trinity were building an outstanding combination of players which would take the club to heights it had never previously reached. By 1958/59 most of the cast for the enfolding dramas had been assembled. Ken Traill's career as a wonderfully brainy loose-forward ended in November 1958 but he continued as coach and was a major driving force at Belle Vue for over a decade. There were some excellent young backs, apart from Neil, in Fred Smith (wing), Gerry Round (full-back) and a trio of half-backs, Ken Rollin, Harold Poynton and Keith Holliday, who were all going to play major roles. Albert Firth, Geoff Oakes and Les Chamberlain were forwards who were developing well. All that was needed was a few sparks of experience to kick-start Trinity's renaissance as a rugby league power. They came in the form of international forwards Don Vines and Derek Turner from Oldham, who also provided winger John Etty later in the season.

Wakefield rose to fifth in 1958/59, won the Yorkshire League Championship and reached the Yorkshire Cup final. The latter was Neil's first major final but ended in disappointment at Headingley on 18 October when Leeds beat Trinity more easily than a 24-20 scoreline suggests. Neil contributed two goals. His performances were certainly getting him noticed, however. On 15 September he won his first Yorkshire cap, kicking a couple of goals, as Yorkshire fell away alarmingly to lose 7-29 to Cumberland at Whitehaven. By the end of the campaign he had added a test cap to his collection, replacing the injured Eric Ashton for the game against France at Grenoble on 5 April 1959. Again the result, a 15-24 defeat in scorching conditions, was a disappointment. Neil and fellow debutant, Hunslet stand-off Brian Gabbitas, were exonerated from blame, both having good games. Even Jack Bentley (*Daily Express*), an early critic of Neil as a test player, conceded, 'In his debut he … showed determination, bumping off a couple of defenders and handing off another to score Great Britain's first try after 47 minutes. He gave a repeat performance six minutes later.' Those two tries brought him the first six of a record 228 test points over the next ten years.

In domestic rugby Neil broke his own club records in 1958/59, kicking 146 goals and scoring 370 points for Wakefield. His outstanding feat came in a 39-12 defeat of Workington Town on 25 October when his haul was five tries and four goals. However, a couple of his club records also fell to right-winger Fred Smith, who scored seven of Trinity's ten tries in a 38-0 home rout of Keighley on 25 April, beating Neil's six the previous season. Smith's third try took him past Neil's and Dinny Boocker's old record of 32 tries in a season and he finished the campaign with 38. Christmas Day, 1958 was also a significant occasion for Neil, for he played alongside Springbok centre Alan Skene for the first time in a 19-7 win at Castleford. For the next four years the pair formed as effective a centre partnership as ever played for Trinity. They complemented each other perfectly. Skene, blond, agile, sinuously smooth in action and three-and-a-half stones lighter than Neil, was the perfect foil for him. Such partnerships hardly exist any longer.

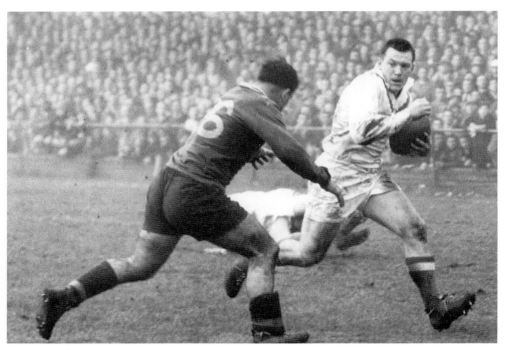

Action from the 1959 Ashes Test at Headingley. Above: *Neil Fox prepares to fend off Australian hooker Ian Walsh.* Below: *The flying Fox – Neil in action during Great Britain's 11-10 victory.*

The 1959/60 season was Wakefield Trinity's most successful of the twentieth century – at least until then. Neil's own achievements were extraordinary. Trinity finished second behind St Helens, their highest position in peace-time rugby league, and retained the Yorkshire League Championship. They reached both major domestic finals and went into the last Saturday of the season seeking the Cup and League double. For his part, Neil equalled his own club record with 370 points (30 tries, 140 goals) and in all games he rattled up 453 points (37 tries, 171 goals) He finished as the game's leading scorer, 54 points ahead of Austin Rhodes (St Helens), and was joint-leading kicker with Rhodes. Trinity's three-quarter line, usually Smith, Skene, Fox and Etty, rattled up 136 tries, yet the only significant addition to the team had been Halifax's ferocious test prop Jack Wilkinson.

Neil won his second Yorkshire cap against the Australians at York on 28 September and celebrated by grabbing 23 points in a 47-15 rout, his ten goals equalling the county record and his 23 points beating the old one. It was not enough to get him into the first test team, however, although he was selected as reserve back. Australia won that test 22-14 and looked world-beaters, particularly at centre with Reg Gasnier and Harry Wells truly exceptional players. Neil was drafted into the team for the next test at Headingley on 21 November along with team-mate Don Vines. Ten days previously at Leigh he had taken Lancashire to the cleaners with 17 points, including a first-minute interception try, in Yorkshire's 38-28 victory.

Great Britain ground out an 11-10 win. It was by no means a pretty game for the 30,029 crowd but it was intensely gripping – 'the match of a life-time between two brilliant sides', according to Harold Mather (*Manchester Guardian*), although others disagreed. Neil scored a try after 34 minutes, after taking Ashton's reverse pass to give Britain a 6-2 interval lead. By the 64th minute Australia led 10-6, when one of the most famous but simple tries in Ashes history fell to Britain. From a scrum close to Australia's line, scrum-half Jeff Stevenson worked an exquisite back flip for loose-forward Johnny Whiteley to score under the posts. Neil was left with a simple but nerve-wracking conversion, which gave Britain a one-point victory.

He got some more practice against the Kangaroos a week later, when Wakefield beat them 20-10 before a crowd of 17,615. A try and four goals reinforced the tourists' growing respect for the young giant. The third test at Wigan on 12 December saw Gerry Round make his test debut and there was a recall for Jack Wilkinson. The star, however, of a tight, combative encounter in muddy conditions, was Neil Fox. Neil opened the scoring with a 50-yard penalty and by half-time he added another couple to give Britain a 6-2 lead. A fourth penalty soon made it 8-2 and then he lofted a huge up and under, which no one seemed to want to collect. The ball bounced and there was Neil steaming in for the first try, which he converted, before potting another penalty – Neil Fox 15 Australia 2! The Aussies fought back to 15-12 but a late Ike Southward try brought Britain an 18-12 triumph. Astonishingly, 1959 remains the last time Britain have won the Ashes on home soil. Neil certainly played his part in that historic series.

In March 1959 Neil played in both Great Britain's test matches against France. At Toulouse Britain went down 18-20 in a fluctuating game filled with good football but marred by the dismissal of Derek Turner after one of the most spectacular fist-and-feet brawls in the history of Anglo-French tests. Neil gave his usual good value with two fine tries and three goals. In the rematch at St Helens, he was the outstanding back, making a try for winger Sullivan, going over himself after a Turner break and booting four goals. Britain squandered a ten-point lead, however, and were lucky to draw 17-17.

Celebrating with the Challenge Cup after beating Hull 38-5 at Wembley in 1960. From left to right, standing: Chamberlain, Holliday, Firth, Etty, Wilkinson, Turner, Vines, Fox, Smith. Front: Skene, Rollin.

Wakefield, meanwhile had embarked on their Challenge Cup quest. Drawn at favourites St Helens in the first round, they stunned Saints with a 15-10 victory. Before the game their coach, Alan Prescott, said, 'Neil Fox never did anything against us', Saints having beaten Trinity easily twice in the league. After the game he admitted, 'Fox was brilliant'. Neil kicked three goals, while his winger John Etty crashed through for two super tries. The second round was equally tight, if not as spectacular, Trinity edging out Widnes 5-2 at Naughton Park, thanks to Neil's penalty and another Etty try from 35 yards out. Whitehaven drew a ground record 18,650 for their third round tie against Trinity but were ousted 21-10, Neil's contribution being a series of blockbusting runs and three goals. The semi-final against

Derek Turner, Keith Holliday and Neil Fox display the spoils of 1959/60 – the Challenge Cup and the Yorkshire League Championship Trophy.

Featherstone at Odsal was another triumph for John Etty, who blasted through for two tries in a comfortable 11-2 victory. Neil landed a late penalty.

The season climaxed with three memorable Saturdays in May. On 7 May Wakefield beat Hull 24-4 in the Championship semi-final at Belle Vue. Jack Bentley wrote, 'If any one man sparked this Trinity win it was Neil Fox, who has had his share of criticism from me this season … It was burly Neil who swivelled from behind a scrum to drop a towering 30-yard goal and edge Trinity ahead at 4-2. It was Neil who powered through four defenders in a 40-yard burst to kick ahead for Skene to score as Wakefield struggled for the first try, and it was this mighty 21-year-old who hustled in for a try of his own and landed another five goals.'

The game had been a dress rehearsal for Wembley on 14 May. Trinity had lost Harold Poynton through injury in the previous game, but Hull were cruelly hit by injuries for the Cup final. In the event they gave Trinity a hard time in the first half, after which they trailed 5-7. In the last quarter Wakefield ran riot to win 38-5, spectacular tries coming at regular intervals. Neil scored two belters and landed a record-equalling seven goals. His 20 points was a record for a Challenge Cup final and he was a very happy man, when he followed skipper Derek Turner to collect his first Challenge Cup-winners' medal from the Queen. Harry Sunderland eulogized, 'Wakefield's moves of majestic magnificence made Neil Fox into a Prince of Points'.

The crowd at Wembley had been 79,773. The following Saturday 83,190 flocked to Odsal for Trinity's Championship final clash with Wigan. Wakefield had never won the Championship and this fixture promised to be a classic. It began well enough for Trinity with Fred Smith scoring in the corner after exquisite passing. It was Smith's 38th try of the season, beating his own club record set in 1958/59. That was as good as it got, however. Fred Griffiths made it 3-2 with a penalty and then disaster struck. Neil took the ball hard into a tackle, got a knee in his left thigh and spent the last 66 minutes hobbling on the wing. Four painkilling injections at half-time failed to make him any more comfortable. Wigan played brilliantly and raced away to win 27-3. Trinity's double hopes vanished with Neil's injury. On a personal level, the injury ended Neil's wonderful record of having scored in his last 95 games (87 for Trinity, eight representative matches). Neil had now just turned twenty-one. His playing record in first-class rugby read: appearances 150; tries 107; goals 503; points 1,327.

Wakefield slipped to seventh in 1960/61, when the only significant signings were second-rower Brian Briggs, who had been a 1954 Lion, and, later in the season, the Springbok wingman Jan Prinsloo, both from St Helens. Prinsloo would eventually take Etty's place as Neil's wing partner.

The World Cup was scheduled for England in late September 1960. On the previous season's form, Neil could surely not be left out of Britain's squad. He played in both of Yorkshire's matches, kicking four goals against Lancashire at Wakefield and five against Cumberland at Whitehaven. However, the games were lost 20-21 and 19-43. He played for Great Britain in their trial against the Rest of the League at St Helens on 12 September and kicked two goals in a 21-16 win. When the World Cup squad was announced he was named only among the reserves, Ashton, Davies and Challinor winning the centre berths. Trinity's Jack Wilkinson and Derek Turner were in the squad that went on to lift the trophy.

There was some consolation for Neil as Wakefield fought their way to the Yorkshire Cup final. His match-winning propensities were amply demonstrated *en route*. He scored the only try of the game to knock Halifax out 3-0 in the first round and in the semi-final against Keighley at Odsal, he coolly converted Les Chamberlain's 78th-minute try for Trinity to scrape through 5-4. The second round had been somewhat easier – a 40-6 rout of Bramley, Neil contributing a try and eight goals. The final at Leeds against Huddersfield was notable for Dave Valentine's reappearance at loose-forward for the Fartowners after four years' retirement. It was Neil who made all the difference in a dour struggle, however. Trinity led 10-3 at half-time, Neil having converted two tries, one scored by himself after he had collected his own towering up-and-under. Huddersfield fought back to 10-10 with only six minutes remaining but a try from Etty restored the lead and Neil capped a 16-10 victory, when he intercepted a sloppy pass and raced over from 15 yards.

Neil was restored to the test team when Ashton withdrew from the side to meet France at Bordeaux on 11 December 1960. Neil partnered Billy Boston for the first time and claimed two tries and two goals in a 21-10 victory. Injury kept him out of the return test at St Helens and dogged the latter half of his season. His returns of 18 tries and 81 goals (216 points) for Trinity seemed small beer in comparison to previous seasons – a telling reflection of the high expectations now placed on him.

It was back to normal service for Neil and Wakefield in 1961/62. Trinity had added to their forward strength by buying back Don Vines, who had spent a season at St Helens, and acquiring hooker Milan Kosanovic from Bradford and Dennis Williamson from Whitehaven. A third Springbok was added in centre/winger, Colin Greenwood.

Neil enjoyed a fantastically prolific season – his best, in fact. He topped the points scoring lists with a massive 456 (until then the second highest ever recorded behind Lewis Jones's 496 in 1956/57). Even today, it is the fifth highest total in history. He was also joint leading goal-kicker with Wigan's Fred Griffiths on 183. He extended his club records for Wakefield to 163 goals and 407 points in a season and they have yet to be broken. He equalled the club record for the second time, when he landed 11 goals in a 58-5 win over Dewsbury on 23 December 1961.

Such form inevitably made him a favourite with the representative selectors. He played for Yorkshire against the New Zealanders, Cumberland and Lancashire but, surprisingly, was only made travelling reserve for the first test against the Kiwis at Headingley on 30 September. New Zealand easily beat Britain 29-11 and Neil was recalled to play alongside Mick Sullivan, who had been dropped from the test team at Leeds for the first time in seven years. The second test

at Odsal on 21 October squared the series with a 23-10 win for the British, Sullivan scoring twice and Neil putting over four goals, including a monster 55-yard penalty – which even some of the Kiwis applauded. The following week the New Zealanders were beaten 20-7 by Wakefield, Neil picking up nine points but suffering a leg injury. Fortunately, it did not stop him turning out in the third test at Swinton on 4 November. Britain played dazzling football to win 35-19, thereby taking the series. Neil was in prime form and his kicking yielded seven goals to equal the record for Anglo-Kiwi test matches. Later in the season he played in two tests against France, both of which were lost.

A week after the third New Zealand test, Neil was again in top form with his boot. Trinity beat Leeds 19-9 at Odsal in the Yorkshire Cup final. They were made to fight hard to retain the trophy, however. Five goals, three from long distances and a final killing drop goal, were crucial. Smith, Skene and Turner scored tries.

Trinity's form was superb throughout 1961/62. Between 2 September and 17 March they went unbeaten for 28 games, only Batley taking a point off them in a 0-0 draw, which Neil missed. They finished second to Wigan on points averages, losing only 3 out of 36 league fixtures. In the Challenge Cup they disposed of Warrington 40-18, Neil being in coruscating form with four tries and five goals, Blackpool 16-4 (two tries and five goals), Wigan 5-4 (a goal) and Featherstone 9-0 (three goals). Their Wembley opponents on 12 May were Huddersfield, but prior to that they met Featherstone at Belle Vue in the Championship semi-final. Neil had an excellent game, making tries for Round and winger Ken Hirst but with five minutes remaining Rovers were level at 8-8. Wilkinson then crossed for a try from a pass that everyone on the ground, except the referee, thought was forward. Neil converted and Trinity progressed to the Championship final. Again their opponents were to be Huddersfield, who had sprung a huge surprise in winning 13-11 at Wigan.

Having won the Yorkshire Cup and the Yorkshire League, Wakefield entered the last two weekends of the season with a real possibility of winning All Four Cups and joining Hunslet (1907/08), Huddersfield (1914/15) and Swinton (1927/28) as history makers.

Huddersfield – solid, organized and high on team spirit – would prove tough opponents. At Wembley Neil Fox turned on one of his most memorable performances in a game that never hit the heights but held the attention of a crowd of over 81,000. Both sides scored two tries and for the only time in history no placed goal was kicked in a Challenge Cup final. Neil opened the scoring in the 17th minute by dropping a goal from 35 yards. A minute later Neil burst away down the left and sent Hirst flying down the wing. As he was clattered down by Frank Dyson, Hirst turned the ball back to the supporting Fox, who loped the final 35 yards to score at the flag. A try by scrum-half Tommy Smales brought Huddersfield back into the game. In the 63rd minute Neil dropped a second goal from 25 yards. That was immediately followed by a superb try from Hirst, following good work by Brian Briggs, and Trinity led 10-3. Huddersfield got back into the game with a try from Peter Ramsden but Neil settled the issue when he lashed over a third, 20-yard drop goal with the last act of the match. Trinity's 12-6 victory had been hard won. Neil had been the match-winner yet again and this time he won a prize – the Lance Todd Trophy.

According to many, Wakefield only had to turn up at Odsal the following week to take the Championship and complete their grand slam. They were undoubtedly the faster and cleverer side. Huddersfield were not going to lie down though and the weather on the day suited them just fine – lashings of wind and rain, which helped to churn up the pitch. The Fartowners tackled like demons, harried and frustrated Trinity, and got their reward, a 14-5 victory and the Championship. Neil had given Trinity a 5-2 lead. Jack Nott (*News of the World*) wrote, 'Fox, that young giant in physique and heart, cleaved out an opening and put Fred Smith through. This dynamic winger had a half-chance to make the flag but, shunning self-glory, he returned the ball inside for Fox, striding up in support, to go unopposed between the posts'. He converted his try but that was as good as it got for Wakefield.

Neil soon had other things to consider. A week later he was in Bathurst, adding another nine points to his record as Great Britain beat Western New South Wales 24-10. Also in the Lions XIII were fellow Trinitarians Round, Poynton, Wilkinson and Turner and his brother Don, who scored two tries. Unfortunately, Don's tour was curtailed through injury and he only played in five matches. Neil had a sensational tour. He played in 21 fixtures in Australasia – more than any other back – and he played in all five tests: 19 tries and 85 goals made him the leading scorer with 227 points. In the 56-13 victory over Northern New South Wales at Tamworth, Neil set a personal best of 32 points (4 tries, 10 goals).

Neil only made one Lions tour but it was one of the most successful and he played a big part in Britain's retention of the Ashes. The three-quarter line of Boston, Ashton, Fox and Sullivan remained intact throughout the Ashes series. It was a rare combination of intelligence, power, bellicosity and speed. Out of 13 tries in the series, 9 came from the three-quarters and Neil kept the scoreboard ticking with a dozen goals, as Britain won 31-12 at Sydney and 17-10 at Brisbane before being robbed 17-18 in the third test at the SCG by a last-minute try and goal from Ken Irvine. After losing the test series 0-2 in New Zealand, the injury-hit Lions visited South Africa and played three exhibition games against RL South Africa, which were won 49-30 (Pretoria), 39-33 (Durban) and 45-23 (Johannesburg). Neil's contributions were 22, 15 and 13 points respectively.

Wakefield's personnel underwent some changes in 1962/63. Neil acquired a new centre partner in the speedy Ian Brooke, Alan Skene leaving for Australia. Another South African arrived towards the end of the season in Gert Coetzer, who made an excellent finisher outside Neil. Trinity finished fifth in a newly formed First Division but continued their love affair with Wembley. This time their road was a hard one and unconvincing. A 15-3 win at Bradford was followed by a desperate 14-12 home defeat of Liverpool City, while the third round produced a 9-9 draw at York and a 25-11 replay victory. Warrington fell 5-2 to a try and a goal from Neil in the semi-final. On 11 May Trinity met Wigan in the final. Compared to the previous year, it was a spectacular affair, incident-packed and full of beautiful

Wembley, 1963. Neil Fox (extreme right) joins his team-mates Keith Holliday, Derek Turner and Gert Coetzer as they parade the Cup after Wakefield Trinity's 25-10 victory over Wigan.

movements. In the end Trinity won well, 25-10. Neil kicked five goals and earned his third and last Cup-winners' medal.

Earlier in the season he had won his first County Championship medal with Yorkshire, who beat Cumberland 11-2 and Lancashire 22-8. There were further honours and plenty of points against the French, when he played for an Eastern Division XIII in a 23-16 win at Carcassonne; for England who beat them 18-6 at Leeds; and for Great Britain who lost 12-17 at Perpignan but triumphed 42-4 at Wigan. In the latter test Neil scored 21 points (a try, nine goals) to equal the record for Anglo-French tests.

If Neil's experiences with the 1962 Lions represented the zenith of his test career, his encounters with the 1963 Kangaroos must have plumbed the depths. He had enjoyed an 11-5 victory with Yorkshire on 18 September at Craven Park, Hull, his four goals being decisive. The first test, however, at Wembley – his last appearance there – was a disaster as Britain were hammered 28-2. Neil scored Britain's points, a 50-yard penalty which bounced on the cross-bar. The second test at Swinton was even worse, finishing as a 50-12 runaway for the Kangaroos. Neil kicked three goals and made a thunderous 60-yard run to set up a try for Stopford. In both games injuries hit Britain hard and no substitutes were allowed. The Aussies were, nonetheless, just brilliant. Neil also played in the Trinity team which lost 14-29 to them, his seven goals providing his side's points.

On 18 March 1964 Neil had more luck, when he equalled his own record in scoring 21 points in a 39-0 test victory over France at Leigh. At the season's close he had scored 313 points to top the scoring list. Remarkably, Don Fox was runner-up on 301.

Neil succeeded Derek Turner as captain at Wakefield in 1964/65. It was his tenth season in senior rugby but he was only twenty-five. In a period of change he led Trinity to fourth place in the league, to the Challenge Cup and Championship semi-finals and to an 18-2 victory over Leeds in the Yorkshire Cup final, in which he scored 12 points. Despite added responsibility and nagging injuries, he scored 262 points for Trinity and for a third time equalled the club record by landing 11 goals against Keighley. He also passed the 1,000 goals mark for his club, was a member of Yorkshire's Championship-winning team and won a test match (17-7) against France at Swinton by kicking seven goals.

Neil took a benefit in 1965/66 but missed the early weeks of the season with appendicitis. Trinity again finished fourth but had tangible reward in winning the Yorkshire League. On 25 September Neil made his first appearance of the season at Doncaster, an occasion made special by his brother Don's debut for Wakefield. Neil's representative rugby was restricted to a winning Roses Match and a losing test in Perpignan, when he was captain.

In 1966/67 Neil gave up Trinity's captaincy, Harold Poynton taking over. He did, however, skipper Yorkshire for the first time, earned another County Championship-winners' medal and was restored to the test team for two games against France. Wakefield made history by winning the Championship for the first time, beating St Helens 21-9 in a replayed final at Swinton after a 7-7 draw at Leeds. After eleven years Neil had now won every honour in the game.

The following season he added a few more as Trinity retained the Championship, beating Hull KR 17-10 in the final at Leeds. Unfortunately, a groin injury kept him out of the Wakefield side that attempted to win the double at Wembley a week later. He consequently missed the notorious 'Watersplash Final' against Leeds, immortalized by Don Fox's last-minute

Neil Fox runs in the ball in Wakefield's 18-5 third round Challenge Cup victory against Castleford in 1968.

miscued conversion. That injury also forced him to give up the captaincy of Great Britain's 1968 World Cup squad down under, reinforcing the disappointment of never having played in such a tournament. His form had been good enough to bring him a place in the second Ashes test and he had given one of his virtuoso displays in captaining Yorkshire against the Australians at Belle Vue. He had scored a try, made two, and kicked three goals, including a last-minute effort which won the game 15-14. He had also captained Britain to victory in two tests against France. On 26 August 1967 Neil had finally broken his own records in kicking 12 goals and scoring 33 points in a 78-9 swamping of Batley.

Neil's representative career ended at Toulouse on 2 February 1969, when he kicked three goals in a 9-13 loss to France. A few months later the rugby league world was shocked when he transferred from Wakefield to Bradford. He only remained at Odsal for a season before returning as player-coach to Trinity. He put in four more seasons at Wakefield, adding 890 points to his mammoth tally. No trophies were won but Trinity were beaten finalists in the inaugural Players Trophy final in 1972 and the 1973 Yorkshire Cup final.

In 1970 Neil began to play at loose-forward but did not convert fully to the pack until he transferred to Second Division Hull KR for the 1974/75 season. There, as a second-rower, Neil had a new lease of life. He broke the club points record with 333, topping the league's scoring list, and his 146 goals was also the season's best. Ironically, he landed two goals as Rovers beat Wakefield 16-13 in the Yorkshire Cup final and Rovers won promotion. In his second season with Rovers he won the White Rose Trophy in their 11-15 defeat by Leeds in the 1975 Yorkshire Cup final.

Spells at York, Bramley and Huddersfield followed, promotion being won with the latter pair. It was as a Fartowner that Neil finally broke Jim Sullivan's seemingly impregnable world record of 6,022 points on 2 January 1978. With his third of four goals in a 22-15 home victory over Oldham, he became the most prolific scorer in history – although sadly no one knew it at the time. Neil's final port of call was Bradford Northern, whom he joined for a second time in February 1978. His brother Peter was coach and was fully aware of how useful Neil, now thirty-eight, could still be, if used judiciously. Neil repaid him handsomely, figuring as a substitute in Northern's 17-8 Premiership final victory over Widnes at Swinton on 20 May 1978 and kicking three conversions a few months later in yet another Yorkshire Cup final victory (18-8) over York. That was his last final, although, but for injury, he could have played in Northern's Premiership final against Leeds in 1979. At the age of forty, Neil Fox played his 828th and last game as a professional on 19 August 1979, kicking two goals in Bradford's 22-7 victory at Huddersfield in a first round Yorkshire Cup-tie.

His playing career continued, however, with the amateurs at Underbank Rangers, where, by a delightful coincidence, that other master centre and Hall of Famer, Harold Wagstaff, had begun his career. Neil was awarded the MBE in June 1983 and has for several years served on the Advisory Panel of the Rugby Football League.

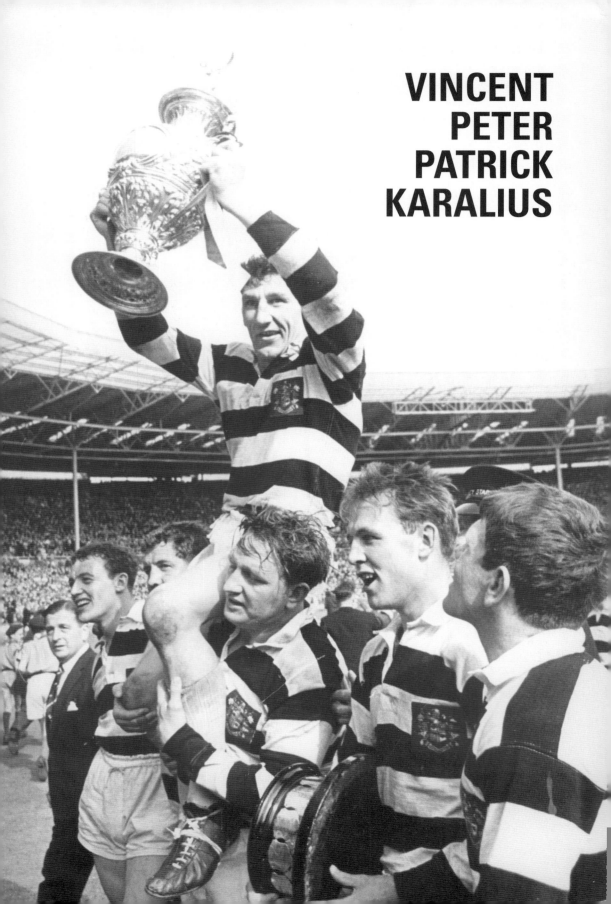

VINCENT PETER PATRICK KARALIUS

ST HELENS

Debut: 2 April 1952 v Warrington (h)
Last game: 13 January 1962 v Leeds (a)

	A	T	G	P
1951/52	6	-	-	-
1952/53	15	1	-	3
1953/54	19	1	-	3
1954/55	2	-	-	-
1955/56	31	8	-	24
1956/57	38	18	-	54
1957/58	33	6	-	18
1958/59	34	5	-	15
1959/60	30	-	-	-
1960/61	32	2	-	6
1961/62	12	-	-	-

WIDNES

Debut: 17 March 1962 v Barrow (h)
Last game: 19 March 1966 v Bradford
Northern (h), cup

	A	T	G	P
1961/62	10	2	-	6
1962/63	44	3	-	9
1963/64	35	-	-	-
1964/65	25	-	-	-
1965/66	18	1	-	3

TESTS (12)

Great Britain	25	Australia	18	1958	Brisbane
Great Britain	40	Australia	17	1958	Sydney
Great Britain	10	N Zealand	15	1958	Auckland
Great Britain	32	N Zealand	15	1958	Auckland
Great Britain	50	France	15	1959	Leeds
Great Britain	23	N Zealand	8	1960	Bradford*
Great Britain	33	France	7	1960	Swinton*
Great Britain	10	Australia	3	1960	Bradford*
Great Britain	21	France	10	1960	Bordeaux
Great Britain	27	France	8	1961	St Helens
Great Britain	2	Australia	28	1963	Wembley
Great Britain	12	Australia	50	1963	Swinton

* World Cup

LANCASHIRE (10)

Lancashire	42	Cumberland	21	1956	Wigan
Lancashire	60	Cumberland	12	1958	Wigan
Lancashire	19	Yorkshire	35	1958	Hull KR
Lancashire	15	Yorkshire	16	1958	Leigh
Lancashire	8	Cumberland	14	1959	Workington
Lancashire	28	Cumberland	8	1962	Widnes
Lancashire	8	Yorkshire	22	1962	Wakefield
Lancashire	45	Yorkshire	20	1963	St Helens (1 try)
Lancashire	13	Australians	11	1963	Wigan
Lancashire	8	Cumberland	13	1963	Whitehaven

CAREER RECORD

	A	T	G	P
St Helens	252	41	-	123
Widnes	132	6	-	18
Tests	12	-	-	-
Lancashire	10	1	-	3
Represent	4	-	-	-
1958 Tour*	13	3	-	9
TOTALS	423	51	-	153

* Excluding tests

VINCENT PETER PATRICK KARALIUS
The Wild Bull

Vince Karalius was admitted to the Rugby League Hall of Fame in November 2000, along with his former St Helens team-mate Tom van Vollenhoven and Roger Millward. As a player Vince was both fearless and fearsome, one of the greatest loose-forwards rugby league has ever produced. However, his election to the Hall of Fame was probably the most contentious of the thirteen so far inducted into this illustrious band of immortals. Prior to Vince's elevation, no forward had entered the Hall of Fame. Theoretically, therefore, Vince must be regarded as the pre-eminent forward in the history of British rugby league.

Players and fans who remember the era in which Vince played will certainly argue the toss as to whether he was a better loose-forward than Hull's elegant and athletic Johnny Whiteley or the ferocious, footballing Derek 'Rocky' Turner (Hull KR, Oldham and Wakefield Trinity). The three were almost exactly contemporary and all three captained Great Britain and, indeed, once played together as a back-row unit in test rugby. Others will ask was he better – whatever that means – than earlier giants of forward play such as Frank Gallagher, Joe Egan, Dave Valentine or those wonderful Cumbrians, Douglas Clark and Martin Hodgson ... and what about Alan Prescott and Brian McTigue, his colleagues in several hard-fought tests? Observers of more recent times would probably ask if he was superior to Malcolm Reilly or Ellery Hanley because, if he was, he must have been one hell of a forward.

The truth is that Vince Karalius *was* one hell of a forward. Alex Murphy, who played at scrum-half with Vince more than any other man, has no doubt as to Vince's status. In 1967 Alex wrote, 'No scrum-half ever received the same perfect cover from his loose-forward as I did from Karalius ... He was like a father, a James Bond, and a lion looking after his offspring when it came to protection for his little 'un, either round or away from the scrum ... Believe me, you had to play alongside Karalius to value him to the hilt. You soon appreciated that there was more, far more, to his magnificent play than just first-time, tremendous tackling. There was his leadership ... all that courage which was almost too much to be wrapped in one man ... his streamlined pass work ... his almost frightening 'killer' instinct ... his power on that vital short burst ... Vinty took some batterings throughout his career. He didn't always have things his own way. But never once did I hear him "squeal".'

In discussing the loose-forward position in his imaginary best ever team in 1993, Murphy said, 'Sorry, I can't find room for Ellery Hanley. Vince Karalius and Johnny Raper were both better in this role. If Vince and Ellery were marking each other, it would be no contest. Vince would win every time. He was so fit he used to run fourteen miles before training.'

Johnny Raper, one of five original and official Australian rugby league 'Immortals', agreed with Murphy, when he picked his own dream team for his autobiography, writing, 'In the position I played and loved, loose-forward, Vince Karalius would be my choice – an irresistible force, and behind him in the second-row would be Derek Turner. Turner was remarkable, tough and mean on the field, capable of handing out terrific punishment and then, in the blinking of an eye, doing something fantastic with a ball on attack.'

For his part, Vince selected Johnny Whiteley as his loose-forward in his own ideal World XIII in his autobiography (1964). As recently as 16 December 2002, Whiteley repaid the compliment in *League Weekly* by choosing Vince for his Dream XIII of the last half-century. His verdict on Karalius ran, 'Johnny Raper and Ray Price were strong contenders for the No.13 jersey but Vinty, fearless and destructive, is my choice because, together with Alex Murphy, he would lock the whole thing together. Feared and respected by the Australians, Vinty had enormous strength and his tackling was devastating. An inspirational figure, who had skill as well.'

Vince was a good man to have on your side but an implacable opponent. He played the game as hard as he could but within the rules. His defence was cruel and he was famous for his crushing bear-hugging, ball-and-all tackles. No opponent was too big or strong to escape his clutches and he revelled in the fiercest of confrontations. Vince admitted that he psyched himself up for games by developing a type of hate complex, instilling in himself the absolute belief that he would dominate the opposition. No one would, as the Australians say, monster him. Allied to his aggression and self-belief was a lifelong obsession with fitness. Not even the most gifted player in the game would be fitter than him. As a ball-handler, too, Vince could cut the mustard. He had enormous hands which enabled him to get the ball away even when apparently overwhelmed by tacklers. Some of the best running forwards in world rugby benefited prodigiously from Vince's dexterity.

By any standards in any era, Vince Karalius would have stood out as an exceptional forward. He is one of the few players who could genuinely claim to have become legends in their own times. Yet he came comparatively late to the game.

Born in Widnes on 15 October 1932, Vince Karalius was one of seven brothers, who had a solitary sister. His grandparents were Lithuanian but his mother was Irish-born and his father was born in Scotland. He grew up with an avid interest in sport but his main interest was soccer and his position was goalkeeper. Rugby was not on his agenda until he was sixteen when he went to watch a local game at West Bank Juniors and was persuaded to make up the numbers, as West Bank were a man short. He loved the game from the off and soon attracted attention. Quickest off the mark were St Helens, whose trainer Peter Lyons recognized a good 'un when he saw one. Lyons had been trainer for Lancashire, England and Wales. Ironically, Lyons, a native Widnesian and a former Widnes and Salford scrum-half, had left Widnes after more than two decades as their trainer and joined St Helens. Otherwise Vince might have joined Widnes. In August 1951 Saints took him on a six-match trial but quickly decided he was good enough and Vince was given a £200 signing-on fee. Sadly, Peter Lyons died on 10 October 1952 and did not see his protégé fulfil his expectations.

Vince made his first-team debut on 2 April 1952, when 13,054 saw Warrington beaten 13-5 at Knowsley Road. He played loose-forward in the last half-dozen games of the season, four of which were lost, as Saints plummeted from sixth in the league in 1950/51 to a lowly twentieth in 1951/52. That performance was a sign of massive underachievement at Knowsley Road, for the available players were of a high calibre. The three-quarters, for example – Steve Llewellyn, Duggie Greenall, Don Gullick and Stan McCormick – were arguably as good as any other back line in the league, while there were some talented half-backs on the books in Todder Dickinson, Tommy Finn, Peter Metcalfe and George Langfield, and a sound full-back in Jimmy Lowe. The pack, led by test prop Alan Prescott, had plenty of firepower in Bill Bretherton, George Parr, George Parsons, Bill Whittaker, Max Garbler and Ray Cale.

The underachievement was banished when Jim Sullivan took over as coach for 1952/53. Saints gelled immediately and finished the season at the top of the league, never suffering defeat in an away league fixture, a unique achievement at the time. Jim Sullivan was a huge influence on Vince, who displayed two of the cardinal virtues the coach revered – courage and dedication to fitness. However, it took Vince a few years to establish himself as a regular in the Saints first team. During 1952/53 he played in only 15 games but qualified for four medals. Saints reached the Lancashire Cup final, only to lose surprisingly to Leigh 5-22 at Swinton before more than 34,000 spectators. Vince earned his medal in this competition by appearing in first and semi-final rounds. Saints won the Lancashire League Championship by ten clear points from Leigh and reached the Challenge Cup and Championship finals. Vince played in first and second round Cup-ties against Oldham and Belle Vue Rangers but was not required for the Wembley final in which Saints went down fighting – literally according to an enraged press corps – 10-15 to Huddersfield. They made some amends two weeks later in beating Halifax 24-14 in the Championship final at Maine Road. Vince played in neither final, being understudy to Welsh RU International Ray Cale. Bizarrely, Cale, regarded as the best back-rower in European rugby union, was left out of the 1950 British Isles squad for Australasia because he was regarded as too rough for New Zealand sensibilities! No wonder Vince had to wait a while to claim the No.13 jersey.

One of the highlights of the season for Vince was an appearance against the touring Kangaroos, who were beaten 26-8 before a crowd of 18,000 at Knowsley Road on 27 September 1952. The Australians lost only that game in 22 fixtures against club sides. Vince had stood up well to all that was thrown at him and laid down a marker for what would occur six years later.

Saints dropped to third in 1953/54, by which time Vince had been called up for National Service. His posting did not allow him to play much rugby but he relished the physical training involved in service life and came out of the Army fitter, stronger and weighing over 14st – well over a stone heavier than when he went in. A notable occasion for him in this period was his first appearance in a major final on 24 October 1953. Saints, under skipper Duggie Greenall, met Wigan at Swinton with a record 42,793 in attendance in the Lancashire Cup final. A pulsating game saw Saints turn a 4-8 half-time deficit into a 16-8 victory, their first in the Lancashire Cup since 1926. It was Vince's and his pack-mates' superior stamina and stand-off Peter Metcalfe's dead shot goal-kicking, which finally killed off the Wigan challenge.

Vince was only available for a couple of games in 1954/55 but returned to big-time action at the start of a momentous 1955/56 season. He played much of the season in the second-row until taking over from Garbler as loose-forward for the last three months. It was as a second-rower that Vince won his first representative honour, playing alongside Harry Bath for a Northern Rugby League XIII, which defeated the New Zealanders 24-11 at Odsal on 7 December 1955. David Nicholls (*Daily Express*) gave his verdict on Vince's performance, 'Established performers like Harry Bath, Albert Naughton, Brian Bevan and Jack McLean did all we expected, and there was rich promise in the first game outside club rugby for Vincent Karalius'. Vince's winning pay amounted to £10 and it was probably the first time he had appeared in a televised match, although technical hitches and scheduling difficulties reduced viewing time to only ten minutes.

Vince and St Helens hit top form when the 1956 Challenge Cup got underway. In the first round they had a magnificent 15-6 home victory over the reigning Champions, Warrington, before a crowd of 24,230. Castleford (48-5) and Bradford Northern (53-6) were annihilated in the following rounds but things were decidedly harder against Barrow in the semi-final on 7 April at Swinton. Saints salvaged a 5-5 draw through an Austin Rhodes penalty goal in the last ten minutes. The replay at Wigan the following Wednesday meant that Vince had to forego reserve duty for Great Britain against France at Odsal on the same evening. The replay proved to be one of those unforgettable games. At the end of eighty minutes there was no score but the teams received a standing ovation for their efforts. Saints eventually pulled clear with tries from Llewellyn and Parsons, plus two goals from Rhodes, to win an epic encounter 10-5. Vince was packed off to hospital clutching part of his ear, which had to be sown back on – never mind, Wembley awaited.

Vince was kept out of action for Saints' last three league games to allow the wound to heal. He was desperate to play in the final against Halifax and there was talk of him playing in a scrum-cap to protect his ear. He did not fancy that and Jim Sullivan agreed, feeling that it would actually draw attention to the injury. By coincidence, Saints had to visit Halifax on 21 April the week before Wembley, in the Championship semi-final. Vince emerged unscathed and scored a try but Saints were trounced 23-8 and lost Todder Dickinson through an injury, which cost him a Wembley place.

The St Helens team which lost at Halifax in the 1956 Championship semi-final. From left to right, back row: Silcock, Rhodes, McIntyre, Terry, Parsons, Llewellyn, Greenall. Front: Carlton, Moses, Prescott, Dickinson, Finnan, Karalius.

Panic stations for Workington Town as Vince Karalius plunges through their defence before a packed Knowsley Road.

Saints went into the Challenge Cup final on 28 April as second favourites but were confident they could reverse the previous week's result and become the first team to bring back the Challenge Cup to St Helens. Their biggest problem would be to subdue the Halifax pack, one of the toughest to have played the game. They had also done their homework. Almost at the kick-off Alan Prescott clattered loose-forward Ken Traill, whose cleverness had tormented Saints in the Championship semi, and he was not his usual self thereafter. For 66 minutes there was no score for the crowd of almost 80,000 to cheer as a war of attrition raged between the packs. The stalemate was finally broken when Vince began the move which launched winger Frank Carlton on a wonderful 70-yard run to the line. The floodgates opened and Llewellyn went over on the other wing before Vince crashed through in the final minute to send Prescott over for a third try. Saints had won 13-2 and finally broken their Challenge Cup hoodoo. Tom Longworth (*News Chronicle & Daily Dispatch*) summed up Vince's display succinctly: 'Vince Karalius was wonderfully effective'. Coach Jim Sullivan (*News of the World*) concurred, writing, 'Young Vince Karalius had a magnificent match' … and he should know!

In 1956/57 Vince began to make further inroads into representative rugby. He won his first Lancashire cap on 6 September when Cumberland were beaten 42-21 at Wigan and was selected to play for Great Britain against The Rest of the League on 3 October. The game was a virtual test trial for the forthcoming Ashes series. Britain won 26-23 but when the test team was chosen, York's Edgar Dawson, who had played for The Rest, got the nod for the first test, while Derek Turner played in the remaining two tests. Vince had also been outshone by Turner on 20 October when Saints lost 3-10 to Oldham in the Lancashire Cup final. There was, however, a rebuke for the selectors, when Saints completely overran the Kangaroos on 24 November inflicting a record 44-2 defeat. Vince was among the try-scorers on that memorable occasion. He scored no fewer than 18 tries for St Helens in 1956/57, including hat-tricks against Whitehaven and Barrow. Try-scoring was not, however, one of Vince's specialities or priorities. Stopping and making them was his business. He would never get into double figures again in a season. In fact his remaining 141 games for Saints would only yield another 13 tries.

A couple of other notable occurrences took place for Vince in that season. On 27 October Saints lost 9-11 to Workington Town at Knowsley Road and for the first time Alex Murphy played at scrum-half in combination with Vince, the start of a truly dynamic partnership. Later, on 2 and 9 March 1957, Vince had the unusual experience of playing in the centre against Halifax and Wigan – an experiment which was never repeated.

The following season saw St Helens finish second in the table to Oldham, losing only 6 of 38 league games. No trophies were won or finals reached, however, and, on a personal level, Vince was overlooked by Lancashire, who preferred Leigh's Peter Foster, and by Great Britain, who chose Derek Turner for all three tests against France. By the turn of the year Vince was not happy with his standard of play and considered taking a break from playing. He persevered, however, but had a jolt when he was sent off in a hectic 15-0 victory in a first round Challenge Cup tie at Hunslet on 12 February. Sending off sufficient was the verdict of the disciplinary committee and he breathed more easily. The selectors were preparing to select the 1958 Australasian tourists and any substantial suspension could have seriously threatened Vince's remaining hopes of touring. He finally got his chance when he was picked to play in the second and final tour trial at Leeds on 19 March in partnership with Murphy in the Green XIII. He took his opportunity with both those huge hands, figuring in several scoring moves as the Whites were overwhelmed 41-18.

Three days later the touring party was announced and there for the first time was the holy trinity of Derek Turner, Johnny Whiteley and Vince Karalius. It was quickly dissolved as Turner withdrew for business reasons. The original 26-man party did not, in fact, include Vince but when the selection panel's list of tourists was presented to Tom Mitchell, the tour team manager, he insisted that he be included, knowing that he was exactly the type of forward needed for the furnace of Ashes rugby. So the selectors added Vince to the list and omitted Brian Edgar, who, ironically, played for Mitchell's club Workington Town. Fortunately for Edgar, he was restored to the Lions party when Oldham's Syd Little withdrew.

Mitchell's faith in Vince was eventually fully validated. In his memoirs (1998), Tom wrote of him, 'Vince Karalius (was) the protector of the best half-back in the world on the 1958 tour. He was dynamite, a perfect physical specimen who tackled forwards much bigger so hard you'd think his muscles were made of steel. A man who showed incredible bravery and lifted the Lions by just being on the field. The three-quarters knew the Australian back-row forwards would behave themselves with Vince on the field. Without him I'm sure we would never have won the Ashes in 1958 yet he nearly didn't make it. The tour selectors left him out because one said he was hard to handle. What rubbish! I insisted he went and, thank goodness, I got my way. He was one of the easiest men to get along with in terms of conduct. The Australians nicknamed him the Wild Bull of the Pampas. Yet he wasn't wild. Vince was controlled and measured; everything was done with a purpose. And he wasn't a bull either. If you had to compare him to an animal it would be a tiger.'

Vince played in five of the first seven tour fixtures and was soon established as one of the men the Aussies would have to tame. He was a certainty for the test team. Then, on 7 June, a week before the first test, disaster struck. Britain beat New South Wales, a virtual test in itself, 19-10 before a rabid crowd of almost 53,000 at the Sydney Cricket Ground. The game was brutal and finally exploded in the 51st minute when winger Peter Dimond – his middle name should have been Rough – hit Vince with a late tackle. Vince hit back, laid Dimond out and was sent off. He was eventually followed by three New South Welshmen – Rex Mossop, Greg Hawick and Peter Dimond. Vince was charged with kicking Dimond, an offence to which he would never stoop, although he did admit to punching in retaliation. Amazingly, Vince's punishment was a suspension until 22 June, which effectively meant three matches, including the first test. Most tourists down the years in both hemispheres received sending off sufficient verdicts. Ironically, Dimond was found guilty of kicking British winger Mick Sullivan.

Britain were trounced 25-8 in the first test but from then on did not lose again in Australia and only once in New Zealand. Frustratingly, Vince suffered an injury in training, causing fluid on his knee, and did not appear again until 29 June when Britain massacred North Queensland 78-17 at Townsville. His knee stood the test and the following Saturday Vince took the field at loose-forward for his debut in test rugby. The game, played at Brisbane Exhibition Ground, has gone down in the annals of test rugby league as 'Prescott's Match' or 'Prescott's Epic' – an encounter Britain won despite mind-boggling odds.

After only two minutes the Lions captain Alan Prescott broke his right forearm but fearlessly and miraculously carried on propping for the whole game. After 17 minutes stand-off Dave Bolton was taken to hospital with a fractured collar-bone and was joined there after the game by full-back Eric Fraser (elbow), centre Jim Challinor (shoulder) and Vince (spine). Vince found himself pressed into service at stand-off following Bolton's departure. His half-back pairing with Murphy was a big factor in Britain's play. The Lions simply refused to be cowed and continued to play open rugby so effectively that they led 10-2 at half-time and denied Australia a try until the 55th minute. Late in the game the Australians hit back to trail 13-20 but the makeshift St Helens halves drove the final nail into their coffin. One report ran, 'Murphy and Karalius made an extremely fine pair of half-backs. Time after time they dazzled the Australian defence with the brilliance of their moves. The last try was a gem. It started on the 25-yard line when Murphy broke neatly away from a scrum and threw an accurate pass to Karalius. The big forward slipped inside, drawing the defence before handing back to Murphy, who went like a hare for the Australian line and touched down between the posts.' That took the score to 25-13 and even a late converted try to Australia could not remove the lustre from one of Great Britain's most famous test victories. The crowd of 32,965 Queenslanders could scarcely believe what they had seen.

Tom Mitchell's report to the RFL on the second test at Brisbane lavished praise on Vince: 'Vincent Karalius, playing magnificently and tackling everything in sight, suddenly appeared to lose some of his fire. It transpired that he had strained his back in such a fashion that he had not the full use of his legs. Up to this time – twenty minutes – he had engaged in destroying half the Australian pack and the half-backs. Nothing questionable, just ferocious tackling at its very best. He completed the game, playing himself into the ground in the process. Karalius has been playing better here in Australia than in those games I saw him playing in back home. He is just the inspiration the team needs against the Aussies. I rather fancy that O'Shea and Provan don't like him very much, and sending him out here was an inspired move by the home selectors. He is a hard and conscientious trainer.'

The third test at Sydney on 19 July was another triumph although this time there were no serious casualties. Vince remained in the pack throughout, forming a virile and devastating back three with Johnny Whiteley and Dick Huddart. In the second half Britain were simply scintillating and ran out easy winners 40-17, a record Ashes score at the time. The Australian crowd, 68,720 of them, were nonplussed. The referee, Jack Casey, bore the brunt of their displeasure when he awarded Britain a dubious try, not that it made any difference to the result. He was pelted with all kinds of fruit and rubbish, provoking much heated discussion in the Australian newspapers about the lack of sportsmanship in Sydney crowds.

Although Phil Jackson was captain for this Ashes-clinching test, the Lions players chaired stricken Alan Prescott around the SCG with the Ashes cup (supported by his one good arm) after the game. Prescott wrote in the *Daily Express*, 'Our forwards! They were magnificent. Vince Karalius has been the key man in this series and I can't praise his play highly enough. In this match Brian McTigue was almost as outstanding.'

Moving on to New Zealand Vince scored his first tour try in the opening match, a 59-7 victory over the Maoris at Huntly on 23 July. Three days later Britain went down to their second defeat of the tour with a 10-15 reverse to New Zealand at Carlaw Park, Auckland. Tiredness – Vince, Dick Huddart, Tommy Harris, Alan Davies and Eric Ashton were all playing their third game in seven days – and understandable reaction to the rigours of the Ashes-clincher probably accounted for a below-par performance. The second and final test, before a second 25,000 crowd at Carlaw Park, saw a return to swashbuckling rugby league as Vince and his colleagues ran away with the game 32-15, after trailing 10-12 at the interval. The tour ended with three more games in Australia, Vince playing in all of them. The last game of the tour, at Perth on 24 August, saw Vince score his second and third tries for the Lions in his nineteenth tour match. However, it was Mick Sullivan, playing at stand-off, who took all the honours in the 69-23 romp against Western Australia. His seven tries gave him an all-time Lions record of 38 tour tries.

Vince, now almost twenty-six, returned from Australasia with a sky-high reputation and a tour bonus of £567. He returned to action for St Helens in a 12-2 second round Lancashire Cup victory at Leigh on 8 September 1958. Two days later he was reunited with seven of his tour colleagues at Wigan, where Lancashire inflicted a 60-12 humiliation on Cumberland, an all-time record score for the County Championship. He also played twice against Yorkshire, who beat Lancashire 35-19 at Craven Park, Hull and 16-15 in a play-off final at Leigh.

St Helens topped the league table but lost 2-12 in the Lancashire Cup final to Oldham on 25 October and Vince had to be satisfied with a runners-up medal. His performances in a red-hot Saints combination continued to be top-notch and he was selected for the test against France at Headingley on 14 March 1959. Twelve of the 1958 Lions were in the side plus Wakefield Trinity second-rower Don Vines. Britain gave a magnificent display of open rugby, although there were quite a few flare-ups, and won 50-15. Alex Murphy was the star with four tries. Vince provided him with the first and 'was always there, backing up, prompting and combining with the little St Helens crackerjack', according to one report. There was also a magical rapid passing duet between Vince and Vines, which led to the latter scoring. Unfortunately, Vince had to withdraw from the return test at Grenoble, which was lost 15-24.

Saints continued to set the pace in the race for the Championship, although they did come unstuck on 27 March against their closest rivals Wigan at Central Park. Despite scoring four tries to three, they lost 14-19 but Vince, and his brother, Dennis, shared the distinction of playing before the largest crowd ever to attend a league fixture – 47,477. When Saints finished first in the table and Wigan second, it seemed odds on that they would contest the Championship final but Wigan surprisingly lost 11-22 to Hunslet in the semi-final. Saints cruised through their semi-final, crushing Oldham 42-4.

The final, at Odsal on 16 May, was a truly exceptional game, punctuated by a series of spell-binding tries, the famous Vollenhoven wonder-try being merely the best of many. Saints eventually pulverized gallant Hunslet 44-22 but not before they had fallen 4-12 behind in the first quarter. The Saints pack of Terry, McKinney, Prescott, Briggs, Huddart and Karalius – all test men – was outstanding. Vince was in his element and once again his linking with Murphy in mid-field operations was crucial. It was the only Championship final in which Vince would ever participate and poignantly it was the finale of his mentor Jim Sullivan as coach of St Helens.

After a tremendously successful couple of years, Vince found the 1959/60 season somewhat trying, despite the facts that Saints were again runaway league leaders at the season's close and that he earned another Lancashire League Championship winners' medal. Trouble with fluid on the knee really dislocated the first half of Vince's season. The only representative football he played was for Lancashire against Cumberland – an 8-14 defeat at Workington on 31 August. He played only intermittently for Saints and missed their Lancashire Cup final defeat against Warrington on 31 October. Ironically, his brother Dennis had joined Warrington and he too missed the final with a knee injury. Even more disconcertingly, Vince was denied any opportunity to test himself against the 1959 Kangaroos, for Saints, Lancashire or Great Britain, although the selectors did hold a place open for him in the second test in the forlorn hope that his injury might clear in time.

By Christmas he had played in only 11 of St Helens' 25 fixtures but when he did squeeze in appearances he was often a dominant figure. A typical press notice from a 29-11 victory over Hull on 24 October (*Sunday People*) read, 'The presence of Vinty Karalius – in only his second game after injury – made me think of test victories at Brisbane and Sydney and a probable test win at Headingley on November 21. Great Britain's almost certain loose-forward choice was the personality of the match as he pugnaciously stalked his prey around the scrums. How he made little Alec Murphy play. The teenaged scrum-half was in his most scintillating mood alongside Karalius.' Sadly, his knee flared up again and put him out of seven of the next eleven games. Even so, the test selectors picked him as a second-rower for the third Ashes test at Wigan on 12 December. His ill-luck continued to dog him and he withdrew on the morning of the match with a back injury.

The 1960/61 campaign began with some trouble at St Helens. Alex Murphy requested a transfer, Austin Rhodes wanted to be relieved of the captaincy and Vince was unavailable for the first month. Happily, all three problems were sorted out and Murphy, Rhodes and Karalius won the biggest honours the game had to offer in the course of the season. Vince took over the captaincy on 3 September in his first match of the season, a 5-18 home loss to

A ferocious Vince Karalius heads for Wigan prop John Barton in a second round Lancashire Cup tie in 1960. St Helens won 7-4.

Wakefield, but four days later, with 29,000 in attendance, inspired his side to a 7-4 victory over Wigan in the second round of the Lancashire Cup. His captaincy reaped immediate dividends as Saints won their next fourteen games, which included their 15-9 victory over Swinton at Wigan in the Lancashire Cup final on 29 October.

Much water passed under the bridge before then, however. Vince's late start to the season could have jeopardized his chances of making the Great Britain World Cup squad. He was, however, chosen for the World Cup trial at Knowsley Road on 12 September. He was named as second-row alongside Johnny Whiteley with Derek Turner at loose-forward for Great Britain against The Rest. Vince had a habit of turning up just before kick-off for games as part of his ritual, an unusual procedure, especially now that he had embarked upon a career in captaincy, but it worked for him in those less regimented, part-time, days of the 1950s and '60s. On this

Vince Karalius strides past the Warrington half-back Bobbie Greenough, a colleague in the 1960 World Cup squad.

Great Britain's victorious 1960 World Cup squad. From left to right, back row: Fallowfield (manager), McTigue, B. Shaw, Turner, Davies, Fraser, Boston, Wilkinson, Challinor. Seated: Sullivan, Whiteley, Ashton, Harris, Murphy. Front: J. Shaw, Rhodes, Geenough, Myler, Karalius.

occasion his time-keeping went awry and he missed the trial. The selectors must have realized his full value and overlooked the incident. He was picked along with fellow Saints, Rhodes and Murphy, and his cousin, the Widnes stand-off, Frank Myler, in the eighteen-man squad. His great rivals, Turner and Whiteley, were also selected.

On 24 September all three played in Britain's opening 23-8 victory over New Zealand at Bradford, Vince in the second-row with Whiteley. A week later France were beaten 33-7 at Swinton in a heated game. Vince and French skipper Jean Barthe were sent off in the 65th minute after a stand-up fight at a play-the-ball. Fortunately, neither received a suspension and Vince was able to take his place at loose-forward – replacing the injured Whiteley – for the deciding game against Australia at Odsal on 8 October. In terrible conditions Vince played one of the most outstanding games of his career. His tackling was cruelly efficient and his passing sparked the two tries scored by Billy Boston and Mick Sullivan, which gave Britain a 10-3 victory and the World Cup.

Vince retained his place in the tests against France at Bordeaux (won 21-10) and St Helens (won 27-8) in December and January, being easily the game's best forward in the latter. In domestic football Vince led Saints all the way to Wembley, dismissing Widnes, Castleford, Swinton and Hull. He had an almighty scare along the way, however. On 31 March Saints lost 2-12 at Wigan and Vince was taken off after 19 minutes with torn knee ligaments. The injury kept him out for a month, causing him to miss the 26-9 semi-final win over Hull. He returned in the last league game of the season and scored one of his rare tries in a 38-0 home rout of Featherstone. A fortnight later, on 13 May, he led Saints out against Wigan at Wembley before

Halifax forward Jack Scroby runs into trouble in the shape of Vince Karalius and Tom van Vollenhoven at Thrum Hall in 1961.

Vince Karalius receiving the Lancashire Cup in 1961 after captaining St Helens to a 25-9 victory over Swinton at Wigan.

Vince Karalius raises the Challenge Cup after St Helens' 12-6 success against Wigan. Also pictured are Alex Murphy, Cliff Watson, Dick Huddart, Bob Dagnall and Abe Terry.

94,672 spectators. Saints won 12-6 on a sweltering afternoon. Vince was commanding. He had a hand in both tries, scored by Murphy and Vollenhoven. In fact if Vince had not had the wit to open out play near his own line by passing to Large, Voll's try of the century would not have occurred. Jack Paul (*Sunday Express*) wrote, 'There was always "King" Karalius to worry Wigan with his prompting and probing, and his lovely passes which, time after time, sent lanky Dick Huddart striding into the open spaces, cracking tackle after tackle.'

Wembley 1961 was the pinnacle of Vince's career with St Helens but, within a year, he had moved to his native Widnes for a fee of £4,500. He missed the first eight games of the season but returned to lead Saints to another Lancashire Cup final victory over Swinton and to a 25-10 defeat of the Kiwis. December 1961 saw matters unravel for Vince at Knowsley Road. On 9 December he missed the train to Saints' game at Wakefield and was relieved of the captaincy. Ten days later Saints dismissed coach Alan Prescott and by 13 January Vince had played his last game for the club. Pressure of work – he was building up a highly successful welding, scrap and

Widnes, 1963/64. From left to right, back row: Gaydon, Bate, Measures, Hughes, Hurstfield, Kemel, Myler. Front: Chisnall, Lowe, Thompson, Karalius, Briers, Owen.

haulage business with his brothers – contributed to the rift and he had from time to time contemplated giving up the game.

His enthusiasm was re-ignited, however, when Widnes tempted him back to playing in March 1962. He gave the Chemics four years of good service, proving a charismatic pack leader and taking the club to its greatest triumph in almost thirty years. In his first season at Naughton Park Widnes finished third in Division One, their highest position since 1946/47. Moreover, they reached the final of the new Western Division Championship, losing 0-10 in a replay to Workington at Wigan, after a 9-9 draw.

In 1963/64 he took over the captaincy from Frank Myler and played well enough to win three more Lancashire caps and two final test caps against Australia. However, there was no fairytale ending as Australia eclipsed Britain 28-2 at Wembley and 50-12 at Swinton – a somewhat incongruous finale for such warriors as Vince, Eric Ashton and Mick Sullivan.

The 1964 Challenge Cup offered Vince a massive boost but what a struggle Widnes experienced in their progress. In the first round they beat Leigh 14–2 at St Helens after two replays and then despatched Liverpool City 16–6. The third round again required two replays before Swinton were ousted 15–3 at Wigan. Unbelievably, the semi-final with Castleford ended 7–7 at Swinton before Widnes scraped a 7–5 replay victory at Wakefield. It took Widnes a record nine games to reach Wembley, but no one was complaining. The final against Hull KR was no classic but Widnes were happy with a 13–5 victory. Vince rolled back the years, making the first try for centre Alan Briers, spraying out an abundance of telling passes and was 'always the leader, always the man making ground and requiring at least two defenders to halt him'.

Wembley 1964 was his last hurrah in big-time rugby league as a player, although he did not retire until 1966. Vince was as successful off the field as on it. His business enterprise enabled him to 'retire' to the Isle of Man but he made good as a coach with Widnes in the early 1970s and, more briefly, in 1983/84, taking them to Wembley triumphs in both spells. He also coached Wigan between 1976 and 1979.

Let's allow Alex Murphy the last word on Karalius: 'He is the hardest player I have ever seen on a rugby field – and the nicest, most gentlemanly guy to meet off it'.

ROGER
MILLWARD

CASTLEFORD

Debut: 3 October 1964 v Dewsbury (a)
Last game: 30 April 1966 v Hull KR (h),
Championship play-off

	A	T	G	P
1964/65	3+3	1	-	3
1965/66	31+3	15	35	115

HULL KINGSTON ROVERS

Debut: 15 August 1966 v Hunslet (a)
Last game: 3 May 1980 v Hull (Wembley),
Challenge Cup final

	A	T	G	P
1966/67	39	25	3	81
1967/68	42+1	32	38	172
1968/69	29+1	15	75	195
1969/70	39	21	99	261
1970/71	12	3	4	17
1971/72	22	3	41	91
1972/73	23+1	18	86	226
1973/74	25	14	62	166
1974/75	41	28	16	116
1975/76	31	15	63(2)	169
1976/77	26+1	7	43(1)	106
1977/78	30	14	32	106
1978/79	31+1	11	40(2)	111
1979/80	10+2	1	5(5)	8

CAREER RECORD

	A	T	G	P
Castleford	34+6	16	35	118
Hull KR	400+7	207	607(10)	1825
Tests	28+1	17	15	81
England	16+1	3	10	29
Yorkshire	12	8	22	68
Under 24	1	1	3	9
1970 Tour*	9+2	12	12	60
1974 Tour*	8+1	8	18	60
1979 Tour*	3	-	4	8
1968 W/Cup*	3+1	4	2	16
1975 W/Cham*	3	2	-	6
1977 W/Cup*	3+1	1	-	3
Represent	2	-	-	-
TOTALS	522+20	279	728(10)	2283

* Excluding tests

Millward appeared as a substitute for The Rest against Great Britain at Leeds on 6 November, 1966, kicking two goals. This game is not included in the above figures, being classed as a non-first class fixture. He also made 14 appearances for Cronulla in 1976, scoring one try and 17 goals (37 points). These are not included in the above figures. Figures in brackets represent one-point drop goals, which are included in the total of goals preceding them.

TESTS (29)

Great Britain	4	France	8	1966	Wigan
Great Britain	16	Australia	11	1967	Leeds (1 try, 3 goals)
Great Britain	11	Australia	17	1967	White City
Great Britain	3	Australia	11	1967	Swinton
Great Britain	22	France	13	1968	Paris (1 try)
Great Britain	19	France	8	1968	Bradford (1 try)
Great Britain	10	Australia	25	1968	Sydney*
Great Britain	2	France	7	1968	Auckland*
Great Britain	38	N Zealand	14	1968	Sydney*
Great Britain	28	Australia	7	1970	Sydney (2 tries, 7 goals)
Great Britain	21	Australia	17	1970	Sydney (1 try, 3 goals)
Great Britain	19	N Zealand	15	1970	Auckland (1 try)
Great Britain	23	N Zealand	9	1970	Christchurch (2 tries)
Great Britain	33	N Zealand	16	1970	Auckland (1 goal)
Great Britain	24	France	2	1971	St Helens (2 tries)
Great Britain	13	N Zealand	18	1971	Salford
Great Britain	14	N Zealand	17	1971	Castleford (1 try)
Great Britain	12	N Zealand	3	1971	Leeds
Great Britain	5	Australia	15	1973	Warrington (1 try, 1 goal)
Great Britain	6	Australia	12	1974	Brisbane
Great Britain	16	Australia	11	1974	Sydney
Great Britain	18	Australia	22	1974	Sydney**
Great Britain	23	France	4	1977	Auckland* (1 try)
Great Britain	30	N Zealand	12	1977	Auckland* (1 try)
Great Britain	5	Australia	19	1977	Brisbane* (1 try)
Great Britain	12	Australia	13	1977	Sydney*
Great Britain	9	Australia	15	1978	Wigan
Great Britain	18	Australia	14	1978	Bradford
Great Britian	6	Australia	23	1978	Leeds (1 try)

* World Cup
** Substitute appearance

Millward was a non-playing substitute in eight test matches – twice against New Zealand in 1965, against France in 1966 (1), 1967 (2), 1968 (1) and 1969 (1), and against Australia in 1970.

INTERNATIONALS (17)

England	40	Wales	23	1969	Leeds (1 try, 7 goals)
England	11	France	11	1969	Wigan (1 goal)
England	26	Wales	7	1970	Leeds**
England	9	France	14	1970	Toulouse
England	11	France	9	1975	Perpignan
England	12	Wales	8	1975	Salford
England	20	France	2	1975	Leeds* (1 try)
England	7	Wales	12	1975	Brisbane*
England	10	Australia	10	1975	Sydney*
England	22	Wales	16	1975	Warrington*
England	48	France	2	1975	Bordeaux* (2 goals)
England	27	N Zealand	12	1975	Bradford*
England	16	Australia	13	1975	Wigan*
England	2	Wales	6	1977	Leeds
England	15	France	28	1977	Carcassonne
England	13	France	11	1978	Toulouse
England	60	Wales	13	1978	St Helens (1 try)

* World Championship
** Substitute appearance

YORKSHIRE (12)

Yorkshire	15	Australians	14	1967	Wakefield (1 try)
Yorkshire	34	Cumberland	23	1967	Castleford (1 try, 3 goals)
Yorkshire	17	Lancashire	23	1968	Widnes (1 try)
Yorkshire	23	Cumberland	10	1968	Whitehaven 1 try, (4 goals)
Yorkshire	10	Lancashire	5	1968	Hull KR (2 goals)
Yorkshire	12	Lancashire	14	1969	Salford (2 goals)
Yorkshire	42	Cumberland	3	1969	Hull KR (2 tries, 6 goals)
Yorkshire	42	Lancashire	22	1971	Leigh (1 try, 4 goals)
Yorkshire	17	Cumberland	12	1971	Wakefield (1 goal)
Yorkshire	14	Cumberland	23	1972	Whitehaven
Yorkshire	20	Lancashire	14	1974	Keighley (1 try)
Yorkshire	10	Cumbria	7	1975	Dewsbury

ROGER MILLWARD
The Dodger

'The greatest player I've seen since the war and a complete footballer, Roger Millward could play in any of the back positions, was the best cover tackler of any back I've ever seen, could kick with either foot and land goals from the touchline when the balls were much heavier. He was also the smallest player on the field but made it big and won the respect of every Australian'

Johnny Whiteley, *League Weekly*, December 2002

Probably uniquely, Roger Millward's was a face famous to rank and file rugby league supporters before he had ever played a game as a professional. A happy accident of history occurred when ABC TV decided to screen a season of junior rugby league matches on Sunday afternoons, beginning on 23 October 1963. They featured the inter-town under-17s and under-19s semi-finals and finals, as well as inter-county finals and county matches. At their inception Roger had barely passed his sixteenth birthday but he looked more like a cherubic twelve-year-old. Yet he was the captain of the Castleford Under-17s team, which beat Hull Under-17s 32-13 in their final on 24 November and went on to beat Widnes 25-3 in the inter-county final. He also played for the Under-19s.

The TV commentator was the RFL Secretary, Bill Fallowfield. The viewers did not, however, need to be told that the tiny half-back, who made monkeys out of the much bigger boys and young men, some of whom also became top professional players, was a genius. He was everywhere, darting through slivers of gaps, dancing away from tearaway teenage tacklers, snapping at the heels of his forwards and bringing down the biggest of his opponents, scoring outrageous tries and kicking goals with balls that appeared almost as big as him. Anyone who knew anything about rugby league recognized that only one thing would prevent Roger the Dodger – even his name was a gift to the copy-writers – from becoming one of the game's legendary half-backs. That was his size, or lack of it. Maybe the professionals would kill him!

Why Roger's lack of poundage should worry the *cognoscenti* of the game was a recurring mystery. Rugby league had always catered for pocket genii. That was one of its great charms and eccentricities – a feature which is sadly vanishing from modern rugby league, where power and weight appears to be paramount. The game had produced little masters by the score. A few years before Roger came on the scene, Leeds scrum-half Jeff Stevenson, all nine stone-odd of him, had captained Great Britain to Ashes success in 1959. Dicky Williams, barely a stone heavier, had led the 1954 Lions and Hunslet's Oliver Morris, a Welsh international stand-off, who many thought might have become one of the game's immortals had he not been killed in the Second World War, failed to make the ten stones mark. As far back as 1901/02 when Broughton Rangers became the first team to perform the double, their half-backs, Sam and Will James, ran the best show in town at less than nine-and-a-half stones each. Hull's Yorkshire and England half-back Harry Wallace weighed in at 8st 10lbs a few years later. Roger Millward's playing weight was around 10st 4lbs and he stood 5' 4", perhaps. Whatever his vital statistics, they were quite enough for the toughest of defences. The bad guys did finally finish him off but it took them sixteen years. The amount of pleasure he gave to lovers of the beautiful side of the game can hardly be measured.

Roger Millward was born in Castleford on 16 September 1947 and began playing rugby league at Wheldon Road Junior School, just down the road from the Castleford RLFC ground. He later attended Castleford Grammar School, which played rugby union but he continued to play league outside school. By fourteen he could run 100 yards in 10.3 seconds and was in the Castleford Under-17 side. Two years later he was a televisual treat.

On 8 November 1963, Raymond Fletcher gave Roger his first name-check in the wider world of rugby league, when he wrote in his 'Keeping In Touch' column in *The Rugby Leaguer*, 'Sunday is now window-shopping day for senior club officials on the look-out for junior talents. That's what the televising of amateur matches has brought about. It could mean big money for some lucky youngsters as several clubs try to outbid each other for them. Players already attracting particular attention are Meekin and Lunn (Hull) and Millward (Castleford).'

Three weeks later he was reporting on a feature in *TV Times* – a double page photo-story of 'Boys who shine in a he-man's game', which focussed on a day in the life of Roger. Raymond wisely remarked, 'It must have done more good towards showing the real side of "This Rugby League Life" than any single thing I can think of'.

There was no doubt which club Roger would join. After signing on temporary amateur forms, Roger signed as a professional for Castleford on his seventeenth birthday, 16 September 1964. He had already made his 'A' team debut on 22 August at Bramley, scoring a try in a 28-4 victory. The following week he made his home debut before a crowd of almost 1,000 and ran in a hat-trick in 24-8 win over Wakefield Trinity 'A'. In his first four games he bagged nine tries. Included among them were four tries, and two goals, in a 39-0 win against Batley 'A' – one of them a thrilling 75-yard interception, which highlighted his devastating pace off the mark and over a distance.

Roger made his first-team debut for Castleford in a 15-9 win at Dewsbury on 3 October 1964 at stand-off to Keith Hepworth, Alan Hardisty having withdrawn after injuring an ankle playing for Yorkshire. Also making their debuts were teenagers Brian Appleyard (17) and Trevor Waring (19) and Abe Terry, the former St Helens, Featherstone and test prop. Abe only lasted ten minutes, suffering a broken nose and being replaced under the new substitution law. Roger scored his first try in a 17-0 home victory over Wigan on 5 December, again deputizing for Hardisty, who was on test match duty in France. His first-team appearances were strictly rationed in that debut season – just six matches, three as a substitute. It was remarked, however, that for one so young and inexperienced, opposing teams were marking him heavily, his reputation as a TV star clearly preceding him.

Castleford had their best season for many years, finishing third in the league, winning the Yorkshire League Championship and reaching the Top Sixteen semi-finals. Hardisty and Hepworth, Yorkshire's current half-backs, would take some shifting. In the meantime, Roger carried on thrilling the Wheldon Road crowds, which had doubled for 'A' Team games. Castleford 'A' won the Yorkshire Senior Competition Championship Shield by beating Hull 'A' 9-0 in the final and Roger's record for the Reserves that season was: 23 appearances, 35 tries, 42 goals, 189 points.

Roger Millward at the start of his professional career at Castleford.

The 1965/66 season presented Castleford with a pleasant problem – how to accommodate three gifted half-backs – four, if Derek Edwards was brought into the equation. Edwards was shifted to full-back, ultimately to represent Great Britain. Injuries and representative calls helped alleviate the problem. Roger played thirteen games at stand-off, eight at scrum-half and ten at left wing. Excluding substitutions, he made 31 appearances to Hardisty's 26 and Hepworth's 33 and he rapidly became a crowd-pleaser. On 6 October he got his first taste of international opposition, playing scrum-half against the New Zealanders. Fog delayed the start by ten minutes and the Kiwis defended relentlessly to win 7-6 but Roger still shone through the murk, winning the Castleford man-of-the-match award and kicking three penalties. A fortnight later he was at stand-off when Britain beat France 12-5 in a stormy Under-24s international at Oldham. Three men were sent off and Roger was the match-winner with a try and three goals.

Although Roger might not have always been assured of a first-team place at Castleford, he was clearly doing enough to be noticed at the highest levels. For the second test against New Zealand at Odsal on 23 October he was selected as substitute, Hardisty being the stand-off. Unfortunately, he never got on the pitch, as no one was injured. Had he done so, he would have been the youngest player ever to have represented Britain at 18 years and 37 days old. He was also a non-playing substitute for the third test and for Britain's game with France at Perpignan on 16 January. He finally won his test cap at Wigan on 5 March 1966 against France. He partnered Alex Murphy but the two had a horrendous time behind a well-beaten pack in a game which won universal derision for its lack of spectacle as Britain succumbed 4-8. It was an inauspicious start to an international career that had another twelve years to run.

Castleford's season was pretty successful. They finished fifth and were runners-up in the Yorkshire League. On 14 December, however, they made a small piece of history, when they visited St Helens and beat the home side 4-0 to win the first BBC2 Floodlit Trophy final. Roger played scrum-half but it was to be his only appearance in a final for Cas. When the season ended Roger was the club's joint leading try-scorer, with Ron Willett, on 15 and had landed 35 goals, one of which was kicked in the last game of the season in a 10-13 home defeat by Hull KR in the Top Sixteen play-offs. It proved his last game for Castleford and, ironically, it was against the club with which he would spend the rest of his career.

By the start of the next season Roger had signed for Hull Kingston Rovers. The fee of £6,000 was big for an eighteen-year-old but ultimately proved to be a giveaway. Castleford had decided to stick with Hardisty and Hepworth, who were still only twenty-five. (Indeed 'Heppy' was still playing for Bramley in 1982, two years after Roger retired.) Roger made his debut on 15 August 1966 in a 28-11 win at Hunslet. There was no messing about with his position at Craven Park, where he played stand-off, usually as partner to Arthur Bunting. Rovers were a similar club to Castleford in that they had progressed from rubbing rags in the 1945-60 period into contenders for honours who played entertaining rugby. Roger found himself behind a formidable pack in Frank Fox, Flash Flanagan, Brian Tyson, Bill Holliday, Frank Foster, and Terry Major – four test men and two county players. Cyril Kellett, at full-back, was one of the greatest goal-kickers the game has ever produced and the three-quarter line of Chris Young, Alan Burwell, John Moore and Mike Blackmore would claim 98 tries in Roger's first season prompting them.

Under the newly introduced four-tackle rule, Rovers enjoyed a most successful season, finishing second in the league and runners-up in the Yorkshire League, both to Leeds. They pushed Leeds into second place, however, in winning the Mackeson Trophy by scoring 888 points in 44 games at an average of 20.18, Leeds's average being 19.78. No Rovers side had ever scored more than 800 points in a season – an indication of just what an entertaining team Roger had joined. Two months after his debut he lined up in the Yorkshire Cup final against Featherstone Rovers at Headingley. *En route* he had claimed his first hat-trick for the club, when Hunslet were beaten 29-3 in the second round, and had grabbed two more in a 27-7 defeat of Huddersfield in the semi-final. He did not score in the final but set his team on the victory path by sending Blackmore over for the opening try that led to a 25-12 success.

There were a couple of major setbacks, however. In the Challenge Cup second round Rovers met Castleford at Craven Park before a post-war ground record crowd of 15,830. They looked like winning at 9-5 but two late drop goals from Hardisty forced a draw. The replay drew an official crowd of 22,582 to Wheldon Road but there were probably 30,000, after perimeter fencing was torn down and the gates opened on police orders. Cas won a splendid game 13-6. In the Championship semi-final Rovers went down 6-18 to Wakefield Trinity before 13,000 at Craven Park. Roger finished his first season at Hull with 25 tries in seventh position in the try-scoring charts, two tries behind Hardisty. Rovers' winger Chris Young finished joint leading try-scorer with Castleford winger Keith Howe on 34, and Blackmore, Burwell and Moore also finished in the top ten try-scorers.

Roger's second season at Craven Park was a triumph. His form was devastating and he played in every possible representative fixture. He tore up the record books by scoring 38 tries from stand-off, beating Frank Myler's record of 34 set in 1958/59. In addition he became the highest try-scoring half-back in history, passing the 37 scored by Alex Murphy, also in 1958/59. A third distinction came in the shape of the leadership of the league's try-scoring list for the season, the first time the feat had been achieved by a non-three-quarter.

October was particularly productive for Roger. On the 4th he made his debut for Yorkshire in a breathtaking 15-14 victory over the Australians at Wakefield. Neil Fox was the undoubted star but Roger could hardly have had a more satisfactory start to his county career. Yorkshire trailed 10-14 with less than a minute remaining, when Fox crashed through the defence but lost the ball when tackled. Roger was on to it in a flash, hacked it on and won the race for the touchdown. Fox converted with the last act of the match. Four days later the Kangaroos were again sorely afflicted when they went down 15-27 to Hull KR. Roger ran them ragged for three tries, one an interception from halfway. The *Manchester Guardian* said, 'The Australian half-backs simply had no answer to the swerve, speed and general dexterity of the little man'.

Roger Millward, supported by Alan Burwell, dashes away from the Bradford Northern defence at Craven Park in 1966.

Hull KR's 1966 Yorkshire Cup-winning team. Captain Frank Foster has the ball at his feet. Roger Millward is seated on the ground to the right of the trophy.

On 14 October there was icing on the cake for Roger and Rovers, when a dramatic Yorkshire Cup final at Headingley resulted in an 8-7 victory against deadly rivals Hull. Roger performed his party piece in the ninth minute by intercepting veteran loose-forward Cyril Sykes's pass 45 yards out, before racing round full-back Arthur Keegan to level the scores at 3-3.

The following Saturday Roger was back at Headingley, representing Britain in the first Ashes test, his third appointment with the Kangaroos in seventeen days. It was a case of three in a row, as Britain won 16-11 with Roger playing a leading role. His scrum-half partner was St Helens' Tommy Bishop, physically a clone of Roger, but temperamentally on a different planet to the quiet, sportsmanlike stand-off. Together, however, they were a constant irritant to Australia. At half-time it was 7-7, Bishop having scored a drop goal and Roger a conversion of a brilliant try from Chris Young. After 44 minutes Roger scored the crucial try, taking a dodgy pass from John Mantle before skedaddling inside Gasnier and away from Langlands for a magnificent try – which he duly converted. Five minutes later he kicked a penalty and two minutes from time skipper Bill Holliday landed another penalty, after Australian prop Dennis Manteit attempted grievous bodily harm on Millward.

On 25 October Roger partnered Keith Hepworth in Yorkshire's 34-23 defeat of Cumberland at Castleford and gave a dazzling performance, contributing three goals, a try and making a mockery of the Cumbrian defence. He retained his place in the second and third Ashes tests at London's White City Stadium and Swinton but they were lost, 11-17 and 3-11, respectively. He made the only British try for Malcolm Price at Swinton, and was the main attacking threat but missed several kickable goals on a snow-strewn pitch.

Two further test match appearances against France enhanced his reputation. On 11 February at Paris's Parc des Princes Britain played superbly to win 22-13. Although Roger

Roger Millward scoots through the Australian defence for his first try in test football during Britain's 16-11 victory at Leeds in 1967. A trio of great Kangaroos – Reg Gasnier, Graeme Langlands and Billy Smith – can do nothing to stop him.

missed the second half with a stomach injury after being kicked, he had already scored a try through 'magnificent anticipation and backing up of a move by Arnie Morgan'. He was also a try-scorer in the return fixture, a 19-8 success, at Odsal on 2 March.

Meanwhile, Hull KR concluded another eventful season in third position and advanced to the Championship final via home play-off victories over Swinton 17-2, Leigh 22-3 and St Helens 23-10, in which Roger registered 13 goals and a try. The final, at Headingley on 4 May, was against Wakefield Trinity. Rovers had already met Trinity six times that season, winning three and drawing three. Much to the chagrin of the Robins' supporters, Sod's Law decreed that they would lose the seventh and most important. A crowd of 22,586 were treated to an exciting encounter, however, which Trinity just about deserved to win 17-10. Roger landed a penalty and a drop goal. He would have to wait another eleven years for a Championship-winners' medal.

Compensation came in the form of a trip to Australasia in the summer of 1968 with the Great Britain World Cup squad. He played in all seven tour fixtures, including the three World Cup matches. The form of the tourists was a let-down, Australia beating them 25-10 before a crowd of 62,256 at Sydney. A trip across the Tasman Sea saw a disastrous 2-7 defeat by France at a mud-bound Carlaw Park, Auckland. A 38-14 victory over New Zealand in Sydney in the final game was small consolation. Britain then played four games in five days, beating Toowoomba 28-10, Queensland 33-18, North Queensland 15-2 and North West Queensland 33-5. Roger scored a try in all four games, plus a couple of goals at Toowoomba. The World Cup may have been a disappointment but the experience was all useful grist to the mill for the little half-back, who had still not reached his twenty-first birthday.

The 1968/69 season was relatively uneventful at Hull KR, who fell to tenth in the league and were in a process of team rebuilding. The pack had been more or less disbanded, apart from Flanagan. Phil Lowe was now established as the hardest running second-rower in the business, Terry Clawson and Brian Mennell were the established props and 1962 Lion Peter Small and short term signing Artie Beetson, the Australian test star, were also drafted in. Unfortunately, Beetson's English experience ended on Christmas Day, when he broke his leg playing against Hull at Craven Park. Roger continued to sparkle and was entrusted with the goal-kicking duties, landing 75. His only representative calls were for Yorkshire but they did bring him his first County Championship-winners' medal. He scored a try and four goals in a 23-10 win over Cumberland at Whitehaven and two goals in a 10-5 Roses Match victory at Craven Park.

There was nothing uneventful about 1969/70 for Roger. Rovers improved to fifth in the league but had the mortification in losing in the semi-finals of the Yorkshire Cup, the Challenge Cup and the Championship. Roger's responsibilities were increased in November 1969, when he was given the club captaincy – a position he kept until he retired. He led Rovers' scoring in both tries (21) and goals (99) and in all matches he claimed a career-best of 302 points. 16 goals in representative matches took his total to 115, the only century of goals he achieved.

Roger played in all six representative matches for which he was eligible, two for Yorkshire and four for England, who won the newly revived European Championship. Roger had a big say in a couple of England's games. At Headingley on 18 October he partnered Alex Murphy again in a 40-23 win over Wales. This time the combination worked sweetly. Roger was in his element, scoring one try, kicking seven goals and creating havoc in the Welsh defence. A week later in a drab game at Wigan, Roger saved England's bacon with a last minute 20-yard drop goal to earn an 11-11 draw against France. His last international of the season, on 15 March, was less happy. For some reason the selectors played him at centre in Toulouse, with the much more robust Mick Shoebottom at stand-off. England lost 9-14.

Fortunately, 21 of 26 of the 1970 Lions had already been chosen before the Toulouse debacle and Roger was one of them. The final party contained an embarrassment of riches at half-back. Apart from Roger, the Castleford pairing of Hardisty and Hepworth and the Leeds duo of Mick Shoebottom and Barry Seabourne were included. The tour captain Frank Myler, selected at centre, was also a former test stand-off of high quality. In the final analysis Roger outshone them all and returned from the tour heralded as the best stand-off in world rugby.

Britain won the first five games of the tour, four by big margins, Roger playing in four of them. When the team for the first test at Brisbane was selected, he was on the bench as the back substitute and never got on the field. The selectors chose to play the Castleford scrum-base trio of Hardisty and Hepworth, and Malcolm Reilly at loose-forward. Britain left the pitch shell-shocked at a 15-37 loss. Six changes were made for the second test at Sydney on 20 June with Roger displacing Hardisty. Alan had not really done anything wrong and his class often showed through on the tour – his 12 tries in 14 games being ample evidence.

Roger was just happy to be trotting out onto the Sydney Cricket Ground before a crowd of 60,962, most of whom expected a repeat of the Brisbane test. What a shock they got. By half-time Britain led 11-2 and Roger had scored all their points. After three minutes he gave the Lions the lead when he followed a Reilly bomb and took it on the bounce to score a try, which he also converted. Four minutes later he piloted a 40-yard penalty and after 12 minutes he bisected the posts with a 30-yard drop goal. On the half-hour he landed another penalty, as Australia struggled in vain to contain him and a rampant British pack. Centre Syd Hynes dropped a goal to stretch the lead to 13-2 after 53 minutes but was then sent off, after clashing with Arthur Beetson, leaving Britain with twelve men for the last 24 minutes. Nothing could stop Britain, however, who ran in another three tries, including another from Roger five minutes from time. Roger's kicking was immaculate and he finished with 7 goals from 7 attempts. His 20 points equalled the Ashes record held by Lewis Jones (1954) and Graeme Langlands (1963), and was not beaten until 1986. Harold Mather (*Manchester Guardian*) summed up Roger's inspirational display in the 28-7 victory: 'Millward was a willo'th'wisp that Australia could not contain, for he was much too nimble of foot and quick in thought for their often flatfooted defence'.

The third test, also at the SCG, aroused massive interest. Roger would later recall waking at 7 a.m. on the morning of the match, 4 July, at the team hotel overlooking the ground and seeing people already camped out ready for the test. There were 61,258 paying spectators, who saw a much closer score-line but just as comprehensive a victory for the Lions. At half-time they led 15-10. Roger had landed two conversions and a penalty to augment tries by Hartley, Atkinson and Hynes. Australia had been completely outplayed but remained in touch thanks to five goals from full-back Allan McKean. Britain continued to dominate, Atkinson scoring his second try and the lead was 18-12 after 53 minutes. Beetson was sent off on the hour after punching Cliff Watson and Britain, so superior that they should have been out of sight, relaxed a little. McKean kicked his seventh penalty and, unbelievably, four minutes from time Australia finally scored a try at the corner through Bob McCarthy to make it 17-18. McKean's conversion attempt failed and justice

Roger Millward (extreme left) with his 1970 Lions tour colleagues.

was done when Roger supplied the *coup de grace* in the last minute. Reilly carved out an opening for Duggie Laughton, who found Roger scurrying up in support 40 yards out. Eddie Waring remarked, 'Millward seemed to be skipping with joy as he scampered past four opponents to score'. The Lions had won 21-17, although 21-0 would have been a fairer representation of the play, and Roger had clinched the Ashes. It was his finest hour. No Briton has emulated his inspiration subsequently and in 2003 the Ashes remain firmly in Australia's possession.

The respected Australian broadcaster and writer, Frank Hyde said in the NSW *Rugby League World*, 'When the Great Britain party was being selected to tour, Millward was in the first batch of names, but we were still told that the selectors were afraid the big Australian forwards might batter him and that the hard Australian grounds could complete his disintegration. It is history now that the big Australian forwards could not catch him to batter him, and that the hard grounds assisted his twinkling feet to dominate the matches in which he played.'

The Lions continued their triumphal march in New Zealand. The crowds loved Roger, although the New Zealand forwards did not share their affection for him. Britain completely outclassed the Kiwis, winning the tests 19-15 (five tries to one), 23-9 and 33-16. Roger scored a try from a smart piece of dribbling in the first test, nabbed a couple in the second and dropped a goal in the third. He was described as 'an elusive, crafty tactician at half, who survived some severe buffeting and was always a move ahead of his opponents'. In the last match of the tour against Auckland, Roger signed off in style with a hat-trick. Britain won 23-8 and a New Zealand racehorse owner was so impressed that he announced that he was going to call one of his colts Roger Millward! Roger's last try brought his points tally for the tour to exactly 100 (18 tries, 23 goals in 14 appearances). Only Syd Hynes scored more tries (19) and only Terry Price claimed more points (117).

Fortunes in sport can fluctuate wildly. For Roger, at the height of his powers and fame, things suddenly went pear-shaped. Returning to England he twice asked to be placed on Hull KR's transfer list but was refused. On the field he was quickly back into form and selected to play for Yorkshire against Cumberland on 14 September 1970. Tragedy struck ten days before the county match in a home fixture against Warrington. Twenty-two minutes into the game Roger made a glorious run which ended in him being tackled two yards from the Wire line. Roger could not get up. His left leg was broken. He would not play again until 23 January 1971. Not only did he miss most of a disappointing season for Rovers, he missed Great Britain's World Cup campaign in England in the autumn.

When he returned to action, he was restored to the test team after only five games. His new half-back partner for the game against France at Knowsley Road on 17 March was Featherstone's Steve Nash, making his debut in international rugby. The two complemented each other well in many subsequent representative games, while Roger's comeback test provided him with two typical tries in a 24-2 victory.

Hull KR had another mediocre season in 1971/72, although it began well enough with Roger captaining them to victory in the Yorkshire Cup. The competition was played earlier than ever before, the final against Castleford being played on 21 August at Wakefield. Roger kicked two penalties in the first half, after which Rovers led 7-3. Castleford levelled at 7-7 but were despatched by two more penalties from Roger in the last 15 minutes. On 8 September Rovers beat the New Zealanders 12-10 but Roger was taken off after eight minutes with a thigh injury.

Fortunately, Roger had recovered in time to face New Zealand in the first test at Salford on 25 September when he was made Great Britain captain for the first time. A 13-18 defeat was not a good start to his leadership, however, and most of his involvement was as a tackler. The second test at Castleford three weeks later ended in a controversial 14-17 reverse and the series was lost. Roger scored a spectacular solo try from a scrum and was again required to tackle his socks off. The final test at Leeds saw Roger partnered by his third scrum-half in the series, Huddersfield's Ken Loxton. His previous partners had been Nash and Murphy. Some pride was regained with a 12-3 victory, Roger engineering one of John Atkinson's two tries but having to retire badly winded after 65 minutes. He had more luck as captain of Yorkshire, who took the County Championship, hammering Lancashire 42-22 and Cumberland 17-12. Injuries bedevilled him in the second half of the season, however, and he missed the last nine games.

Season 1972/73 was another of lost opportunity, although Roger began with a flourish. In consecutive games in August he scored nine goals and two tries in a Yorkshire Cup tie against Bradford, and eleven goals and three tries against Hunslet. Playing for Yorkshire against Cumberland, however, on 13 September he left the field after 39 minutes with a hamstring injury. Even so, he was selected for Great Britain's World Cup squad for France. A further leg injury ruled him out of the tournament, which Britain won against long odds. Roger was certainly having a hard time with injuries in this period and was losing the edge on his hitherto blinding pace. Yet he was still scoring plenty of points, as 226 for Rovers in 24 games proved.

Two divisions were reintroduced in 1973/74. Rovers finished fourteenth and were relegated. Roger was surprisingly restored to the test team at scrum-half for the third and decisive Ashes test at Warrington on 1 December. On a frost-bound pitch Australia won 15-5 but Roger put on a brilliant display of tackling and scored Britain's five points before yet another leg injury forced him to retire after 59 minutes. Despite Rovers' dismal form and his persistent injuries, Roger forced his way into Chris Hesketh's 1974 Lions tour party.

The tour was not as successful as in 1970, but the Lions did much better than anticipated, winning 21 of 28 fixtures. The Ashes series was hotly contested and a 1-2 defeat was reversed in the New Zealand series. Roger played in 12 games and scored 60 points. He figured in all three tests against Australia, playing stand-off in the first test 6-12 defeat, left wing in a wonderful 16-11 victory in the second and substituted for Ken Gill for the last ten minutes in the decider, which was lost 18-22. In the last game in Australia, against Southern New South Wales, he received a rib injury that restricted him to just two appearances in New Zealand.

Hull KR had a highly successful 1974/75 season. They won promotion, finishing one point behind champions Huddersfield. The Yorkshire Cup was won, Wakefield Trinity being beaten 16-13 at Headingley in the best final for many years. Roger was in superlative form, taking the White Rose Trophy. Rovers also reached the semi-finals of the BBC2 Floodlit Trophy, the Players Trophy and, bizarrely, the Premiership, which comprised the top twelve First Division clubs and the top four from Division Two. Roger was far too good for Second Division defences. He finished fourth in the try-scoring lists with 30, Rovers' winger Ged Dunn being the leader with 42, while Clive Sullivan, the other winger, bagged 28. Roger was perhaps relieved to have relinquished the goal-kicking to Neil Fox, while from November he had moved from stand-off to scrum-half.

The season was a quiet one on the representative front as there were no tests or tours. Roger captained Yorkshire in a 20-14 victory over Lancashire and led England, from scrum-half, to the European Championship, which was revived after a five year abeyance. It was now known as the Jean Galia Trophy. After the first match, an 11-9 victory at Perpignan, Harold Mather reported, 'Millward, who had a great game, epitomized what a hard match it was when he remarked, "I'm as tired as two Blackpool donkeys on a bank holiday".' The second game, a 12-8 defeat of Wales at Salford, was almost as close, with Welsh prop Jim Mills being dismissed on the hour.

The Great Britain team was split for the 1975 World Championship into England and Wales and the competition was played on a home and away basis between March and November. Roger captained England in seven of the eight matches and came very close to leading his country to the Championship. His personal performances in adversity were reminiscent of his greatest days. England effectively lost the tournament on 10 June 1975, when they lost to Wales 7-12 in a brutal affair at Brisbane. Roger was knocked out four times, concussed and finally taken from the fray after being kicked on the ankle. The injury caused him to miss England's 17-17 draw with New Zealand at Auckland on 21 June. He was, however, back for England's clash with Australia at Sydney a week later and played heroically in a surprise 10-10 draw, which should have been a victory on the balance of play. Injury again forced him off after an hour. Returning home, Roger enjoyed the distinction of leading England to a 40-12 win in their first ever encounter with Papua New Guinea at Port Moresby.

When the World Championship resumed in Europe, Roger led England to victories over Wales 22-16, France 48-2, New Zealand 27-12 and Australia 16-13. Trevor Watson (*Yorkshire Evening Post*) wrote of his performance against Wales, 'This was Millward at his best – fast, constructive, skilled and brave. His display had everything.' The last game against Australia at

Hull KR beat Hull 12-9 in the second round of the Challenge Cup in 1977. Here, Roger Millward runs past Chris Davidson, followed by Rovers' loose-forward Len Casey.

Roger Millward prepares to kick as Steve Rogers approaches during Britain's 18-14 win against Australia at Odsal in 1978. John Joyner is to Millward's left.

Wigan on 1 November provoked headlines such as 'Millward towers over champions' (*Guardian*) and 'Millward the magnificent' (*Daily Mail*). He was simply stunning in a tremendous match and took the £50 man of the match award. England had taken three out of four points from the Australians but had lost the Championship to them by a solitary point.

Eleven days later at Headingley England met Australia in a challenge match requested by the Australians. Both teams were much changed and three England players had played in a cup-tie the previous night. What should have been a celebration turned into a nightmare, particularly for Roger. His opposite, Tommy Raudonikis, who had not played at Wigan, had one thing in mind – belting Roger off his game, or out of it. At the first scrum Raudonikis cracked Roger. At the second he did it again and in a flurry of punches Roger was out cold. Referee Fred Lindop sent Raudonikis off but then astonished everyone by dismissing Roger too – for retaliation. It was like saying that St Francis of Assisi was cruel to animals. Roger was in tears. The crowed booed Raudonikis all the way off. When Roger had recovered his senses they cheered him to the echo. It was no consolation. He had never been sent off in his life and England lost 0–25.

Hull KR finished eighth on their return to Division One and reached the 1975 Yorkshire Cup final, Roger's fifth and last. The game against Leeds, at Headingley, was lost 11–15 in the last five minutes. In a first round tie against Wakefield on 31 August he scored two tries, the first of which took him past Gilbert Austin's club record of 159 tries.

Although he was approaching thirty, Roger remained England's captain and scrum-half for the 1977 games against Wales and France. He was duly selected to lead the Great Britain World Cup team to Australia but ended up reverting to stand-off, playing in all four of Britain's matches including the final, which was agonizingly lost 12–13 at the SCG. His representative career stretched on to 1979, including captaincy of Great Britain in the Ashes tests of 1978, and a record-equalling third Lions tour in 1979.

In domestic rugby, Roger's last three years were blessed and brought him the major honours which had so long eluded him. He led Rovers to victory over St Helens in the 1977 Floodlit Trophy final and to the Championship in 1978/79. Most romantically of all, however, he finally played at Wembley in 1980, when Rovers beat Hull 10–5. There was never a more popular captain of a Challenge Cup-winning side. Sadly, it was to be his last first-class appearance. After 13 minutes his jaw was broken – the third time that season. Courageously, he lasted the match, dropped a goal and received the trophy from the Queen Mother. He was bludgeoned into retirement on 4 October 1980, when his jaw was broken again in a reserve game against Batley.

Roger coached Hull KR (1977-1991), Halifax (1991-92) and York (1994). He was awarded the MBE in 1983 and an honorary MA by Hull University in 1991. In 1998 he was the first recipient of the Tom Mitchell Trophy as 'Lion of the Year' and in 2003 Hull KR named a stand in his honour.

ALEXANDER
JAMES MURPHY

ST HELENS

Debut 16 April, 1956 v Whitehaven (h)
Last game: 28 May 1966 v Halifax (Swinton),
Championship final

	A	T	G	P
1955/56	1	-	-	-
1956/57	18	10	-	30
1957/58	38	27	5	91
1958/59	36	31	-	93
1959/60	35	21	1	65
1960/61	33	23	10	89
1961/62	30	11	6	45
1962/63	24	11	2	37
1963/64	36	17	3	57
1964/65	31	12	10	56
1965/66	37	12	5	46

LEIGH

Debut: 19 August 1967 v Oldham (a),
Lancashire Cup
Last game: 15 May, 1971 v Leeds
(Wembley), Challenge Cup final

	A	T	G	P
1967/68	25	6	9	36
1968/69	27+1	9	15	57
1969/70	27+2	6	42	102
1970/71	34+2	12	30	96

WARRINGTON

Debut 6 August 1971 v Whitehaven (h),
Lancashire Cup
Last game: 21 September 1975 v Keighley (h)

	A	T	G	P
1971/72	29	6	17	52
1972/73	20	2	13	32
1973/74	12+1	1	10	23
1974/75	4	-	-	-
1975/76	1	-	-	-

CAREER RECORD

	A	T	G	P
St Helens	319	175	42	609
Leigh	113+5	33	96	291
Warrington	66+1	9	40	107
Tests	27	16	-	48
England	2	1	1	5
Lancashire	14	12	2	40
Represent	4	4	-	12
1958 Tour*	16	18	3	60
1962 Tour*	8	7	-	21
TOTALS	569+6	275	184	1193

* Excluding tests

TESTS (27)

Great Britain	8	Australia	25	1958	Sydney
Great Britain	25	Australia	18	1958	Brisbane (1 try)
Great Britain	40	Australia	17	1958	Sydney (1 try)
Great Britain	32	N Zealand	15	1958	Auckland (1 try)
Great Britain	50	France	15	1959	Leeds (4 tries)
Great Britain	15	France	24	1959	Grenoble
Great Britain	14	Australia	22	1959	Swinton
Great Britain	23	N Zealand	8	1960	Bradford* (1 try)
Great Britain	33	France	7	1960	Swinton*
Great Britain	10	Australia	3	1960	Bradford*
Great Britain	21	France	10	1960	Bordeaux (1 try)
Great Britain	27	France	8	1961	St Helens (2 tries)
Great Britain	11	N Zealand	29	1961	Leeds (1 try)
Great Britain	23	N Zealand	10	1961	Bradford
Great Britain	35	N Zealand	19	1961	Swinton (1 try)
Great Britain	15	France	20	1962	Wigan
Great Britain	31	Australia	12	1962	Sydney
Great Britain	17	Australia	10	1962	Brisbane (1 try)
Great Britain	17	Australia	18	1962	Sydney (1 try)
Great Britain	2	Australia	28	1963	Wembley
Great Britain	12	Australia	50	1963	Swinton
Great Britain	8	France	18	1964	Perpignan
Great Britain	17	France	7	1965	Swinton
Great Britain	9	N Zealand	9	1965	Wigan
Great Britain	13	France	18	1966	Perpignan (1 try)
Great Britain	4	France	8	1966	Wigan
Great Britain	14	N Zealand	17	1971	Castleford

* World Cup

ENGLAND (2)

England	40	Wales	23	1969	Leeds (1 try, 1 goal)
England	11	France	11	1969	Wigan

LANCASHIRE (14)

Lancashire	60	Cumberland	12	1958	Wigan (1 try)
Lancashire	19	Yorkshire	35	1958	Hull KR (2 goals)
Lancashire	15	Yorkshire	16	1958	Leigh (1 try)
Lancashire	8	Cumberland	14	1959	Workington
Lancashire	30	Australians	22	1959	St Helens
Lancashire	28	Yorkshire	38	1959	Leigh (2 tries)
Lancashire	21	Yorkshire	20	1960	Wakefield
Lancashire	32	Cumberland	18	1961	Salford (1 try)
Lancashire	15	N Zealand	13	1961	Warrington (1 try)
Lancashire	18	Cumberland	21	1961	Workington
Lancashire	14	Yorkshire	12	1961	Leigh (1 try)
Lancashire	45	Yorkshire	20	1963	St Helens (2 tries)
Lancashire	30	Cumberland	10	1969	Workington (3 tries)
Lancashire	12	Yorkshire	32	1971	Castleford

ALEXANDER JAMES MURPHY
Alexander the Great

'Talking of great players, more than one veteran, under the influence of nothing more stimulating than a cup of tea, was prepared to go on record as saying that Murphy is the best scrum-half ever. Rogers, Parkin, Watkins, Adams, Thornton, McCue, Bradshaw, Helme, Stevenson – they went through the illustrious list and still put this irrepressible 19-year-old on top'

Alfred Drewry, the *Yorkshire Post*

If Billy Batten was the most controversial rugby league player of the first half of the twentieth century, Alex Murphy was the most controversial of the second half – by a long way.

No one in their right mind doubted Murphy's abilities. As scrum-halves go, there has probably never been a quicker number seven. His acceleration from a standing start was practically unrivalled and at his peak he could run in tries from anywhere on the field. He could handle and pass as well as anyone, had an excellent kicking game and was an artiste when it came to dropping crucial goals. Alex was an out and out match-winner and he desperately wanted to win – everything and any way he could. So, while he won the accolades – he was called a genius, the greatest, a magician, the best thing since sliced bread – he was also called every nasty name under the sun by supporters of opposing teams. He was arrogant, cocky, loud-mouthed, selfish, dirty, a niggler, and he thought he was the ref. At least, that is how many fans saw him. He clashed with referees and he was no stranger to the early bath. His will to win seemed to rule and galvanize all his actions. Often he seemed to be the only centre of attention and crowds were agog as to what he would be up to next. He could infuriate and captivate, scowl and smile, but he could not be ignored. He was hero and villain, he was loved and loathed. There was something theatrical, even pantomimic, about him. He was God's gift to journalists, always good for a spicy comment, and to television cameras. If he was not producing moments of sublime skill, he was arguing the toss with the opposition or berating his less talented team-mates and it was all riveting.

The thing about Alex Murphy was that he knew he was good – well, a lot better than good – so why pretend otherwise? In his first autobiography in 1967, when he was twenty-eight, he stated, 'I have always had confidence in my own ability. I couldn't care a tuppenny damn whether it sticks out a mile or not. I play this game of rugby league to win. If I am playing "jacks" or crib in the snug of my local, I would still play to win… Any talk about good losers is sheer rubbish. I will shake hands with the opposition after a game. That's only natural. Yet while I'm doing it I'm already plotting how to beat them the next time we meet. Yes, I'm the worst loser in the business. I make no secret about it, and I offer no excuses. On the other hand, I never hold a grudge against any player. I have taken some awful hammerings in my time. As a scrum-half … you are the most marked man on the field.'

There are probably more stories and myths in rugby league about Alex Murphy than anyone else. Some are true, some apocryphal, some perhaps invented by himself. A recurring tale goes thus: a young Alex was playing in an away match. As the players came on to the field, the local hard man trotted alongside the good-looking, boyish and Brylcreemed scrum-half in the white jersey with the broad red band and snarled, 'Don't try anything clever today, Murphy. If you do, you'll wish you hadn't cos I'll have you'. The hard man could have been Frank Foster or Jack Wilkinson or Bill Drake or any one of a host of such characters. A few minutes into the game Alex sees an opening and flies through it, with 70 yards to go. He hears the footfall of someone chasing him and for a split second he wonders if the hard man is about to pounce. The moment passes, as he remembers that he is Alexander the Great and no one tells him what to do. He steps on the accelerator, beats three defenders, throws a couple of dummies and heads for the goal-line. Behind him, his loose-forward, probably Vince Karalius, screams, 'Spud, whatever you do, don't go behind the sticks!' 'Why not?' yells Murph. 'Because you'll never get your head between the posts!' ... And then there are the tales of his altercations with Mick Sullivan at Central Park in the 1960 Championship semi-final, with Syd Hynes at Wembley in 1971, with referee Eric Clay, whenever they met, and with Wigan boss Maurice Lindsay in 1984. All wonderful copy, cementing his place in rugby league folklore.

Casting aside all the ballyhoo, there was never any question that Alex would be among the first batch of inductees into the Hall of Fame. His track record as a player was phenomenal – 27 test caps, two Lions tours, World Cup winner, captaincy of Lancashire, England and Great Britain, winner of every medal available, and the status of a legend at his three professional clubs, St Helens, Leigh and Warrington.

Alex Murphy was born on 22 April 1939 at 25 Sunbury Street in Thatto Heath, St Helens. His parents, James, a boiler-stoker at the local mental hospital, and Sally had three daughters and two sons, Alex being the younger. It was clear from an early age that Alex was going to be a rugby league player. He attended St Austin's, a prolific producer of good teams and players. Alex graduated through the school, town and Lancashire schools teams and was quickly spotted as a treasure trove by St Helens, and a few other clubs. Saints' coach Jim Sullivan recognized his potential and took him under his wing, inviting him to train at St Helens while still at school. Saints signed Alex just after midnight on his sixteenth birthday in 1955. His signing-on fee was £80.

Alex began playing for the 'A' team in the 1955/56 season but when he did not get picked for several games he displayed his impetuosity by demanding a transfer – a precursor of things to come. Alex finally got his chance in the first team on 16 April 1956, six days before his seventeenth birthday. It was the last league fixture of the season and Saints fielded a team almost entirely comprised of reserves, as their next two games were both against Halifax in the Championship semi-final on 21 April and at Wembley the following week. Whitehaven, at Knowsley Road, were Saints' opponents on Alex's debut and his stand-off partner was Wilf Smith, an underrated player, who would enjoy many successes with Saints in a variety of positions. Saints won 22-7, with wingers Alec Davies (3) and Eric Ledger scoring all the tries.

By the time Alex got his next first-team game, on 27 October, Saints had won the Challenge Cup for the first time in their history. They had also lost in the final of the

Lancashire Cup to Oldham the week previously. Workington Town were Alex's second opponents and left Knowsley Road with an 11-9 victory. Alex scored the first of his 275 tries in senior football but was back in the reserves the following Saturday. Jim Sullivan might have been his biggest fan and his most inspiring mentor but he was a hard taskmaster, constantly making Alex train for speed, the be-all-and-end-all for any half-back who aspired to survive and prosper in such an unforgiving arena as rugby league.

Alex kissed goodbye to 'A' team football in January 1957, establishing himself, firstly at stand-off – as half of the regular Saints half-back pairing, with Austin Rhodes, another former pupil of St Austin's. It was about this time that Alf Ellaby, the legendary St Helens winger of the 1920s and 1930s, first got a glimpse of Alex and remarked prophetically that 'he will be as good as any scrum-half has ever been', a statement which Alex would no doubt have heartily endorsed.

Saints finished fifth in the league in Alex's first season, consecutive losses at Barrow, Wigan and Workington in April costing them a top four spot, and were booted out of the Challenge Cup in the first round at Whitehaven. The 1957/58 season, however, proved a triumph for Alex, even though Saints did not win anything. They finished second in the league and runners-up in the Lancashire League, both to Oldham, who also knocked them out in the semi-final of the Lancashire Cup. Alex was in a good team, though, and having a whale of a time. He had Vince Karalius to protect him at loose-forward and had test men all around him in Glyn Moses, Duggie Greenall, Ray Price, Tom McKinney, Nat Silcock and skipper Alan Prescott. He played in 38 of Saints' 45 fixtures and ran in 27 tries, including hat-tricks against Leeds on Tom Vollenhoven's debut, Swinton and Liverpool City. In all games he scored 28 tries, more than any other half-back that season.

By the time the Challenge Cup came round, Alex was running very hot. On 12 February 1958 he scored an astounding try straight from a scrum in a 15-0 first round win at Hunslet and was described as 'a dashing, dancing delight at scrum-half'. Saints won their second round tie at Keighley 19-4, when Alex kicked the first two goals of his professional career. The third round brought disappointment, however, with a 0-5 loss at snow-flecked Featherstone on 8 March.

Four days later, the weather was much worse but Alex was happy enough as he took the field in the first Australasian tour trial at Swinton. The current Great Britain scrum-half was Leeds's Jeff Stevenson, a brilliantly inventive and quick player, whose place on tour was assured. Facing Alex was Oldham's whippet-quick Frank Pitchford, who was favourite for the second scrum-half berth. Both had good games. Alex's Green XIII lost 10-22 to the Whites but he scored a try. Unfortunately, the game had to be abandoned after 68 minutes because of a snowstorm. The selectors obviously wanted to see more of Alex and a week later he was on duty again in a second trial at Headingley opposite Johnny Fishwick of Rochdale Hornets. This time the Greens won 41-18 with Alex's stand-off Harry Archer grabbing a hat-trick.

When the touring party was announced Stevenson and Alex were named as the scrum-halves but Stevenson withdrew for business reasons and Pitchford took his place. Five other St Helens players were also in the party – props Alan Prescott, chosen as captain, and Abe Terry, full-back Glyn Moses, winger Frank Carlton and loose-forward Vince Karalius. Alex was just nineteen years and a month old when the Lions played their first match, making him the youngest Lion up to that date. Before going on tour Alex and his fellow Saints/Lions had a date with

Workington Town at Knowsley Road in the Championship semi-final on 3 May. A remarkable match was lost 13-14 but Saints came back from 0-9 to 7-9, at which point Alex dropped three goals – an almost unheard of feat at that period – to give his team a 13-9 lead, only for a late try to dash his hopes of a Championship medal.

The 1958 tour was perhaps the most celebrated and contentious of all Lions tours and Alex was one of the key figures. Jim Brough, the coach, wrote, 'As for individual players, there is no doubt that young Murphy, at scrum-half, was the presiding genius of a back division which never failed to play up to his lead'. Alex's vital statistics in 1958 were recorded as 5ft 7½ins and 11st. He was the lightest man in the squad bar Pitchford. Despite his youth and lack of poundage, only second-row sensation Dick Huddart played more games than Alex, who scored 21 tries and 3 goals in 20 appearances, and established a reputation which still resonates in Australian rugby league circles. Remarkably, Alex scored at least one try in 18 of his 20 games, failing to score only in the first Ashes test and against New South Wales Colts almost at the close of the tour.

Britain played seven games prior to the first test at Sydney on 14 June winning six and drawing the other. Confidence was high and 68,777 fans expected a close encounter. Alex was given the scrum-half spot, alongside Dave Bolton, another lightning fast runner. Unfortunately, Alex's test debut was a disaster. Australia walloped the Lions 25-8 and veteran scrum-half Keith Holman played Alex off the park. Alex and Mick Sullivan both received warnings from referee Darcy Lawler. Fortunately, Alex and Britain digested their lessons and came back stronger. Of the remaining 22 tour fixtures only one was lost, and none in Australia. Alex drew constant rave reviews, such as the following by Vic Simons after a 50-25 victory over Wide Bay at Bundaberg, 'Aussie fans are all talking about British rugby league tour half-back Alex Murphy. They call him "Iron man" Murphy. And no wonder! He had already played in eight of the eleven tour games when he was asked to stand in today for Frank Pitchford (muscular trouble). He was told to take it easy in what turned out to be little more than a training run for Great Britain … but chipped in with a try and a dynamic burst or two. He has not played one bad game in his nine … and he is only nineteen, the "baby" of the British party'.

The second test at Brisbane (dealt with more fully in the chapter on Vince Karalius) saw Murph at his best. He revelled in the mayhem and adversity, as Britain's depleted XIII performed heroics to win 25-18. He was instrumental in creating Britain's first three tries and added his own first try in test rugby, a bobby-dazzler in conjunction with Karalius, which finally killed off the late Australian challenge. The third test at Sydney, before another 68,000 crowd, saw Australia humiliated 40-17. Alex was superb. One report ran, 'Murphy was the wizard of the match, cutting great gaps in the Australian defence. He scored a brilliant try to put Britain further ahead. Twice he beat Wells on the edge of the Australian "25" and with startling acceleration he flashed past Clifford and over the line to a terrific ovation from the crowd.'

An infected knee kept Alex out of the first New Zealand test, which was lost 10-15 at Carlaw Park, Auckland, but he was back for the second at the same venue. Britain squared the series with a comprehensive 32-15 success before 25,000 fans. Alex displayed his full repertoire and crowned it with a devastating 70-yard interception try.

Alex's form was luminescent in the domestic season of 1958/59. He ran in 37 tries in all games to set a record for a half-back in English rugby league and there were occasions when

The price of fame? Alex Murphy took some fearful hammerings. Here, he is carried from the field at Swinton in the first Ashes test of 1959.

it seemed impossible for opponents to lay a finger on him. St Helens topped the league throughout the season but were beaten 12-2 by Oldham in the Lancashire Cup final, while Featherstone again dumped them out of the Challenge Cup. Alex won his first three caps for Lancashire but they lost the County Championship in a play-off to Yorkshire. He also retained his place in the test team for games against France at Leeds on 14 March and Grenoble on 5 April. At Headingley he equalled the British try-scoring record with four in a 50-15 win. Jack Paul (*Sunday Express*) wrote, 'A mastermind behind the scrums, a darting demon in the loose, Murphy ripped the French defence to tatters. Four tries were chalked up by this scrum-half superb – one with an electric burst from half-way; another with a pulverizing break around the blind-side of a scrum: and two more from lightning pickups as the demoralized Frenchmen flung the ball about wildly.' However, the vicissitudes of playing tests against France in the 1950s was amply illustrated at a scorching Grenoble, where Alex played well enough but was in a team that lost 15-24.

Observers of rugby league were struggling in Murphy's early days to compare him to anyone they had ever seen before. There were immediate comparisons of him with Jonty Parkin, the undisputed best until then, but Jonty was a scrum-half of different talents to Alex. What really set him apart was that debilitating pace off the mark and over a distance. No one had seen a half-back who could score so often and so easily from static positions such as scrums and play-the-balls. Moreover, he was strong as well as fast.

The 1958/59 campaign climaxed marvellously for Saints who took the Championship, overrunning Hunslet 44-22 in style at Odsal in the final (a game immortalized by Vollenhoven's wonder try). Even so, Alex was the Saints' mainspring, collecting two cracking tries himself, the second a stupendous 75-yarder which rivalled even Voll's gem.

Although St Helens topped the league again in 1959/60 and won the Lancashire League, Alex suffered some setbacks. He played three times for Lancashire, who lost to both Cumberland and Yorkshire, but beat the Australians 30-22 at Knowsley Road. On 10 October they returned to St Helens and beat the home team 15-2 before a stunned crowd of over 29,000. Alex had a tough time against half-backs Barry Muir and Brian Clay, who repeated the dose in the opening Ashes test the following Saturday at Headingley. Murph was hampered by a knee injury and, like the rest of the British team, did not come up to expectations as Australia won 22-14. He was replaced by Jeff Stevenson for the remaining tests, which Britain won. A fortnight later there was more disappointment when he had to settle for a second successive Lancashire Cup runners-up medal, as Warrington dramatically beat Saints 5-4 in the final.

His season was rounded off in controversial style, when Saints met Wigan in the Championship semi-final on 7 May 1960. Alex had been playing stand-off since December and Wigan moved fiery winger Mick Sullivan to number six. Inevitably, the two clashed repeatedly and after 36 minutes Eric Clay marched the pair off after they had stood toe to toe slugging. Wigan prospered from the ruckus and won 19-9. Clay had a great deal of respect for Alex. In 1972 he wrote in *Yorkshire Sports*, 'Alex Murphy and I had several brushes on the field. I sent him off three times; he reported me for calling him a "yapper". I think we finished with a sensible relationship – I wouldn't upset him if he didn't upset me … Murphy is the most professional of all players I have handled. If he can use the rules to win he will. If he is playing for the team you support, he is the greatest. If he is against you, he is the biggest rogue unhung.'

The 1960/61 season was certainly one of Alex's most memorable. At the lower end of the scale he won his first County Championship medal with Lancashire and at the higher end he was a Challenge Cup and World Cup winner. The World Cup was staged in England in September and October and Alex was a major figure. Some critics noticed that he was more prepared to submerge his individualism for the good of the team and certainly his partnership with stand-off Frank Myler proved to be a key element in Britain's successes. He was the first try-scorer in Britain's 23-8 opening victory over New Zealand, and finished with a couple in Britain's 33-27 win over the Rest of the World in the tournament finale, both games staged at Odsal. In between he helped destroy the French 33-7 at Swinton and was the outstanding

One of Alex Murphy's trademarks was his searing speed – well exemplified in this break for St Helens against the 1961 Kiwis.

A slashing dash by Alex Murphy takes him through the New Zealand defence in the first test at Leeds in 1961.

back in the effective decider, when Britain beat Australia 10-3 in a ferocious encounter at Odsal on 8 October. Oddly enough, Alex never played in another World Cup.

Two weeks later Alex had been called up for service with the RAF but it did not stop him playing in the Lancashire Cup final on 29 October when Swinton were beaten 15-9 at Wigan. Murph definitely flew that afternoon, making the first try for Vollenhoven and the winning try for Rhodes, while collecting his first Lancashire Cup winners' medal and a £40 pay packet. National Service did not prevent Alex from regularly appearing for Saints – he was stationed in nearby Haydock – and he was available for test match victories against France at Bordeaux and St Helens in December and January in which he gathered three tries.

Alex's days in the RAF gave rugby union people a taste of genius. He did not play scrum-half as a union player. It would have been a waste of his talents. Often Alex was barely containable and earned rave reviews. In 1961 Pat Marshall (*Daily Express*) reported on his performance in the RAF's 18-6 victory at Cambridge University, 'This was Murphy's day. This rugged league man is one of the truly great rugby players of our time. He made the first try with a brilliant side-stepping burst – first outside, then back inside – before slipping the pay-off pass to unmarked Bryn Morgan. Next, he worked a perfect scissors with Williams, then popped up for the return pass to score under the posts. And the third try was Murphy's alone. From midfield, 45 yards out, he gathered a loose ball and moved for the left corner flag at a pace Cambridge cover defenders could not match. A final deft dummy, a side-step and he was over for as magnificent and individual try as I've seen this season.'

Alex actually played at Twickenham before he played at Wembley, when he represented the RAF in the inter-services tournament in both their games in 1961. Even he, however, could not stop the Royal Navy when they beat the RAF 9-3 on 11 February. He had better luck on 26 March playing opposite the England RU fly-half Richard Sharp, when the Army were defeated 19-11.

Wembley did beckon Alex on 13 May 1961, when Saints downed Wigan 12-6 in a tensely fought encounter. Alex was in the wars throughout, losing a tooth, getting a kick on the leg and being laid out twice, none of which stopped him from scoring the only try of the first half when he supported Dick Huddart's scything break and scampered the last few yards for a try which gave Saints a lead they never lost.

Alex finished fifth in the leading try-scorers lists with 31 in 1960/61. He would never again score as many as 20 in a season. In just four and a half seasons with St Helens he had scored 112 tries, an unprecedented rate for a half-back. His last five seasons at St Helens produced only 63 tries; as his style of play altered, opponents paid ever more attention to containing him and his pace inevitably declined. However, it would be a long time – more than a decade in fact – before any opponent could relax when Alex Murphy was on the field.

St Helens dropped to ninth in the league in 1961/62, but Alex's star remained undimmed. He played for Lancashire in their 15-13 victory over the New Zealanders at Warrington and in Saints' 25-10 win against the tourists. He also figured in all three tests against the Kiwis. He was a try-scorer in the first at Leeds but Britain were thrashed 29-11. The second at Odsal was won 23-10, although Alex followed it with an outburst against a perceived lack of support from the Yorkshire 'speckies'. He was much happier after the third test on Lancastrian soil at Swinton. Britain clinched the series with a convincing 35-19 triumph and Alex was in his element, claiming two tries and this eulogy from Jack Bentley (*Daily Express*), 'Murphy

Alex Murphy leaves Kangaroos Dick Thornett and Ken Irvine trailing in the second Ashes test of 1963.

Great Britain's first test team against Australia in 1963 contained three Hall of Famers. From left to right, back row: Armour (physiotherapist), Measures, Tembey, Bowman, Field, Tyson, Sayer, Burgess. Front: Bolton, Gowers, Karalius, Ashton, Murphy, Fox, Fallowfield (manager).

One of Alex Murphy's 175 tries for St Helens. The victims this time were Widnes at Knowsley Road.

was at his mightiest. Baffling, bewildering, like a swiftly flowing blob of human mercury, and just as difficult to grasp, as he ripped the uncertain New Zealand mid-field defence to shreds.'

A week later, on 11 November Alex picked up a try and a winners' medal as St Helens beat Swinton 25-9 in the Lancashire Cup final before a 30,000 crowd at Wigan. There was disappointment, however, on 11 February at the same venue when Great Britain surrendered a 13-2 lead to lose 15-20 to France. French scrum-half Louis Verge spent most of the afternoon offside at the scrums, giving Alex a frustrating time. Alex missed the return at Perpignan through injury and on 3 March was sent off by Mr Clay as Saints crashed out of the Cup 2-13 at home to Huddersfield. By now Alex was temporarily captain of Saints, as Vince Karalius had played his last game for St Helens. There was joy, however, when he was named in his second Lions tour party as first-choice scrum-half.

The 1962 tour was another tremendous success for Great Britain, who won the Ashes 2-1. Alex scored 9 tries in 11 tour games and proved to the Australians that he was still the world's best. He played in all the Ashes tests, completely overshadowing Barry Muir in the first at Sydney, where Britain triumphed 31-12. In the second at Brisbane the Lions won 17-10 and Alex was carried off after 55 minutes with an ankle injury, just eight minutes after he grabbed the decisive try with a characteristic score straight from a close-in scrum. Britain lost the last test 17-18 after Murph seemed to have clinched the game with a magnificent 50-yarder, again from a scrum. His next game, a 33-5 victory over Sydney's champion club, St George, on 18 July was his last ever in Australia. Typically he scorched over for two tries but injured his arm, preventing him from playing on the New Zealand section of the tour.

From 1962 to 1964 the RFL introduced two divisions and those years were relatively unproductive for St Helens and Alex. The only tangible rewards were consecutive Lancashire Cup wins, although Alex missed the 1962 final as he was still recovering from his tour injury, and the lifting of the Western Division Championship in 1964, when old rivals Swinton were beaten 10-7 in the final. Alex's representative career stuttered too. The only tests he played in the period were the disastrous first two tests against the 1963 Kangaroos, who destroyed Britain 28-2 at Wembley and 50-12 at Swinton.

The return to a single division for 1964/65 coincided with a return to normal. Alex was now captain and led Saints to the top of the league, the Lancashire League Championship and the Lancashire Cup – their fifth consecutive success in that competition. He also won back his test place and was awarded the captaincy in the season's two tests against France, the first being lost 8-18 in Perpignan and the second won 17-7 at Swinton. Saints reached the Championship final but Alex, playing at stand-off, failed to get an adequate response from his team, who went down 7-15 to underdogs Halifax at Swinton.

The 1965/66 season was one of St Helens' finest and Alex was in super form. Saints again topped the league and this time took the Championship with a 35-12 revenge victory over Halifax in a bruising encounter at Swinton. The Lancashire League was won and the Challenge Cup was taken at Wembley, where Wigan were demolished 21-2. Alex employed one of his most cynical game plans, not that such an expression existed then, by constantly having his team run offside, in order to win the scrums following Wigan's penalty kicks to touch, as they had no recognized hooker. It was not a pretty tactic, nor really in the spirit of sportsmanship, but it was within the rules and it worked a treat. Alex's tactics were the catalyst for a subsequent rule change, reintroducing the tap penalty, following a successful penalty kick to touch. In this great season Saints were also runners-up in the inaugural BBC2 Floodlit Trophy.

By any standards Alex's captaincy of Saints in 1965/66 had been phenomenally successful. Yet it proved to be his last season at Knowsley Road. Saints had played Alex at stand-off for some of the pre-Christmas period with Welshman Prosser at scrum-half. They then signed Tommy Bishop, a great scrum-half, from Barrow and moved Alex out to centre, from where he operated for the second half of the season. The test selectors continued to choose him as a half-back, playing him at stand-off in the final test against New Zealand and at scrum-half in the two tests against France, restoring him to captain for the second French test.

Alex was not at all happy at centre. He was not built for it, was a natural scrum-half and needed to be at the hub of play. The Great Britain selectors complicated his life by choosing him at centre for the 1966 Lions tour. It would have been his third tour, equalling the Lions' record and a huge distinction. Murph turned the tour down, admitting later that he was piqued at not getting the captaincy, which went to loose-forward Harry Poole (who missed all the Ashes tests anyway). It was not one of Alex's better decisions.

Crunch time had arrived for Alex and Saints. Refusing to play centre any more, he asked for a transfer and was eventually listed at £12,000, a world record fee. Leigh agreed to sign Alex as player-coach but Saints would not play ball. North Sydney and Wakefield Trinity were keenly interested parties, as positions became ever more entrenched and the upshot was that Alex was kept out of the game for a year until sense and a fee of £5,500 sorted out the issue.

Moving from St Helens to Leigh was not generally regarded as a great career move but in Alex's case it worked out well. Leigh had finished thirteenth in the league in 1966/67 but under Murphy they rose to seventh. While Alex had been prevented from playing, the game had introduced the four-tackle rule, which probably suited him. Kicking was more prevalent now and Alex's ability with the boot, both in field-kicking and dropping goals, won many matches for Leigh. Alex Murphy's four-year regime at Leigh brought back good times to Hilton Park and five major finals were reached – unparalleled levels of success at the club. In his first year as a player-coach he took his side to the BBC2 Floodlit Trophy final but Castleford just edged Leigh 8-5 in the final at Headingley. His season ended worryingly, however, as a chest infection turned nasty and he was medically advised to miss the last couple of months of the campaign.

He was back at full throttle for 1968/69, however. Leigh finished ninth but came close to reaching two finals, losing in the Lancashire Cup semi-final to St Helens and to Wigan in the Floodlit Trophy semi-final. The following season saw Leigh reach both finals of the Lancashire Cup and Floodlit Trophy, as Alex's team-building began to show tangible rewards. On 1 November 1969 Alex captained Leigh in the Lancashire Cup final against Swinton at Wigan and at half-time his 24th-minute drop goal had kept Leigh level at 2-2. The second half saw Swinton too strong, however, with Alex's opposite number Peter Kenny out-kicking

Alex Murphy fends off former St Helens colleague Kel Coslett while playing for Leigh in 1969. Note the advertisement on the stand to Murphy's left.

Wembley, 1971. Alex Murphy raises the Challenge Cup after Leigh's crushing 24-7 victory over Leeds.

the maestro with four drop goals in an 11-2 victory. Alex had missed five attempts at drop goals and had come in for some rough treatment. Six weeks later, on 16 December, he felt much better after Leigh had beaten Wigan 11-6 on their own ground in the Floodlit Trophy final. Again he dropped a first half goal but made his most valuable contribution by making the break that gave winger Rodney Tickle the game's only try.

In the first part of the season, until the acquisition of Stuart Ferguson from Welsh rugby union, Alex had been doing much of Leigh's place kicking and had landed a personal best six against Huyton, when he also scored two tries. His form had been good enough to make Lancashire select him at stand-off against Cumberland at Workington on 24 September. It was like old times. Lancashire led 15-2 by half-time and Alex had scored all three tries but in the 39th minute had to retire having been kicked on the elbow. The win gave Lancashire the county title. Even better, on 18 October he was back as captain of England, who beat Wales 40-23 at Leeds. Losing 12-13 at half-time, it was Murph who turned the game for England, shooting straight over from a ten-yard scrum, referee Eric Clay being bowled over as he touched down. A week later at Wigan he led England to an 11-11 draw with France. England won the European Championship but Alex missed the next two internationals and the entire second half of the season.

All Alex's ambitions for Leigh were fulfilled in a remarkable final season at Hilton Park. He now had a team that knew how to win. It was not a team of stars but it was organized, opportunistic and imbued with a soaring team spirit. The forwards could play good football

Featherstone scrum-half Steve Nash throws himself at Alex Murphy's feet during the 1974 Challenge Cup final. Murphy dropped two goals in Warrington's 24-9 triumph.

and/or tough it out when necessary – Chisnall, Ashcroft, Fiddler, Watts, Lester, Grimes, Clarkson and Smethurst (permutations of any six), were a formidable unit. The backs, Dave Eckersley, Tony Barrow, Joe Walsh, Les Chisnall, Stan Dorrington, Mick Collins and goal-kicker extraordinaire Stuart Ferguson became more than the sum of their parts under the orchestration of Murphy.

They began by lifting the Lancashire Cup at Swinton on 28 November 1970. It was a dreadful game, the conditions were wretched and three men were sent off but Alex was gleeful as Leigh beat his old team, St Helens, 7-4. As the game neared its close, Saints led 4-2 but Alex had one last ploy. He hoisted a steepling up-and-under, which bounced fortuitously for Dave Eckersley to snatch the winning try and Leigh had won the Lancashire Cup for the first time in fifteen years.

Leigh had won the Challenge Cup in 1921 but had never been to Wembley. Alex took them there in 1971 and they massacred hot favourites Leeds 24-7. Anyone who knows about

Billy Batten

Billy Boston

Brian Bevan

Neil Fox

Vince Karalius

Roger Millward

Alex Murphy

Jonty Parkin

Gus Risman

Albert Rosenfeld

Jim Sullivan

Tom van Vollenhoven

Harold Wagstaff

J. SULLIVAN

OGDEN'S CIGARETTES

A. J. RISMAN (SALFORD)

A selection of images featuring some of the players from the Hall of Fame. From left to right: Albert Rosenfeld (painted by Stuart Smith), Jim Sullivan *and* Gus Risman.

Two of the many tributes to the immortal Brian Bevan. Below: A stamp featuring the great man. *Right:* The traffic island named after him and featuring a sculpture of him in full flight.

BRIAN BEVAN
RUGBY LEAGUE 1895-1995

BRIAN BEVAN ISLAND

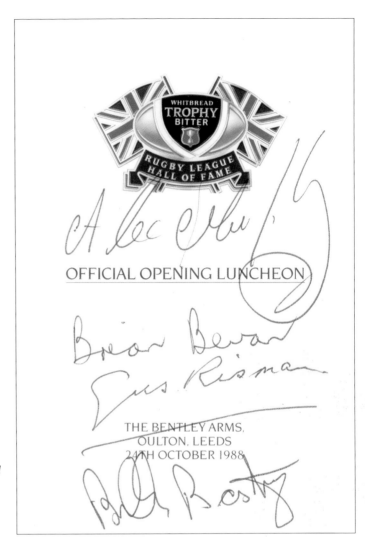

WHITBREAD
TROPHY
BITTER

RUGBY LEAGUE
HALL OF FAME

OFFICIAL OPENING LUNCHEON

THE BENTLEY ARMS,
OULTON, LEEDS
24TH OCTOBER 1988

Right: The menu card from the official luncheon to launch the Hall of Fame.

Below: First day cover issued to commemorate the event.

HAROLD WAGSTAFF
RUGBY LEAGUE 1895-1995

GUS RISMAN
RUGBY LEAGUE 1895-1995

JIM SULLIVAN
RUGBY LEAGUE 1895-1995

BILLY BATTEN
RUGBY LEAGUE 1895-1995

BRIAN BEVAN
RUGBY LEAGUE 1895-1995

FIRST DAY OF ISSUE HUDDERSFIELD · 3 OCT 1995

FIRST DAY OF ISSUE HUDDERSFIELD · 3 OCT 1995

FIRST DAY OF ISSUE HUDDERSFIELD · 3 OCT 1995

**RUGBY LEAGUE
CENTENARY**

Royal Mail First Day Cover

THE
HALL OF FAME
CHALLENGE MATCH

GREAT BRITAIN
V
REST OF
THE WORLD

**WHITBREAD
TROPHY
BITTER**

CHALLENGE

HEADINGLEY LEEDS
29th OCTOBER 1988 2.15 pm

OFFICIAL SOUVENIR PROGRAMME
£1.50

The programme cover for the game at Headingley to mark the opening of the Hall of Fame rugby league is familiar with the dramas of that final. Syd Hynes, the Leeds captain, became the first man to be sent off at the stadium, allegedly for attacking Alex, who was carted off to the dressing-room. Even today no one, apart probably from Alex and Syd, is sure of what happened. What is certain is that Alex played a blinder, kicked two of Leigh's four drop goals and won the Lance Todd Trophy.

... And then he signed a five-year contract with Warrington and more or less repeated the miracles he had performed at Leigh. Warrington had finished twenty-second in 1970/71. Alex took them to fifteenth in 1971/72, to victory over the New Zealanders and to the Challenge Cup semi-final. In 1972/73, under the new six-tackle rule, Warrington were top of the league and Alex was a Wire messiah, along with club chairman Ossie Davies. In 1973/74 Warrington enjoyed an orgy of trophy-winning, although Alex took the field on only 13 occasions. Without him they beat Featherstone 4-0 in the final of the new-fangled Captain Morgan Trophy and defeated Rochdale 27-16 in the Players Trophy final.

Alex made his last appearances in big match action at the end of the season. On 11 May 1974 he popped over two drop goals at Wembley, where Warrington easily beat Challenge Cup holders Featherstone 24-9 in a torrid clash. The following Saturday he captained his team to a sweet 13-12 win over St Helens at Wigan to take the one-off Club Championship. That game effectively signalled the end of his magnificent playing career, for he appeared in only five more games for Warrington.

Almost all rugby league players, no matter how great and charismatic, quickly fade from view when they cease to play. Perhaps one of Alex's most remarkable achievements was his ability to remain in the public glare for the quarter century after his retirement from playing. His coaching career (1967-94) was long and varied, taking in Salford, Leigh, Wigan, St Helens and Huddersfield, as well as Lancashire and England in the 1975 World Championship. Beyond playing and coaching, however, his activities in the media became an extension of his on-field persona. For many years he was the BBC's television summarizer alongside his former St Helens playing partner, Ray French, and was also given a platform to pronounce on the game in his long-running column in the *Daily Mirror*, under the all-too-predictable byline 'Murphy the Mouth'.

Alex was awarded the OBE in 1999 and was voted the Player of the Millennium in a *Rugby Leaguer* poll. Perhaps his old adversary Eric Clay got it dead right thirty-odd years ago when he wrote, 'No matter how sternly I treated him on the field, there was never any personal animosity. He was only another player to me, but I can't help thinking that, with twenty more Murphys playing, the game would be in a vastly different shape'.

JONATHAN PARKIN

WAKEFIELD TRINITY

Debut: 19 April 1913 v Bradford Northern (a)
Last game: 26 April 1930 v Halifax (h)

	A	T	G	P
1912/13	1	-	-	-
1913/14	17	2	2	10
1914/15	30	6	-	18
1918/19	9	6	4	26
1919/20	24	5	5	25
1920/21	20	9	16	59
1921/22	32	11	28	89
1922/23	20	9	3	33
1923/24	28	10	5	40
1924/25	27	8	5	34
1925/26	28	7	2	25
1926/27	33	8	1	26
1927/28	29	9	1	29
1928/29	29	1	19	41
1929/30	22	5	3	21

HULL KINGSTON ROVERS

Debut: 4 October 1930 v Leeds (h)
Last game: 23 April 1932 v Hunslet (h)

	A	T	G	P
1930-31	28	7	25	71
1931-32	29	4	2	16

CAREER RECORD

	A	T	G	P
Wakefield Trinity	349	96	94	476
Hull KR	57	11	27	87
Tests	17	9	-	27
England	12	6	5	28
Yorkshire	17	8	2	28
Represent	3	2	-	6
1920 Tour*	8	15	1	47
1924 Tour*	9	9	6	39
1928 Tour*	2	1	-	3
TOTALS	474	157	135	741

*Excluding tests

TESTS (17)

Great Britain	4	Australia	8	1920	Brisbane
Great Britain	23	Australia	13	1920	Sydney
Great Britain	31	N Zealand	7	1920	Auckland (3 tries)
Great Britain	19	N Zealand	3	1920	Christchurch (1 try)
Great Britain	11	N Zealand	10	1920	Wellington
Great Britain	6	Australia	5	1921	Leeds
Great Britain	2	Australia	16	1921	Hull
Great Britain	22	Australia	3	1924	Sydney (2 tries)
Great Britain	5	Australia	3	1924	Sydney (1 try)
Great Britain	11	Australia	21	1924	Brisbane (1 try)
Great Britain	31	N Zealand	18	1924	Dunedin
Great Britain	28	N Zealand	20	1926	Wigan
Great Britain	21	N Zealand	11	1926	Hull
Great Britain	8	Australia	0	1928	Sydney
Great Britain	6	N Zealand	5	1928	Christchurch
Great Britain	9	Australia	3	1929	Leeds
Great Britain	0	Australia	0	1930	Swinton

INTERNATIONALS (12)

England	35	Wales	9	1921	Leeds (2 tries)
England	33	Other Nat.	16	1921	Workington
England	5	Australia	4	1921	Highbury
England	12	Wales	7	1922	Herne Hill (1 try)
England	2	Wales	13	1923	Wigan
England	17	Other Nat.	23	1924	Leeds (1 try, 1 goal)
England	27	Wales	22	1925	Workington
England	37	Other Nat.	11	1926	Whitehaven (1 try)
England	30	Wales	22	1926	Pontypridd
England	11	Wales	8	1927	Broughton
England	20	Wales	12	1928	Wigan
England	39	Wales	15	1928	Cardiff (1 try, 4 goals)

COUNTY GAMES (17)

Yorkshire	5	Lancashire	15	1919	Broughton
Yorkshire	27	Cumberland	6	1920	Maryport
Yorkshire	5	Lancashire	2	1921	Rochdale
Yorkshire	30	Cumberland	12	1921	Halifax (5 tries, 2 goals)
Yorkshire	8	Australians	24	1921	Wakefield
Yorkshire	9	Cumberland	4	1922	Maryport
Yorkshire	51	Cumberland	12	1923	Hunslet (1 try)
Yorkshire	5	Lancashire	6	1923	Oldham
Yorkshire	0	Cumberland	20	1924	Whitehaven
Yorkshire	9	Lancashire	28	1924	Halifax
Yorkshire	13	Cumberland	31	1925	Huddersfield
Yorkshire	10	Lancashire	26	1925	St Helens Recs
Yorkshire	13	Lancashire	18	1926	Wakefield (2 tries)
Yorkshire	17	N Zealand	16	1926	Huddersfield
Yorkshire	20	Glam & Mon	12	1927	Hunslet
Yorkshire	5	Cumberland	11	1927	Wakefield
Yorkshire	10	Lancashire	33	1928	Halifax

JONATHAN PARKIN
Jonty

'Jonty was something more than just a scrum-half. He was half the back division, amazingly slick, full of craft … and always the man for the quickest route. Not so much of an artful dodger was Jonty, but so swift as to be there before the other chap had barely moved. Parkin was always thinking a move ahead, and a great little captain, too. Wakefield Trinity have always been well endowed for scrum-halves, though they've never had one to equal Jonathan Parkin, the little man who seemed to have outsize hands when it came to ball manipulation'

Allan Cave, *Rugby League Gazette*, May 1955

Jonathan Parkin was born on Bonfire Night, 1894. He hailed from Sharlston, a pit village with a reputation for producing great rugby players, with a particular specialism in scrum-halves. Jonty was undeniably the most celebrated scrum-half from the village but others have included Herbert Goodfellow (Yorkshire and England), who worthily succeeded Jonty at Wakefield Trinity from 1934 to 1950, Don Fox, Lance Todd Trophy winner with Trinity in 1968 and a 1962 British Lion, and Carl Dooler, a 1966 Lion who also won the Lance Todd Trophy with Featherstone Rovers in 1967. Probably even more amazingly, the village – a community of fewer than 2,500 souls – produced two Hall of Famers in Jonty and Neil Fox.

At school in Sharlston, Jonty played in the forwards before moving to half-back. Jonty played his junior rugby with North Featherstone in the Wakefield & District Intermediate League and signed for Wakefield Trinity on 15 April 1913 for £5, having trialled with the reserves. He followed his brother, Ernest, a strong running forward (who sometimes played full-back) to Belle Vue. Ernest had signed for Trinity on 27 February 1912, having played as an amateur with Westgate. He would play alongside Jonty for the next decade.

Jonty's first-team debut came four days after his signing. The previous week Trinity had been thoroughly whipped, 35-2, by Huddersfield in the Challenge Cup semi-final at Halifax. Trinity had only one more league fixture to fulfil, at Bradford Northern, and so decided to throw in eighteen-year-old Jonty, along with another debutant, winger A.C. Cockroft, whom they had signed from Knottingley Albion on the same day as Jonty. Jonty was up against the wily old veteran, George Marsden, who had played for England at both rugby codes, but had the satisfaction of finishing on the winning side, 7-6.

Tommy Newbould, a Lion in 1910, was Wakefield's resident scrum-half and Jonty could not realistically expect to oust him immediately. He had to wait until 19 November 1913 before he appeared in the first team again, partnering Newbould in an 8-24 home defeat by St Helens. It was not until January 1914 that he really established himself as Trinity's first choice scrum-half. Jonty could play equally well at stand-off and in those pre-Great War days half-backs were often interchangeable. He and Tommy Newbould were such a combination.

Jonty had joined Wakefield as they were entering a decline. Between 1907/08 and 1912/13 they had never finished lower than eighth in the league. They had won the Challenge Cup in 1908/09 and the Yorkshire Cup in 1910/11 and had been Yorkshire League Champions in 1909/10 and 1910/11. Their glory days were now behind them, however, and in 1913/14 they slumped to seventeenth. There was, however, a final fling. In the 1914 Challenge Cup Trinity embarked on a run of agonizingly close-run battles that took them all the way to the final. Jonty missed the first two rounds in which home victories over Swinton (2-0) and Leeds (9-8) were recorded. He was in the team which beat Wigan 9-6 at Belle Vue in the third round and played against Broughton Rangers at Rochdale in the semi-final, which was drawn 3-3. He missed the replay, a 5-0 victory at Huddersfield, but was in the Cup final side against Hull at Halifax on 18 April.

The Challenge Cup final was only Jonty's seventeenth first-team appearance and brother Ernest was also in the Trinity ranks. Hull, having invested in a whole series of expensive signings, including Billy Batten and three notable Australians, were expected to win the Cup for the first time. A crowd of 19,000 saw a mighty struggle in which Jonty and his less expensive team-mates almost drove Hull to despair. At half-time there was no score and after 45 minutes Trinity skipper Herbert Kershaw was sent off. Still Hull could not break Trinity's defence and it was not until the 73rd minute that winger Jack Harrison broke the deadlock with a try, followed five minutes later by another from Alf Francis on the opposite wing. Trinity lost 0-6 and Jonty received his runners-up medal, no doubt dreaming that a winners' version would one day come his way.

It never did and Jonty did not play in another Challenge Cup final. In fact his long career with Wakefield (1913-30) was practically devoid of success in terms of winning trophies. His only other final appearances were a couple of Yorkshire Cup finals, just one producing a winners' medal. In his seventeen years with Wakefield the club only finished higher than tenth in the league on one occasion, usually being a mid-table side, or even lower. While Trinity produced some excellent players, particularly in the pack, Jonty's career at Belle Vue presented a vivid contrast to his career at representative level. At Belle Vue he largely played with and led mediocre personnel but shone like a beacon. With Yorkshire, England and the Lions he was surrounded by and led the finest exponents of the game and still shone like a beacon. Perhaps therein lay his genius. His career was unlike all twelve of his fellow Hall of Famers. Every one of them played in successful teams at one time or another. All figured in teams which won the traditional big four domestic competitions – the Championship, the Challenge Cup, the Lancashire or Yorkshire Cup and the Lancashire or Yorkshire League Championship. They were all intimately acquainted with the thrill of winning finals and trophies – repeatedly. Such thrills were strangers to Jonty Parkin, yet his reputation stood as high as anyone's before or since.

He was clearly a wonderful player. For a scrum-half he was quite sturdy at around 5'6" and 11st 6lbs, being well muscled and a little flamboyant with unusually long, wavy hair. The Australian centre Dinny Campbell described him thus, 'He was of the crafty type, a strategist to the finger-tips, and as cunning as a fox. He had those magnetic hands that allowed him to handle the ball with great dexterity. He varied his play more than any other scrummage-half, and when he turned to the blind-side his work was perfect, for he had a grubber kick through that has never been equalled.'

Jonty could do everything required of a scrum-half. He was tough and masterful in playing to his forwards – as he usually had to with Wakefield. Equally, he was adept at opening out play when he had good players around him. He was a fine tactician with a ploy or a kick for every occasion. He could quickly weigh up the strengths and weaknesses of individuals or teams and would adapt the appropriate measures to undo them. He was an opportunist as well as a creator, and he had a fair turn of pace, as his 157 tries in peace-time football testified. That total stretched to around 220 with his appearances in war-time matches. Harold Wagstaff wrote in 1935, 'The best scrum-halves I have seen in rugby league football have been Chris McKivatt, captain of the 1911 Australians, Johnny Rogers, Jonty Parkin and Fred Smith. McKivatt was a wonderful forager for the ball, and so was Jonty Parkin, and the two, similar in type, were glorious generals, for they controlled the team from the scrum-half position.' Wagstaff knew a good captain when he saw one and Jonty was a natural leader, who spent the last dozen years of his career, at least, skippering every team in which he figured.

In 1914/15, however, he was still establishing himself as Trinity's number one half-back. The Great War brought an end to competitive rugby and in 1915/16 Wakefield did not play any games at all. Jonty, as a pit worker, was not called up and played for Dewsbury that season. It was a good move as many top-class players, including Billy Batten and Wakefield forwards Herbert Kershaw and Nealy Crosland, also went to Crown Flatt. Dewsbury finished top of the unofficial league table and Jonty scored 20 tries in 33 appearances. He was also recognized as a rising talent when he played for a Yorkshire XIII, which beat a Lancashire XIII 27-6 at Halifax on 24 April 1916, 'a brilliantly contested match', which raised £418 for war charities. It was the first time that he appeared in the same team as Harold Wagstaff and Billy Batten, who were Yorkshire's centres. On 6 May they were all together again, along with a fourth Hall of Famer, Albert Rosenfeld – probably a unique occurrence. This was the occasion of a testimonial match for Steve Darmody, Hull's Australian centre, who had lost a foot while serving in Flanders. The four Hall of Famers played in a West Riding XIII against an East Riding XIII.

Wakefield Trinity resumed activities in 1916/17 and Jonty divided his appearances between them and Dewsbury, who again led the unofficial league table, Trinity finishing sixteenth of twenty-six clubs. The war threw up some curious fixtures as services teams played rugby union against all manner of opposition. Jonty was in a Yorkshire Northern Union XV, which beat a New Zealand Military XV 19-8 at Headingley on 7 May 1917. It was reported that the New Zealanders 'found the Yorkshire backs rather too clever for them'.

Wakefield decided not to play again in 1917/18, so Jonty spent the entire season with Dewsbury, who finished second to Barrow in the unofficial league table. Jonty scored 23 tries and a couple of goals in his 24 games for Dewsbury. All games were played twelve-a-side, as the war took its grisly toll. Jonty, as a miner, would hardly have expected to have played for the Navy, but he was drafted into the centre for the Royal Naval Depot team, which beat Leeds 24-3 under Northern Union laws at Headingley on 28 December 1917. On 30 March he played for a second time for a Yorkshire XIII, when a Lancashire XIII were defeated 29-6 at Headingley.

Jonty's temporary career with Dewsbury ended when peace-time rugby was recommenced in January 1919. He had played over 90 games for them – proper records are not available – and scored at least 52 tries and eight goals. He also played as a guest for Hunslet in a 5-5 draw against Leeds on 19 October 1918.

Jonty Parkin.

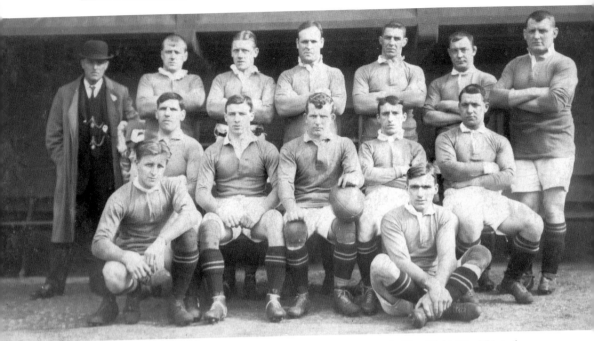

Jonty Parkin and Billy Batten played many games for Dewsbury during the First World War. This is the Dewsbury team which met their most powerful rivals, Leeds, on 25 April 1916. From left to right, back row: Davis, Burton, Rhodes, Dixon, Brown, Kershaw, Crossland. Seated: Batten, Lyman, Price, Farrar, Robertshaw. Front: Parkin, Rogers.

Three immortal Trinitarians – Johnny Rogers, Billy Batten and Jonty Parkin.

In the first properly constituted league season after the war, Wakefield Trinity were placed eighteenth of twenty-five, at first sight not a great platform for Jonty to launch his representative career. He may have been playing in a very ordinary team but his own performances were extraordinary. The Yorkshire selectors recognized his value when they gave him the first of 17 caps in the Roses Match at Broughton on 24 September 1919. It was an unhappy start, though, as Lancashire won 15-5. However, Jonty struck up an effective partnership with Leeds's Joe Brittain, which was to serve Yorkshire well for four seasons.

Injury kept Jonty out of action for the whole of October and November – an unfortunate turn of events which seemed to threaten his chances of a place on the first post-war Lions tour in the summer of 1920. However, he came back strongly and when the first tour trial teams were selected he was in the East team to meet the West at Leeds on 4 February 1920. Several of the tour team had already been chosen before the trials, including two half-backs in Ernie Jones (Rochdale Hornets) and Johnny Rogers (Huddersfield). Consequently, only a good show in the trials would suffice. Jonty was selected at outside-half to Bobby Lloyd of Halifax. The pair had a field day, as East hammered West 37-16, to the delight of a 12,000 crowd. Jonty scored a try and Lloyd got two.

Jonty obviously impressed but was picked to play in the next trial, while Lloyd got a tour place without recourse to a second match. Before the trial, Jonty had a hectic time with Wakefield in the Challenge Cup. On 21 February Trinity went to St Helens in the first round, Jonty's goal securing a 2-2 draw. In the replay four days later another 2-2 draw was the result before Trinity won the second replay 12-2 at Leeds on Friday 27 February. Amazingly, Trinity were forced to play the second round, a home tie against Huddersfield's Team of All the Talents, the following day. Hardly surprisingly, Trinity went down, but only 2-3 to a try by Albert Rosenfeld, in one of the most exciting games ever played at Belle Vue. A ground record of 21,000 attended. Two days later Jonty played his fifth game in ten days in the tour trial at Oldham. His team, The Reds, beat The Whites 21-11 and Jonty's display was good enough to win him the fourth half-back's spot in the tour party.

An indication of just how much Jonty's presence meant to his club side can be gauged from Trinity's final fixtures of the season. Jonty only figured in one of the last four games, a 5-8 defeat by Huddersfield. The other three games, in his absence, resulted in away defeats at Rochdale (0-64), St Helens (2-49) and Halifax (0-41).

His next appearance in a first-class fixture came half the world away on 5 June 1920, when the Northern Union tourists beat Metropolis 27-20 in a tremendous match at the Sydney Cricket Ground. The crowd of 67,859, a world record for a rugby match, dwarfed any he had ever experienced before – 10,000 or so of the spectators spilling over onto the playing area. For the first time at representative level, Jonty partnered Johnny Rogers at half-back, by all accounts a pairing made in heaven. Both were primarily scrum-halves, Rogers being regarded by many as the fastest seen in the first half-century of the sport. Often it was a case of who got there first as to who fed the scrums and their understanding of each other's play became almost telepathic. They would later reunite as club colleagues at Wakefield.

The two were first paired at test level on 26 June when Britain went down 4-8 to Australia before 28,000 at the Exhibition Ground, Brisbane. It was not an auspicious debut. Jonty played well enough, but the Australian forwards were too strong for the Lions and the British half-backs had too little ball. Despite two massive first-half penalty goals from Ben Gronow which gave the Lions a 4-0 lead, Australia scored the only tries of the game through Chook Fraser and Frank Burge, the latter, in the 65th minute, converted by Harold Horder. It was one of the hardest games Jonty ever played in, rough and uncompromising tackling being the order of the day. Jonty was off for several minutes after being hurt in one of the fiercest exchanges.

A week later Britain surrendered the Ashes when they went down 8-21 in the second test at the Sydney Cricket Ground. Jonty missed the game, his place being taken by Lloyd (the only change from the first test team). It was the low point of his tour, but four days later he scored a hat-trick in a 27-10 win against Tamworth and was restored to the test team for the third test at Sydney's Agricultural Ground on 10 July. A much changed side won a pleasantly contested match 23-13, watched by a crowd of 32,000. Jonty moved to scrum-half and was partnered by Ernie Jones, a big and forceful type of stand-off, while Rogers was shifted to the right wing. Jonty was reported to have been 'very lively' and to have fed his backs excellently. It was from a very long pass by Jonty that centre Jim Bacon opened the scoring, receiving the ball direct from a scrummage on the blind-side before strength and some fancy footwork took him over near the left corner flag.

Moving on to New Zealand Jonty enjoyed a fine run of form. He scored two tries in the opening fixture in a 16-24 defeat at Auckland on 24 July (when Johnny Rogers suffered a broken leg). A week later he was at his most devastating at the Domain Cricket Ground, Auckland, where he ran in a hat-trick in a stunning 31-7 victory in the first test before a 30,000 crowd. Hull winger Billy Stone also scored three tries, Jim Bacon one try and Ben Gronow five goals. In the 19-3 second test victory at Lancaster Park, Christchurch, on 7 August he was again among the try-scorers. Britain won the series with a clean sweep a week later at the Basin Reserve, Wellington, although an 11-10 victory was anything but easy. Jonty was this time denied a try but had registered another hat-trick just three days earlier when the Lions crushed West Coast 55-13 at Greymouth.

Jonty had established himself as Britain's premier half-back on tour and launched a test career which would run for a decade. He had made 13 appearances on tour and scored 19 tries and a goal. Only three-quarters Billy Stone (24 tries in 17 games) and Jim Bacon (23 in 17) had claimed more tries. The tour had been a colossal financial success with a profit of £6,700 for the Northern Union. Jonty and his team-mates each received £86/10/- as their share of the profit.

The tourists did not arrive home until mid-October and Jonty did not find things any easier at Belle Vue. Trinity could reach no higher than nineteenth in the league. Jonty finished top of both the try-scoring (9 tries) and goal-kicking (16 goals) for the club, despite missing the season's first two months. Among the debutants in 1920 was a versatile young back, Tommy Pickup, who would often partner Jonty at half-back. The two would become brothers-in-law in 1926. The highlight of Trinity's season was another Challenge Cup tie against Huddersfield, this time in the first round, on 26 February 1921. Although Wakefield succumbed 4-8 after another titanic struggle, the Belle Vue ground record was again broken with 29,466 in attendance – an indication of the possibilities if Trinity were to develop a successful team.

Jonty played in Yorkshire's 27-6 County Championship-clinching victory over Cumberland at Maryport on 6 November 1920, the Tykes' first title since 1912/13. He also appeared in both of England's international matches, his debut being at Leeds on 19 January 1921, when Wales were overrun 35-9. Jonty scored two tries and Joe Brittain, his partner, also scored. Winning pay was a mere £2. A few weeks later, on 5 February, the England players got a rise to £3, when they defeated Other Nationalities 33-16 at Lonsdale Park, Workington (the first international staged in Cumberland). The crowd of 10,000 was thought to have been the largest yet to have attended any type of football match in the county.

Wakefield improved marginally to seventeenth in 1921/22. By now Jonty was captain of the side and again proved its most prolific scorer with 89 points (11 tries, 28 goals). A new arrival was Huddersfield's legendary winger Albert Rosenfeld, whose try-scoring days were long behind him, his only scoring contribution to the season being a goal. Rosenfeld and Parkin actually played together at half-back on two occasions in March 1922.

There was plenty of big match action for Jonty in 1921/22, however. The County Championship proved a triumph for Jonty, who led Yorkshire for the first time, when they defeated Lancashire 5-2 at Rochdale on 4 October. The County Championship was taken for the second year running with a 30-12 beating of Cumberland at Halifax on 14 November. Jonty played one of the games of his life and set his name in the record books. His partner, Joe Brittain, had injured his hand in a Yorkshire Cup tie against Bramley two days earlier and, after the first 20 minutes, it appeared to onlookers that Jonty was doing the work of two men. He was certainly in magnificent form for he bagged five tries and kicked a couple of goals. Those five tries have never been equalled in any County Championship match. The centre-wing pairing of Billy Batten (Hull) and Cyril Stacey (Halifax) was also on top form, one reporter writing, 'The Parkin-Batten-Stacey triangle made the running in the greater part of the match. The inter-passing between these three players illustrated the possibilities of scientific support.' The Yorkshire committee certainly appreciated Jonty's efforts, for he was presented with a diamond studded gold medal in recognition of his deeds.

Jonty saw plenty of the 1921/22 Kangaroos, appearing in five games against them. On 1 October he partnered Johnny Rogers in the first test at Headingley, where 32,000 witnessed a breathtakingly close 6-5 victory for Britain. Jonty had a part in both Britain's tries, charging down a kick to provide Billy Stone with a try to give his side a 3-0 lead. Australia recovered to lead 5-3 at the interval and it was not until the 77th minute that Britain edged ahead, forcing a five-yard scrum, from which Rogers, Jonty and Jim Bacon sent winger Squire Stockwell racing over at the corner.

On Monday 10 October, Jonty had the great thrill of captaining England for the first time, when they beat the Australians 5-4 in another excruciatingly tight match at Highbury Stadium, London – half of the £830 receipts going to the Russian Famine Relief Fund. England's winning points came from a magnificent penalty goal kicked by Leigh's full-back Tommy Clarkson 12 yards in from touch on the halfway line. Jonty injured his knee after 70 minutes but recovered to lead Wakefield against the Kangaroos on 22 October. Unfortunately, Trinity were hopelessly outgunned and went under 3-29.

Jonty celebrated his twenty-seventh birthday, 5 November 1921, with his first captaincy at test level. Sadly, the second test at Hull ended in a 2-16 defeat for his team, as the Australians levelled the series. He was no happier on 7 December when Yorkshire were soundly beaten 24-8 by the Kangaroos at Belle Vue and he was even unhappier when injury prevented him from playing in the deciding test at Salford on 14 January 1922. Missing that 6-5 victory, one of the most celebrated in Britain's test history, was a major disappointment in his career.

The 1922/23 season held some promise for Wakefield, who rose to thirteenth, reached the semi-final of the Yorkshire Cup and set a club record score in beating Hensingham 67-13 in the first round of the Challenge Cup. Jonty, however, was absent from the latter game as injury caused him to miss the last 15 games of the season. Johnny Rogers had joined Trinity at the start of the season and much had been expected of Jonty's partnership with his test colleague. Before being incapacitated, Jonty had figured in Yorkshire's victory over Cumberland and had captained England against Wales at Herne Hill, London and at Wigan. In the former game, which was won 12-7, the players had received gold medals from Lord Colwyn. The match had been staged in aid of St Dunstan's funds for the blind. Jonty's growing stature in the game was underlined in the international at Wigan, a 13-2 victory for the Welsh. Both Harold Wagstaff and Billy Batten, former captains of the national side, were content to play under him – a tremendous compliment. Unfortunately for Jonty, it was in that game that he picked up the injury that finished his season.

Jonty had recovered by the start of the 1923/24 season, when Trinity slipped back down to nineteenth. He was again unlucky, however, to be ruled out (injured) of the season's only international against Wales on 1 October after being chosen as captain. He represented Yorkshire in both their games, however, scoring a try in a 51-12 victory over Cumberland at Hunslet but finishing a loser at Oldham, where Lancashire won 6-5. There was not much doubt that he would be selected for the 1924 Lions tour. He played in the first trial at Headingley on 9 January when he captained the Whites to a 26-18 victory over the Stripes, and was one of his team's six try-scorers.

His selection as captain of the Great Britain touring team was a formality, although there were some surprises in the rest of the party. Full-back Charlie Pollard, his Wakefield Trinity team-mate and a howitzer goal-kicker, was one of those surprises and so was Jonty's reserve scrum-half, chunky Walter Mooney of Leigh, who had not even played in either tour trial at Leeds or Wigan.

The tour was a triumph for Jonty. He began with a hat-trick in the opening fixture on 24 May – a 45-13 win over Victoria at Melbourne. He also ended it with a hat-trick in the final fixture on 16 August when Canterbury (New Zealand) were beaten 47-10. In between he was the dominating figure in the Ashes series, which Britain won 2-1.

A crowd of 50,005 attended the first test at the Sydney Cricket Ground on 23 June and a typically robust and exciting Ashes test ensued, with the result in doubt for the first hour. Britain led 6-3 at that point, when the Australian prop Norm Potter was sent off for punching. Prior to that, Jonty had saved Britain with a brilliant tackle on the flying Harold Horder when the latter looked clear for a try. Once Potter had departed, Britain, and Jonty in particular, turned the screw. His burst from a scrum on halfway was carried on by centre Tommy Howley, who sent forward Jack Price careering under the posts for a try that broke the Australians' hearts and gave Britain a decisive 11-3 lead. Then he broke again from a scrum, using winger Johnny Ring as a decoy, and scored at the corner. The Australians claimed that Jonty had never put the ball into the scrum and had not retired either! That did not bother Jonty and he further infuriated the crowd when he cut clean through another scrum. He was brought down a good foot from the line but lifted the ball over the line with an obvious double movement. The referee ruled a try, however, and, after Syd Rix added a further try, Britain ran out winners 22-3.

Five days later at the same venue, Jonty, suffering badly from an ankle injury, led his team to a 5-3 victory and the Ashes. His unlikely half-back partner was Frank Gallagher, a rotund loose-forward, who looked anything but the part, yet was touched with genius. On a mud-bound pitch Australia led 3-0 from the 8th to the 70th minute. Then Jonty struck. From a scrum 35 yards out he put in a grubber kick past the Australian inside backs. Full-back Frauenfelder misfielded and Jonty hacked on again. The ball stopped dead in the mud as Horder tried to collect it but haplessly slithered past it. Jonty toed it forward again and it came to rest 12 yards from the posts in the in-goal area. Jonty's final surge carried him to the touchdown just before an Australian chaser could retrieve the situation. Jim Sullivan's conversion nailed down the coffin lid. Jonty, battered, exhausted and elated, was carried into the dressing rooms by his team-mates when the final whistle blew. The third test was lost 11-21 at Brisbane and Gallagher and Australia's Jim Bennett were dismissed in a torrid encounter. Jonty made his own little piece of history, however, scoring the last try of the match with a slice of blindside trickery to become one of a select band of players to have scored a try in all three tests of an Ashes series.

In New Zealand, Jonty and his team were not as successful as previous Lions. Both he and Jim Sullivan were diagnosed as having contracted diphtheria and they missed the first two tests, which were lost 8-16 and 11-13. They returned for the third test at Tahuna Park, Dunedin, however, which resulted in a 31-18 victory. Despite a tour blighted by injury and illness, Jonty made 13 appearances for the Lions, scoring 13 tries and 6 goals.

Returning to Wakefield, Jonty, whose tour bonus had been £91, found that Trinity had signed Billy Batten and things looked rosier than for many years. Trinity actually reached the Yorkshire Cup final in 1924, thanks largely to Jonty. Hull were beaten in the first round 20-8, Jonty claiming a try and a goal, and an 8-5 win at Keighley set up a semi-final at Leeds. It was there that Jonty pulled off one of his most (in)famous coups before 27,000 stupefied spectators. There was no score when Charlie Pollard attempted a penalty goal and sent the ball well wide but high. As the ball descended into the crowd, Leeds full-back Syd Walmsley, both feet over the dead-ball line, caught it and tossed it forward to Jim Bacon to take a '25' yard drop-out. Jonty claimed a forward pass and the referee concurred. The touch-judge – only one stood behind the posts in those days – had not signalled that the ball had gone dead. By the time the Leeds players had recovered their senses, a five-yard scrum had been formed and Jonty had skipped through the defence for a try under the posts, which Pollard converted. Despite having Pickup sent off in the first half, Jonty inspired his team to a remarkable 5-4 victory.

Of course, all great scrum-halves have a streak of cockiness, or low cunning, and Jonty was no exception. In 1964 'Knightrider' recalled, 'Parkin's knowledge of the game was matched by his innate football skill and his physical toughness, and he was a fine judge of opposing players and referees. How he revelled in a tussle with a referee who seemed to be paying rather more attention to Jonathan than to the other players. More than once I have seen a zealous official, obviously starting a match with the intention of "watching Parkin", wilt before the end, though I am not inferring that the maestro was allowed undue licence. I believe that mentally he had most of the referees "docketed" as to their strong and weak points and knew better than most just what features of play the different officials were keenest on. However, when all is said and done, it was Jonty's quick football brain, his alertness to seize and profit on the slightest opening or slip of an opponent, plus his understanding with his various half-back partners in club, county and international football that made his name.'

Trinity's opponents in the Yorkshire Cup final at Headingley on 22 November 1924 were Batley and 24,546 saw a gripping tussle. Within two minutes Batley led 5-0, but Jonty dragged Wakefield level when he supported a charge by loose-forward Charlie Glossop and was under the posts before Batley could react. He converted the try too. Batley edged ahead 8-5 at the interval but then Jonty took control of the game, one reporter noting, 'Parkin's leadership was wonderful, and time after time he outwitted the opposition, who failed to accurately guess his intentions ... His short and sharp kicks into touch were very annoying to Wakefield's opponents.' Batley became so frustrated they gave penalties away, two of which Charlie Pollard converted from extremely difficult positions, and Trinity won 9-8. Parkin and Pollard were carried shoulder high by the crowd when the game ended.

The 1924 Yorkshire Cup final was as good as it ever got for Jonty at Wakefield. Two years later he skippered them in a second Yorkshire Cup final only to lose 3-10 to Huddersfield at Headingley, while in 1927 Trinity lost 3-7 to Oldham in the Challenge Cup semi-final.

His international career continued to thrive, however. In 1926 he captained Great Britain to victory in the first and second tests against New Zealand – 28-20 at Wigan and 21-11 at Hull. Moreover, he continued to skipper England and Yorkshire. In 1928 he made history by becoming the first man to tour Australasia three times and emulated Harold Wagstaff by winning a second Lions captaincy.

On a personal level the tour was disastrous. He broke his thumb in the opening game at Cootamundra and was restricted to just four appearances, Jim Sullivan taking over as captain in four tests in his absence. Jonty did, however, play in two crucial tests despite his injury. Britain beat Australia 15-12 at Brisbane and Jonty took his place at Sydney for the second test. Winger Alf Ellaby described Jonty's performance as 'courage personified' in a game played in six inches of mud. Britain won 8-0, Jonty scored the first try and the Ashes were retained, although Jonty's injured thumb was aggravated.

Eddie Waring, in his book *The Great Ones* (1969), tells a nice story of Jonty's determination to get the best out of his team on the 1928 tour, 'Two great forwards made their debut in [tests against] Australia – thanks to Parkin. The two forwards, Bob Sloman of Oldham and Albert Fildes of St Helens Recs, were not in the original team picked for the test. The two managers had disagreed and Parkin was called in as arbiter. It is said that Parkin, when asked about the merits of the players in question, said, "There's no argument. It must be Sloman and Fildes. I'm a Yorkshireman, but I want these two Lancashire lads in the match. You see, Bob knocks the opposition for six one way and Albert knocks them for eight coming back."'

In New Zealand Britain lost the first test but won the second. So it was decided that Jonty should play in the final test at Christchurch, having survived an exhibition match three days earlier. Typically, he led his side to a 6-5 victory and a series triumph.

His last test series was against the 1929/30 Australians. On 28 September Trinity beat the Australians 14-3. The Australian vice-captain Pat Maher said, 'Jonty Parkin played a grand game, clearly proving that he is no back number. His tactics as a leader were the work of a football genius.' Nonetheless, he was left out of the first test, which was lost 8-31. He was quickly restored as captain for the next test at Leeds and adopted the perfect restrictive tactics necessary to beat

Jonty Parkin gained only one winner's medal in his long career. This is the team he led to victory over Batley in the Yorkshire Cup final of 1924. From left to right (players only), back row: White, Abrahams, Blower, Glossop, Horton, Siswick. Seated: Reid, Pollard, Parkin, Batten, Thomas. Front: Jubb, Pickup.

the quicker Australians 9–3. Thirty years later he recalled, 'Before the game I had a word with Arthur Atkinson and reminded him that it would not be nice if he had to go back to Castleford and admit that in his first test he'd taken the dummy from Tommy Gorman. Arthur understood. He made, I have always been told, a very great impression on Australia's captain that afternoon.' Jonty knew that Gorman was the tourists' mainspring.

Alf Ellaby declared, 'That second test in 1929 was the hardest game of football I have known. It was a clash I shall never forget and I've an idea that Gorman agrees with me. I remember talking to him in Brisbane twenty years afterwards and I found then that his memory matched mine. I can still see Sullivan's crash into Gorman when there was defensive work to be done. That is something Gorman has not forgotten.'

Jonty retained the captaincy for the third test at Swinton on 4 January but announced that thereafter he was retiring from test rugby. The game was the only scoreless test in history and one of the most dramatic, Chimpy Busch's disallowed try for the Kangaroos becoming an Antipodean sore point for generations. Uniquely, a fourth test was arranged at Rochdale, which Britain won 3–0, but Jonty held fast to his retirement decision.

Left: *Jonty Parkin skippered Great Britain to a 28-20 victory over New Zealand at Wigan in the first test of 1926. He is pictured with the Kiwi captain Bert Avery (left) and referee Bob Robinson.* Right: *One of Jonty's most memorable games was the Ashes-clinching second test at Sydney in 1928, which Britain won 8-0. Jonty played with a broken thumb. Here, he kicks over a breaking scrum, watched by Oldham forward Bob Sloman. Jonty's Wakefield club-mate Bill Horton is obscured by Parkin.*

The England team which beat Wales 30-22 at Pontypridd in 1926. From left to right, back row: Dannatt, Whitaker. Standing: Whitty, Thomas, Bennett, Burgess, Revd Chambers (referee), Cunliffe, Taylor, Leake, Gabbatt. Seated: Carr, Rix, Brough, Parkin, Evans, Sloman, Gallagher. Front: Fairclough, Bentham.

The Hull KR team which beat Wigan 12-3 on 19 September 1931. From left to right, standing: Saddington, Tattersfield, Williams, Westerdale, Spamer, Britton, Binks, Smith, Sharpe. Front: Osborne, Batten, Parkin, Dale, Hill. To Jonty's right is Billy Batten junior – the son of his old club, county and test colleague.

There was a sensation at the beginning of September 1930. Wakefield's committee announced that all players were to be paid a flat rate. For years Jonty had been the highest paid man and felt unable to accept the new terms. Trinity placed him on the transfer list at £100 on 3 September. The following day Jonty gave the club a cheque to that value and bought his own transfer, subsequently arranging to join Hull KR, where his remuneration was to be £10 per match. Contrary to popular belief, Jonty was not the only man to buy his own transfer but he was the last, as the laws were subsequently tightened up. Jonty was a sharp operator. He had by then become a publican at The Griffin Hotel in Wakefield and had received a benefit of around £700 in 1922. The fact that he went on to play two full seasons with Hull KR, playing 57 games at £10 a time, is ample evidence of his financial acumen. Although Rovers were just as unsuccessful as Trinity, Jonty made good use of his time in Hull, making many contacts in the wholesale fish trade, in which business he became very successful in Wakefield. Jonty Parkin died on 9 April 1972.

AUGUSTUS JOHN FERDINAND RISMAN

SALFORD

Debut: 31 August 1929 v Barrow (h)
Last game: 23 March 1946 v Rochdale (h)

	A	T	G	P
1929/30	42	3	-	9
1930/31	41	2	4	14
1931/32	39	16	13	74
1932/33	34	16	100	248
1933/34	35	15	116	277
1934/35	35	10	89	208
1935/36	39	17	92	235
1936/37	35	16	66	180
1937/38	33	17	96	243
1938/39	47	18	104	262
1939/40	27	11	81	195
1940/41	2	-	-	-
1945/46	18	2	28	62

WORKINGTON TOWN

Debut: 5 October 1946 v York (h)
Last game: 1 May 1954 v Halifax (a),
Championship semi-final

	A	T	G	P
1946/47	32	6	46	110
1947/48	43	2	96	198
1948/49	31	2	65	136
1949/50	42	4	104	220
1950/51	38	7	108	237
1951/52	37	1	87	177
1952/53	33	5	72	159
1953/54	45	6	138	294

BATLEY

Debut: 2 October 1954 v Doncaster (h)
Last game: 27 December 1954 v
Dewsbury (h)

	A	T	G	P
1954/55	9	-	20	40

CAREER RECORD

	A	T	G	P
Salford	427	143	789	2007
Workington	301	33	716	1531
Batley	9	-	20	40
Leeds*	12	6	27	72
Bradford N*	9	4	3	18
Hunslet*	2	-	1	2
Dewsbury*	31	15	55	155
Tests	17	-	12	24
Wales	18	5	6	27
England	1	2	-	6
Glam & Mon	3	2	-	6
Represent	9	1	5	13
1932 Tour**	13	9	-	27
1936 Tour**	10	9	16	59
1946 Tour**	11	3	27	63
TOTALS	873	232	1677	4050

* War-time guest
** Excluding tests

TESTS (17)

Great Britain	18	Australia	13	1932	Sydney
Great Britain	24	N Zealand	9	1932	Auckland
Great Britain	25	N Zealand	14	1932	Christchurch
Great Britain	20	N Zealand	18	1932	Auckland
Great Britain	4	Australia	0	1933	Belle Vue
Great Britain	7	Australia	5	1933	Leeds
Great Britain	19	Australia	16	1933	Swinton
Great Britain	12	Australia	7	1936	Brisbane (2 goals)
Great Britain	12	Australia	7	1936	Sydney
Great Britain	10	N Zealand	8	1936	Auckland
Great Britain	23	N Zealand	11	1936	Auckland (4 goals)
Great Britain	5	Australia	4	1937	Leeds
Great Britain	13	Australia	3	1937	Swinton (2 goals)
Great Britain	3	Australia	13	1937	Huddersfield
Great Britain	8	Australia	8	1946	Sydney (1 goal)
Great Britain	14	Australia	5	1946	Brisbane
Great Britain	20	Australia	7	1946	Sydney (3 goals)

INTERNATIONALS (19)

Wales	18	England	23	1931	Huddersfield (1 try)
Wales	2	England	19	1932	Salford
Wales	19	Australia	51	1933	Wembley
England	32	France	21	1934	Paris (2 tries)
Wales	11	France	18	1935	Bordeaux
Wales	41	France	7	1935	Llanelli (2 tries, 1 goal)
Wales	17	England	14	1936	Hull KR
Wales	3	England	2	1936	Pontypridd
Wales	9	France	3	1936	Paris (1 try)
Wales	7	England	6	1938	Bradford
Wales	18	France	2	1938	Llanelli
Wales	17	England	9	1938	Llanelli (1 try, 1 goal)
Wales	10	France	16	1939	Bordeaux
Wales	16	England	3	1939	Bradford
Wales	5	England	8	1940	Oldham
Wales	9	England	9	1941	Bradford (3 goals)
Wales	9	England	9	1944	Wigan
Wales	8	England	18	1945	Wigan
Wales	11	England	3	1945	Swansea (1 goal)

COUNTY GAMES (3)

Glam & Mon	14	Lancashire	10	1930	Salford (1 try)
Glam & Mon	19	Cumberland	12	1931	Whitehaven
Glam & Mon	12	Yorkshire	33	1931	Halifax (1 try)

AUGUSTUS JOHN FERDINAND RISMAN
Gus

'Risman was an artist, a personality and, withal, an athletic genius, and it is the impact of those things on the game of Rugby football that we shall remember, when his scoring achievements and representative honours are forgotten, or else yellowing lines of print in the record books'

J.R. Jones

According to Bradford Northern and Wales second-rower Trevor Foster, a great leader of rugby players himself, Gus Risman was 'The perfect captain and the greatest footballer I ever played with. He also had the ideal physique.' Tom Mitchell, the grand old man of Cumberland rugby league, said in 1954, 'Gus Risman was unequalled in the realms of rugby football and was by far the best, most complete and gentlemanly player it has been my lot to see. There is hardly likely to be another anywhere in rugby league football who will match the brilliant successes he has achieved on the field both here and in Australia over such a long period.'

Indeed Gus Risman was that rarest of creatures – the natural, all-round rugby footballer. Strategist, tactician, master-tackler, incisive attacker, try-maker, try-scorer, field-kicker, goal-kicker, full-back, centre, stand-off, leader of men – he was all these and more. He played the game fairly and with honour. He conducted himself with dignity, on and off the field. He was God's gift to God's game.

Risman's achievements were extraordinary. He played until he was almost forty-four and his first-class career of 25 years and 4 months was longer than anyone else's until Jeff Grayshon (1969-95) bettered it. He stands third in the all-time scoring list with 4,050 points, fifth in the goal-kicking list with 1,677 and second only to Jim Sullivan in the appearances list with 873 matches. As a test player his career spanned fourteen years (a British record) and he played in five Ashes series, all of which were won. He made three Lions tours, played in 17 tests and 19 internationals, created numerous club records with Salford and Workington Town, and led both clubs to their greatest triumphs.

Yet he did not come from a rugby-playing background. His father, Augustus George Risman, was a Latvian seaman, who settled in Cardiff to run a seamen's boarding house. George and Annetta Risman had three children, Gus and his sisters, Val and Virginia. Gus was born on 23 March 1911 in Cardiff, but the family moved to Barry when he was eleven. He apparently spoke Latvian and English until he was six. His sporting prowess burgeoned at Barry. He was a Welsh Schoolboys soccer trialist at the age of thirteen, while at Gladstone Road School, but on winning a scholarship to Barry County School, he shone at rugby. He played briefly for Dinas Powis and Cardiff Scottish but was persuaded by Frank Young, a 1910 Lion and former Cardiff and Leeds full-back, to give rugby league a try. Leeds did not have an interest so it was arranged for Salford to give him trials. It was just as well, as both Tottenham Hotspur and Cardiff RU were keen to acquire his services.

Salford signed Gus on 31 January 1929. His signing-on payment was £52 at £1 per week. Gus's father was ill, so Lance Todd, the Salford manager, threw in another £25 in cash. The £77 proved a sound investment over the next seventeen years. Gus agreed to match payments of £3 a win and £1/17/- a loss. By 1938 the figures had only risen to £3/10/- a win, £3 a draw and £2/10/- a loss. Those figures related to league matches only. There were graduated bonuses for cup-ties and, down the years, Gus's talents ensured that he would derive more income from rugby-related activities. Most unusually, he kept a diary-cum-accounts book, which is a wonderful source of information, mostly financial. In his first season at The Willows he earned an additional £43/10/- for working on the ground staff and £29/5/- as a clerk with Shell-Mex. These were large sums for a nineteen-year-old, who, however, sent some of his earnings to his family in Barry.

Gus's career at Salford began badly for, playing in the reserves, he broke an ankle. By the start of the 1929/30 season it had mended and he made his first-team debut on the wing in a 16-13 home victory over Barrow on 31 August 1929. His interception try was the first of 143 he would score for the club. Gus missed only one of Salford's 43 fixtures, playing mostly at full-back, apart from eight games on the wing and four at centre. After almost a decade in the doldrums Lance Todd had brought Salford to a level where they were beginning to challenge for honours. He had been a great player for Wigan and a member of the first New Zealand touring team to England in 1907. His managerial skills worked wonders at The Willows, as he built one of the great teams in rugby league history in the 1930s. In 1967, at his famous pub Nont Sarah's high on the Pennines, Risman recalled, 'Todd was a great character … He could walk in through that door, this bar would be full, and within minutes there would be complete silence with everybody listening to him. He let us coach ourselves, but never missed a trick on that field. His half-time round-up was his forte … He'd set about every player … The smallest thing you'd done wrong was brought up and you couldn't say anything. "Shut up!" he'd say, "I've only got five minutes."'

Risman's debut season was eventful. Within a few months he had played in his first major final but Salford made a hard job of reaching the Lancashire Cup final, even after receiving a first round bye. They drew 8-8 at St Helens in the second round, winning the replay 13-3. The semi-final, against their fiercest rivals Swinton at The Willows, was drawn 3-3 and the replay at Station Road finished scoreless. The second replay, at Broughton, finally went Salford's way 8-0. Disappointment followed in the final at Wigan, where Warrington beat Salford 15-2. On 11 January 1930 Gus had his first shot at the Australians, Salford losing 5-21. A third disappointment followed at the end of the season when Salford, who finished third, were beaten at Huddersfield in the Championship semi-final. The future, however, would bring him four Lancashire Cup winners' medals, a plethora of victories over the Aussies and six winning appearances in Championship finals.

Although Gus continued to play full-back in 1930/31, his talents were being noticed by the representative selectors. Jim Sullivan was the incumbent Wales full-back and held that position for the short-lived Glamorgan & Monmouthshire team in the County Championship. There was some surprise then when Gus was picked to play centre for

Glamorgan against Lancashire at Weaste on 22 November, scoring a try in a 14-10 victory. He was retained for the 19-12 win against Cumberland at Whitehaven and for the championship decider against Yorkshire at Halifax on 15 April 1931. He again scored a try but was on the losing side, 12-33, in the Welsh county's ultimate fixture.

On 18 March, three days before his twentieth birthday, Gus had won his first cap for Wales in an 18-23 reverse against England at Huddersfield. Gus scored a try and went on to win 18 caps for Wales, all at centre. In club football Salford dropped to ninth but were steadily building the nucleus of an outstanding team. Already established in the team were Barney Hudson, a block-busting winger from the North-East, who was doing the side's goal-kicking, the extremely versatile Cumbrian back Sammy Miller, and a Welsh stand-off of genius, Emlyn Jenkins, who had a fine understanding with his scrum-half Reg Meek, from Gloucester. The forward pack was already one of the best, having a sterling leader in Billy Williams, a dual Welsh international, who was backed up in the front row by Fred Shaw and Jack Muir. Back-rowers Joe Bradbury, Aubrey Casewell, Teddy Haines, Alf Middleton and the outstanding pair of Paddy Dalton and Jack Feetham ensured that Salford had enough steel to dominate the rugby league world.

The 1931/32 season brought more reinforcements in the shape of little Billy Watkins, a scrum-half from Cross Keys RU, Wales RU hooker Bert Day from Newport, ex-Wigan Highfield and Dewsbury full-back Harold Osbaldestin, and the crowd-pleasing three-quarter Bob Brown from Wigan. In this company, Gus Risman blossomed. Salford again reached the Lancashire Cup final in 1931. This time Gus picked up his first winners' medal, when veteran centre Fergie Southward landed a last-minute penalty to beat Swinton 10-8 before a crowd of 26,471 at Broughton. Gus played for Wales on 27 January 1932, when England comprehensively beat them 19-2 at Salford but the selectors decided to stick with him as a centre in the first tour trial at Warrington on 10 February. He played in the Whites team that beat the Reds 22-3, scoring a try in freezing conditions. Surprisingly he was then selected as full-back in two more trials, facing Jim Brough and Jim Sullivan. He did well enough to push the great Brough out of the tour party and won selection as number two full-back to Sullivan.

Jim Sullivan's 1932 Lions were one of the most successful parties ever to tour down-under, being strong in the forwards and having a sensational three-quarter line. Gus had three Salford team-mates in the squad – Barney Hudson, Billy Williams and Jack Feetham. Gus had a super tour, playing in 17 games and scoring 9 tries. He scored a hat-trick from the wing on his Lions debut, a 50-9 romp against Western New South Wales at Orange. Britain won the first test and lost the second. Gus could not expect to oust Sullivan, or any of the three-quarters, but he was so good that he had to be found a place. He figured at stand-off in victories over Ipswich and Newcastle, never having played in that position in his league career. On 16 July he found himself making his test debut at the Sydney Cricket Ground before over 50,000 wildly enthusiastic Australians as Great Britain's stand-off.

It was a memorable occasion, although it did not begin well. Britain fell behind 3-11 soon after half-time, at which point Gus and the spring-heeled centre Stanley Brogden swapped positions. The move worked like a charm. Brogden sliced straight to the line from a scrum on Australia's '25' to make the score 6-11. Gus then seized a loose ball when Australia's passing faltered on their own '25' and threw a beautiful long pass to winger Stan Smith, who swept in at the corner for a converted try. Each side kicked a goal and the game was tied at

13-13. The game-breaker a few minutes from time came when Brogden kicked into Australia's quarters. Full-back Frank McMillan gathered the ball but was tackled so forcefully by Gus that the ball came loose and was shifted quickly to Smith, who flew to the corner, taking the flag down but scoring the try which won the Ashes.

Having made his debut, Gus was never dropped from the test team and missed only one test through injury. The tour proceeded to New Zealand, where all eight games were won, including the three tests.

Gus enjoyed a wonderful 1932/33 season with Salford, who finished ten points clear at the top of the league. Salford won the Lancashire League and met Swinton in the Championship final at Wigan on 29 April 1933. Salford led from the seventh minute and ran out winners 15-5, earning £15 per man. Gus landed three goals. His conversion of Jack Feetham's last-minute try brought him his 100th goal of the season. He was the first Salford player to have achieved that feat. It had taken Salford three years to recognize Gus's skill at goal-kicking. He would maintain a reputation as one of the game's leading practitioners for the next twenty-one years. On 5 April he kicked a club record 13 goals, and threw in a couple of tries, in a 74-3 butchering of Bramley.

The 1933/34 season brought a Kangaroo tour and Gus Risman found himself opposing them six times. He booted four goals in Salford's 16-9 win on 21 October and his two goals for a Northern Rugby League XIII at York on 1 November helped to beat the tourists 7-5. It was a different story, however, on 30 December when Gus had the thrill of appearing at Wembley for the first time as Australia hammered Wales 51-19. Much more enjoyable were his three appearances in the Ashes tests, which ended in narrow victories at Belle Vue, Manchester (4-0), Headingley (7-5) and Swinton (19-16).

For the first time that season he encountered French opponents. Jean Galia organized a breakaway French rugby league movement and in March 1934 brought a team to England on a six-match tour. Salford were their final opposition and beat the Frenchmen 35-13 with Gus contributing four goals. On 15 April Gus had the novel experience of playing for England at the Stade Buffalo in Paris in the first Anglo-French international match. Two other Welshmen, Jim Sullivan and Emlyn Jenkins, were in the England side which won 32-21, Gus bagging a couple of tries.

Salford were again runaway league leaders in 1933/34, finishing 12 points ahead of Wigan, and retained the Lancashire League title. Gus created new Salford records with 116 goals and 277 points, the latter shattering Jim Lomas's old record of 266 set in 1906/07. However, in the Championship final against Wigan at Warrington, he had a wretched afternoon with his kicking, as Wigan shocked a crowd of over 31,000 with a well-merited 15-3 victory.

In July 1934 Gus wrote to Arsenal asking for a trial. They responded by saying that the peculiar circumstances made it awkward, otherwise they would happily have had a look at him. Whether Gus was really serious about changing over to soccer is a moot point. It would appear that what he really wanted was a better deal from Salford and such leverage undoubtedly helped him in his negotiations with Lance Todd and C.B. Riley, the Salford chairman. A new contract was signed guaranteeing Gus at least a £350 benefit in 1936/37.

Salford fell from top of the league to fourth in 1934/35 but won a third consecutive Lancashire League Championship and took the Lancashire Cup. Gus kicked 15 goals in the three Lancashire Cup-ties prior to the final against Wigan, which was attended by 33,544 at Swinton on 20 October. With six minutes remaining, Salford were clinging to a 14-12 lead, when Gus landed a glorious touch-line penalty to effectively kill Wigan off. His last-minute conversion of a Jenkins try, his sixth goal, crowned a wonderful display of kicking and took Salford to a 21-12 triumph.

Immediately after the Lancashire Cup final, Salford embarked on a six-match tour of France. Within twenty-four hours of beating Wigan, Salford were in Paris, where Gus kicked 9 goals and scored a try in a 51-36 win against a Paris XIII. It was reported that, 'The sporting crowd particularly appreciated Risman's truly amazing place-kicking. Roars of generous applause greeted his penalty goal scored from the centre of the field well behind the halfway line. The ball cleared the dead centre of the cross-bar by about two inches.'

Salford then beat Lyon-Villeurbanne 34-17, Beziers 41-8, Albi 44-5, XIII Catalan 41-16 and Villeneuve 34-10, the last game being played on 4 November. The trip stretched over 2,000 miles and was regarded by Gus as a wonderful experience. The players received £15 for the tour but Shell-Mex stopped Gus a week's wages! Salford were billed as 'Les Diables Rouges' (the Red Devils), a nickname which stuck for the rest of the century. However, it

Gus Risman's Salford team wave goodbye to Jim Sullivan's Wigan, whom they had just beaten 21-12 in the Lancashire Cup final of 1934. Risman's team was leaving for a pioneering six-match tour of France.

is quite likely that Lance Todd, rather than the French, dreamed up the title for publicity purposes.

Gus took a turn for the worse, literally, in January 1935, when he contracted gastric vertigo. He had fourteen teeth filled and one removed. He was off work and rugby for a month. On his return he was given his first taste of captaincy, when the injured Billy Williams missed the game at York on 16 February. Salford lost 0-5 in a mud bath. The Salford management must have been happy enough for they gave Gus the captaincy full-time in 1935/36 and he held it for the remainder of his time at Weaste. In August they also gave Gus and his new wife, Ethel, 10 guineas as a wedding present. By then Gus had given up his job with Shell-Mex and had become a cinema manager for the Luxor Hulme Company. He worked at various cinemas, including the Scala, the Weaste Picture House and the Rex from that time until the war.

Gus was a fine all round sportsman but one sport he probably never expected to be involved with was baseball. The 1930s saw a boom in baseball and semi-professional leagues were formed in Lancashire and Yorkshire. Many footballers and rugby league players were attracted to the sport, which offered them the chance to earn a few extra bob in the summer. Salford had a team in 1935, prophetically known as Salford Reds, for whom Gus turned out regularly for five shillings a game. The Reds lasted only a year, but in 1937 Gus played for Oldham Greyhounds, where the going rate was much better at £1/10/- a game.

The 1935/36 season was one of Salford's least successful of the period. Finishing fifth in the league, they were knocked out of the Challenge Cup by Warrington at the semi-final stage. They did, however, retain the Lancashire Cup defeating Wigan 15-7 at Warrington. Gus kicked three goals, including two from the touch-line. 'Saturn' reported, 'Risman played a captain's part for Salford. He was the complete player and inspired his men by his great work in defence and attack.'

On 21 September 1935 Gus first partnered Salford's new nineteen-year-old winger Alan Edwards, from Aberavon, in a splendid derby match at Belle Vue, where 12,000 saw Broughton Rangers beat Salford 12-10. The pair formed one of the finest centre-wing partnerships the game has seen, both at club and international level. Edwards, tall and skinny, bullet-fast and unpredictable, revelled in the service provided by the robust and guileful Risman. Before the season's close, Edwards and Risman had shared in Wales's annexation of the European Championship, France having been annihilated 41-7 at Llanelli and England pipped 17-14 at Craven Park, Hull. This was a golden age for Wales, who won the Championship three seasons running and lost only one of nine games between 1935 and 1939, with the Risman-Edwards duo on the left wing throughout. The two last played together for Wales when England were beaten 11-3 at Swansea on 24 November 1945.

The brilliance of the Salford back division in this period was sharply illuminated when the 1936 Lions party was chosen. Gus won his second tour, this time as a first-choice centre, and he was accompanied by wingers Barney Hudson and Alan Edwards, and half-backs, Emlyn Jenkins and Billy Watkins. The party was led by Leeds full-back Jim Brough and was away from 17 April to 17 September. The entire Salford contingent returned with reputations enhanced, from a tour containing only 3 defeats in 25 fixtures. Gus, who was contracted to write twelve tour articles for the *Manchester Evening News*, made 14 appearances, scoring 9 tries and 22 goals. Alan Edwards, the youngest Lion ever to tour up to then, topped the try-scorers with 21 in 16 appearances.

Gus missed the first test at Sydney. After scoring two tries in a 39-3 win over North Queensland at Townsville, an ankle injury ruled him out. Australia licked Britain 24-8, with props Ray Stehr and Widnes's Nat Silcock being sent off. A big effort was needed to restore British pride in the second test at Brisbane on 4 July. On a soft, wet surface Swinton hooker Tommy Armitt played a crucial role by winning the scrums 51-25, but the Salford trio of Jenkins, Risman and Edwards also figured prominently in a nail-biting 12-7 success. Both British tries fell to Edwards, who capitalized on deft kicks from stand-off Jenkins, whose policy of kicking to the wings was ideal in the circumstances. Gus kicked an easy penalty in the first half and converted Edwards's second try from a very wide position.

The final test at the SCG drew over 53,000 fans and was a red letter day for Gus. Arthur Atkinson had skippered Britain in the first test and tour captain Jim Brough had been in charge at Brisbane. For the decider the honour was given to Gus and he never played in another test when he was not captain. All five Salford men played in the test, which again ended in a 12-7 victory for Britain. Gus had a part in both tries. For the first, which gave Britain a 5-2 lead just before half-time, a scrum heel wide on the left on the Australian '25' saw Watkins and Jenkins move the ball on to Gus, who punted over the incoming Australian winger. The ball bounced quirkily and in the ensuing race Barney Hudson touched down just before the ball ran dead. Martin Hodgson kicked a wonderful conversion. Britain sealed the game and the Ashes when Watkins grubber-kicked from a scrum 25 yards out. Loose-forward Harry Beverley was first to the ball. He handed it on to Gus who sent Stan Brogden haring for the corner to score the match-winner.

Gus Risman leads out a test team for the first time in the third Ashes test of 1936 at the Sydney Cricket Ground. Britain won the test 12-7 – and with it the Ashes. Gus is followed by four of his Salford team-mates, Alan Edwards, Barney Hudson, Emlyn Jenkins and Billy Watkins.

Gus and the Lions went through New Zealand unbeaten in eight matches. In the first test at Auckland Gus led his team to a 10-8 victory, Jenkins and Edwards scoring the only tries of the game; the following week he kicked four goals as Britain won the second and final test 23-11, also at Auckland. However, his outstanding memory of New Zealand was probably the 17-3 victory over South Island at Christchurch on 1 August. The game was played in the most appalling conditions imaginable. In his autobiography, *Rugby Renegade* (1958), he recalled, 'One half of the ground had been cleared, but the other half was covered in freezing snow and sleet. It was sheer murder to play on that surface, and I felt so cold that I thought I was going to die. Whenever we moved we could feel our boots cutting through the ice and squelching in the water underneath. I was emergency scrum-half and I became so sick and ill with it that I could hardly feel the ball when I handled it, and once when I was putting the ball into the scrum I collapsed. I remember absolutely nothing about it ... The trainers told me that I had collapsed face downwards into the ice, snow and slush, and when I came round they were trying to revive me with sips of brandy. Eventually the blood in my veins thawed and I was able to go back on to the field for the last ten minutes of sheer agony.'

The 1936/37 season saw Salford back at the top of the league, Lancashire League Champions, Lancashire Cup winners and Northern Rugby League Champions. Only the Challenge Cup eluded Gus's boys, Warrington knocking Salford out 10-4 in the first round at Weaste.

The Lancashire Cup final at Wilderspool on 17 October pitted Salford and Wigan together for the third consecutive year. The result was the same each time – Salford were the winners. Gus's team made history by becoming the first team to win the trophy three times in a row, but it was a mighty struggle. The only try of the match was a fabulous solo effort from full-back Harold Osbaldestin in the early stages. He made a thrilling corkscrew run from about 30 yards out, beating four defenders before punting over Jim Sullivan, regathering, and touching down. Sullivan reduced the deficit to 2-3 with a penalty but Gus clinched a 5-2 victory in the closing minutes with a fine angled penalty goal.

The campaign climaxed at Central Park, Wigan on 1 May 1937, when Salford and their bogey team, Warrington, met in the Championship final before a crowd of 31,500. The play was largely desultory but the closeness of the scores kept the fans on tenterhooks. Warrington were handicapped by injuries to full-back Billy Holding and centre Dave Brown, the Australian test captain in the recent Ashes series, both of whom stayed on the field as passengers. Seventy minutes elapsed without a try. Gus had piloted four penalty goals and Warrington had replied with three of their own and a drop goal. 8-8 then became 11-8 to Warrington, when hooker Dave Cotton crashed over following fierce forward play. Warrington probably deserved to win, but four minutes later Alan Edwards made a great left wing dash before four men stopped him. The ball was swept to the right wing and Barney Hudson crashed over near the flag. If ever the pressure fell on a goal-kicker this was the moment, but Gus hit a perfect conversion and Salford took the title with a 13-11 victory.

Earlier in the season both Hudson and Risman had taken benefits. Barney had been fortunate with his match, 13,000 passing through the gates for an 8-8 draw with Bradford Northern on 6 February. Gus's benefit match, a 16-0 win over Halifax on 17 April, was cursed with a foul afternoon, reducing the attendance to 5,000. However, £200 from the Salford Supporters Association swelled his coffers and he was able to go out and buy a Ford 8HP for £70.

There was a Kangaroo tour in 1937, led by the great loose-forward Wally Prigg. Gus was ready for his fourth Ashes series and captained Britain to yet another success. The first test at Headingley on 16 October was won by Emlyn Jenkins's second half try, Britain scraping a 5-4 victory. Two weeks later Gus led Salford to a similarly close victory (11-8) against the Kangaroos and on 13 November at Swinton made it a hat-trick when the second test (13-3) and the Ashes were won. Jenkins and Watkins pulled the strings at half-back and fellow Salfordians, Edwards (2 tries), Hudson (try) and Gus (2 goals), scored all the points. The third test at Huddersfield was lost 3-13, the only losing test Gus ever experienced.

Salford surrendered all three trophies they had won the previous season in 1937/38, but had a huge compensation by winning the trophy they had never held – the Challenge Cup. En route to their first Wembley final, Salford disposed of Hull, Liverpool Stanley, St Helens Recs and Swinton. Their opponents at the Empire Stadium were also first timers there, Barrow, who finished fourth in the league, two places above Salford. It promised to be a tough game and it was. Emlyn Jenkins had been transferred to Wigan and Gus filled in at stand-off in all the cup-ties. After 9 minutes Barrow led through a penalty from Fred French, which Gus emulated after 22 minutes. Just before half-time, Gus put Salford ahead with a lovely drop goal only for Barrow scrum-half Billy Little to equalize on 61 minutes with an almost identical effort. The score remained at 4-4 until the last minute, when Salford centre Albert Gear profited from a Barrow mistake, kicked the ball on and beat three men to score the winning try and give Salford the Challenge Cup for the only time in the club's history. Gus accepted the trophy from another sporting colossus, Don Bradman. The press were almost unanimous in declaring Gus had been the best man on the field.

The 1938/39 season was another memorable affair. Salford finished top of the table and took their fifth Lancashire League title in Gus's time. They did, however, suffer the novelty of losing (7-10) to Wigan in the Lancashire Cup final. Gus led them back to Wembley, St Helens, Hunslet, Bramley and Wigan being their victims along the way. The semi-final, at Rochdale on 1 April, saw Gus score a try and four goals as Wigan were beaten 11-2 but the result appeared insignificant as there were two fatalities and scores of injuries, when a stand roof collapsed five minutes into the game. About 100 of the massive 40,000 crowd had climbed onto it and fell onto the people below. It was the worst accident in the history of the game. Gus's wife Ethel and two friends were in the wrecked stand. Ethel was uninjured but a beam hit the shoulders of the others.

Wembley proved another disaster for Salford, who were affected by 'flu and were well beaten, 3-20, by Halifax. Gus scored Salford's only try. That was enough, however, to earn him a six-guinea suit from Harry Gledhill's Tailors, who had offered the prize to the Salford player scoring most points at Wembley.

A week later Salford had some consolation when they beat Castleford 8-6 in the Championship final at Maine Road before a crowd of 69,504, then the largest attendance for a rugby league match in Britain. Gus received £20, his biggest pay-packet as a Salford player. No one realized that Maine Road represented the end of an era and it would be a long time before Salford would again be a power in the land. Gus had for the only time finished as the league's leading points scorer with 267 – seven more than Jim Sullivan.

Don Bradman presents the Challenge Cup to Gus Risman after Salford's 7-4 win against Barrow at Wembley in 1938. Also on view are Lance Todd (centre, between Bradman and Risman) and Harold Thomas (right).

Salford's 1938 Challenge Cup winning team. From left to right, back row: Feetham, Davies, Thomas, Brown, Bradbury. Standing: Edwards, Dalton, Osbaldestin, Williams, Hudson, Day, Gear. Seated: Todd, Riley, Risman, Goldstraw, Dawson. Front: Miller, Watkins.

Salford carried on playing through 1939/40 but closed down at Christmas 1940 until the end of the war. Gus joined Salford Police War reserve as soon as war was declared and in June 1940 volunteered for the RAF. He was turned down because a new law classed his parents as aliens. Gus instead joined the Corps of Military Police and eventually ended up in the Airborne Division, seeing service in North Africa and rising to lieutenant.

The war provided him with plenty of rugby, however, of both codes. On 9 November 1940 he finally captained Wales, in the absence of Jim Sullivan, when they lost 5-8 to England at Oldham. He led them against the English in wartime internationals again in 1941, 1944 and 1945. After Salford closed down, Gus guested for Leeds, Bradford Northern, Dewsbury and Hunslet. In 1940/41 he played for Bradford Northern in winning Yorkshire Cup and Championship finals and was in Leeds's Challenge Cup-winning team against Halifax in 1942, seven weeks after helping Dewsbury to beat Bradford in the Championship final.

The war provided Gus with the opportunity to show the rugby union world what it had lost. Many judges regarded Gus and Haydn Tanner as the greatest backs in the game during the period. Gus was certainly in demand. He captained the Army and led Wales in Services internationals. He also represented Scottish Command and on 28 April 1945 played for the British Empire *v.* France at Richmond in the last major representative fixture of wartime RU. Eight of the Empire team, which won 27-6, were rugby league men. Gus contributed two tries and three conversions.

Gus's peace-time rugby was hectic. For example, on 3 November 1945 he helped Salford win 3-0 at Barrow. On 9 and 11 November he played for Scottish Command in Hanover, Germany and then captained Wales RL to an 11-3 victory over England at Swansea on 24 November. He played for the Army against New Zealand at Bristol on 1 December and against Ireland at Belfast on 15 December, turned out thrice for Salford over Christmas, led a Rugby League XIII to a 19-6 victory over a French XIII in Paris on 6 January 1946 and was demobbed at Edinburgh on 25 January 1946.

On 4 March he was appointed captain of the 1946 Lions, despite being weeks away from his thirty-fifth birthday. The 1946 tour was one of the most momentous undertaken. Risman's team became known as the Indomitables, after the aircraft carrier on which they sailed to Australia. The Ashes were retained, Britain being undefeated in the three tests – a feat never achieved by any other Lions. Gus played in all three tests and in 14 tour fixtures, scoring 31 goals and 3 tries. Harry Sunderland wrote at the completion of the tour, 'Risman is a personality far above average … He carried the responsibilities of leadership with a graceful calm that has made him as great a figure as has ever toured, whether on the playing field or at the banquet table when making most concise, well-phrased and diplomatic speeches.'

If Gus Risman had retired after the 1946 tour he would undoubtedly have been elected to the Hall of Fame on his record up to that time. When he returned no one could have foreseen what would happen. Gus had played his 427th and last game for Salford on 23 March, having kicked two goals against Rochdale in a 13-6 home win. He still had over 300 games in him but not as a Red Devil.

On 4 October he was transferred to the one-season-old Workington Town for £750 as player-manager, taking up residence at Cockermouth. In Cumberland Gus was in demand.

Gus Risman captained many representative rugby union XVs through the Second World War, including this Wales Services team in 1942. Gus is seated in the centre with the ball. Among his colleagues are Alan Edwards (standing, second left), Trevor Foster (standing, extreme right), Syd Williams (seated, fifth left), Gwyn Williams (seated, extreme right) and Willie Davies (front left) – all of whom were distinguished rugby league players.

He wrote weekly articles for the *Workington Star* and for *Rugby League Review*, he ran coaching sessions for the RFL, opened up a business as a sports outfitters and attended more functions and fetes than royalty.

He also continued to provide the goods on the field. In his first season he played mostly at stand-off but soon settled to full-back. In 1947/48 Gus played in all 43 of Town's games and set new club records with 96 goals and 198 points. He would go on to break both records three times. Town had finished eleventh in 1946/47 but rose to fifth in 1947/48, when they reached the Lancashire Cup semi-final and gave the Kiwis a hard game before losing 7-10. In 1948/49 Workington slipped to eighth but beat the Australians 10-7 in a brilliant affair at Borough Park. Gus missed that triumph, having sustained a double fracture of the jaw in tackling Wakefield winger Duggan a fortnight earlier on 30 October. It was the worst injury he suffered in his career. When he returned to action he reaffirmed the view that he was indestructible by playing 68 consecutive games.

In 1949/50 he raised his club records to 104 goals and 220 points, extending them to 108 and 237 in 1950/51. By 1950, Gus had assembled a formidable team. Native Cumbrians were augmented by top men from Scotland, Wales, Australia and Lancashire and Town regularly drew five-figure attendances. When the 1950/51 league season ended Town were in third place and qualified for a Championship semi-final at Wigan. They stunned the rugby league fraternity by winning 8-5 despite losing their wonderful loose-forward Billy Ivison in the first half.

The final, at Maine Road on 12 May, was against Warrington, who had taken the Lancashire League title on points average from Town. A crowd of 61,618 expected a

41-year-old Gus Risman is chaired by his Workington Town colleagues after their 18-10 victory over Featherstone Rovers in the Challenge Cup final of 1952.

Gus Risman in one of his last games for Workington Town, against Hull on 11 March 1954. He is about to be tackled by Welshman Carl Turner, while another great Welsh player, Tommy Harris (centre) looks on.

Warrington victory and, despite losing test winger Albert Johnson with a broken leg in the opening minutes, the Wire led 8-3 at the interval. Gus had made Town's try for Tony Paskins. The second half was entirely Town's. Gus converted a try by centre Eppie Gibson and then kicked his side into the lead with a penalty. He added two more conversions and Town won 26-11. He was chaired from the field and received the Championship trophy, eighteen years after he had first played for Salford in a Championship-winning side.

Alfred Drewry wrote in *The Yorkshire Post*, 'Cumberland is in such an exalted state of Risman-worship that his opponents would lose to him either as a graceful gesture or for fear of what the rest of Cumberland might do to them for spoiling the hero's happiness. If Risman asks for Workington Town Hall, they will give him that, too.'

The following season, Gus miraculously led Workington to Wembley, where they met Featherstone Rovers before 73,000 – the biggest crowd Gus ever faced. There was no stopping Gus and Town. Gus kicked a 40-yard penalty in the opening exchanges and finished with three goals as Town won an entertaining match 18-10. Gus received the Challenge Cup from Anthony Eden, fourteen years after lifting it for Salford, yet another record to add to his incredibly long list. Gus, at forty-one, remains the oldest man to have played in the Challenge Cup final at Wembley.

Gus played for Town until 1954. Remarkably, in his last season he broke the club records and his own personal records by scoring 138 goals and 294 points, playing in all 45 of Town's games and failing to score only once.

Glorious Gus's career finished with a brief period at Batley, when he admitted that he was having to do too much running and tackling for a man of his age. In the 1950s and 1960s Gus accepted coaching posts at Salford, Oldham and Bradford Northern. Like Billy Batten, Gus Risman left the game a wonderful legacy in his two sons, Bev and John. Bev played for England and the British Lions at rugby union and captained Great Britain at rugby league, while John represented Cumberland and Wales as a league player.

ALBERT AARON
ROSENFELD

HUDDERSFIELD

Debut 11 September 1909 v Broughton Rangers (h)
Last game: 2 April 1921 v Leeds (h), Cup

	A	T	G	P
1909/10	36	22	-	66
1910/11	29	35	2	109
1911/12	40	78	-	234
1912/13	36	56	-	168
1913/14	42	80	-	240
1914/15	40	55	-	165
1918/19	3	-	-	-
1919/20	36	31	-	93
1920/21	25	9	-	27

WAKEFIELD TRINITY

Debut: 17 September 1921 v Bradford Northern (h)
Last game: 20 October 1923 v Batley (h)

	A	T	G	P
1921/22	27	-	1	2
1922/23	38	16	-	48
1923/24	1	-	-	-

BRADFORD NORTHERN

Debut: 15 December 1923 v Wakefield Trinity (a)
Last game: 20 December 1924 v Wigan Highfield (a)

	A	T	G	P
1923/24	16	1	-	3
1924/25	7	-	-	-

CAREER RECORD

	A	T	G	P
H'field	287	366	2	1102
Wakefield T	66	16	1	50
Bradford N	23	1	-	3
Represent	2	3	-	9
TOTALS	378	386	3	1164

Note: Rosenfeld also played 15 games for the Australians in England and Wales in 1908/09, scoring 5 tries. He played 12 games for Eastern Suburbs (1908 and 1909), scoring 6 tries, 18 points.

TESTS (4)

Australia	10	N Zealand	11	1908	Sydney (1 try)
Australia	12	N Zealand	24	1908	Brisbane
Australia	14	N Zealand	9	1908	Sydney
Australia	5	Great Britain	15	1909	Newcastle

NEW SOUTH WALES (4)

NSW	8	N Zealand	12	1907	Sydney*
NSW	18	N Zealand	10	1908	Sydney
NSW	26	N Zealand	21	1909	Sydney (4 tries, 1 goal)
NSW	27	N Zealand	20	1909	Sydney (1 try, 1 goal)

* Played under rugby union laws

ALBERT AARON ROSENFELD
Rozzy

'Rosenfeld was not merely a scoring machine ... He was a complete footballer, and he had the heart of a lion. I never saw a more dangerous wingman.'

Harold Wagstaff, 1935

When Albert Rosenfeld began playing rugby union aged fifteen around 1900 in the eastern suburbs of Sydney, the term rugby league had not yet been coined. Nor was it likely that he would have been aware of the existence of another type of rugby –northern union rugby – on the other side of the world. He would certainly never have imagined that within a few years he would have left Australia forever to take up a career in that unknown game, and that almost a century later records that he created would remain unbroken.

Albert Aaron Rosenfeld was born into a Jewish family on 28 July 1885 and began his working life as an apprentice tailor under his father. His major preoccupation, however, was rugby union, which he played for about seven years. He played for East Sydney Borough and for a couple of other rugby union organizations. When the rugby revolution hit New South Wales in 1907, Rosenfeld abandoned union and joined the new rugby leagueists. In August 1907 the rebel New Zealand touring team, Baskerville's All Golds, who were en route to play the teams of the Northern Union in England, docked at Sydney to play three matches against New South Wales. At that point none of the New Zealanders or the Australians had ever played the new game and the series was played under union laws. Albert Rosenfeld played in the first match at five-eighth (stand-off) on 17 August when NSW lost 8–11 before a crowd of 20,000 at the Royal Agricultural Ground. The Kiwis, billed disparagingly in some papers as the 'Professional All Blacks', won the other games 19–5 and 5–3. By playing in these games Rosenfeld and his team-mates had effectively banned themselves from ever playing rugby union again. They had become outlaws.

By the time the New Zealanders returned triumphantly from the Northern Hemisphere, rugby league football had been established on a proper basis in New South Wales. A nine-team competition had been formed and Albert Rosenfeld had joined Eastern Suburbs. Albert's name went down in history as one of the men to play in the first games of rugby league played in Australia on Easter Monday, 20 April 1908. Four games were played on that momentous afternoon, Albert appearing at stand-off in Easts' 32–16 victory over Newtown at Wentworth Park. A few days previously, Albert and the other players who had figured in the 1907 games against the All Golds were made Life Members of the New South Wales Rugby League and presented with commemorative medallions.

A few weeks later, the All Golds hove into Sydney harbour on their return from Britain to play another three-match series. This time the rules were those of the new rugby and the games were the first test matches to be staged in the southern hemisphere. Rosenfeld played in all three

Albert Rosenfeld played for Sydney's Eastern Suburbs club in their inaugural season of 1908. He sits cross-legged (centre) just in front of the great Dally Messenger.

games, scoring a try at Sydney in the first test on 9 May that New Zealand won 11-10. The second test at Brisbane on 30 May was also lost, 12-24, but the following week in Sydney Australia, wearing sky blue jerseys, won a test for the first time, 14-9.

Easts did well in their first season, losing in the Premiership final to Souths on 28 August but Albert and five of his team-mates, along with six of the Souths club, were missing from that historic encounter. They had left Sydney on 15 August on HMS *Macedonia* bound for England with the first Kangaroos. The tourists were travelling second class and on one-way tickets, hoping that the income from their games would pay for the return fares. Their remuneration was £1 a week but if their tour were to be as successful as the 1907 New Zealanders' there would be a huge profit and a healthy share-out. The tour was managed by the entrepreneurial James Giltinan. The captain was North Sydney's Dennis 'Dinny' Lutge and the vice-captain was Albert's team-mate Dally Messenger, Australia's greatest player, who had also toured as an honorary All Gold and knew what to expect. It was James Giltinan who decided to call the tourists the Kangaroos in preference to the 'All Blues' or 'Cornstalks', as people were referring to them before their arrival in England.

Albert Rosenfeld had not actually been selected amongst the original party of thirty players, which caused a rumpus. He and Tedda Courtney (Newtown) were added to the party and then Alf Dobbs (Balmain) and Jim Abercrombie (Wests) were also drafted in. A thirty-fifth player, Paddy Walsh from Newcastle, joined the party after a few games had already been played. It was not until 27 September that the Kangaroos arrived in England. They were certainly fit, having trained for at least two hours every day, while some members of the party

The York and Australian teams on 14 October 1908. This was Albert Rosenfeld's first appearance in Northern Union rugby in England, the game ending in a 5-5 draw. Rosenfeld is seated in the front row, fourth from the right.

had kept their weight down by helping to stoke the ship's boilers. Incidentally, Albert had won a fancy dress competition masquerading as a nurse.

When Rosenfeld arrived in England he was twenty-three years old, his playing weight was given as 11st 8lbs and his height as 5ft 5ins – there were no shorter men on tour. His tour jersey number was 15 and he had been selected as a five-eighth.

The tour started well enough with an unbeaten opening run of seven matches, but soon things turned ugly. Injuries abounded, the English winter threw its full vicious armoury at the tourists and the folly of insisting on a one shilling admission charge – double the normal cost – was exacerbated by strikes and an economic crisis which hit the north of England hard. The tourists remained in Britain until March 1909, playing 45 games, of which only 17 were won and 6 drawn. Eventually, the players' allowances were reduced from £1 to ten shillings a week and the tour ended with a huge loss of £418, bankrupting James Giltinan.

All things considered, however, Albert Rosenfeld's tour turned out to be not so bad. Early in the tour he suffered his share of injuries, playing in only 15 games and scoring 5 tries, but he was considered to have been one of the side's best performers. Significantly, nine of his games were played as a winger, a portent of what was to come. His first appearance in England was, however, at five-eighth at York on 14 October. He scored the Kangaroos' only try, which looked like being the match-winner until a last-minute goal by York levelled the score at 5-5. He played one of his best games at Everton on 18 November when the Australians beat a powerful Northern Rugby League XIII by 10-9. *The Yorkshire Post* remarked, 'Rosenfeld's play at left wing three-quarter showed that he is more at home in that position than at half-back. His tackling was especially fine.'

On 23 January 1909 he played on the wing opposite Billy Batten in the second test match against the Northern Union. The game was played at Newcastle before 22,000, the largest crowd of the tour. Australia were well beaten 5-15 and went on to lose the series. Rosenfeld had the satisfaction of making some brilliant tackles on the rampaging Batten, but he would never play another test. He was a try-scorer in his next game, a thrilling 8-9 defeat at Hull, where the local paper reported that 'Rosenfeldt (sic) played a romping good game at half-back'.

He was at half-back too when the Australians played at Huddersfield in their forty-first fixture on 20 February. It was reported that on entering the field Huddersfield gave three cheers for the Kangaroos and 'the latter replied with their weird chant'. The game was a good one, always in the balance, before Huddersfield won 5-3. The crowd of 9,677 saw Rosenfeld make some smart runs but the star of the game was his partner at scrum-half, George Anlezark. Many of that crowd would have read 'Football Mems' in the *Huddersfield Daily Examiner* two days later, which ran: 'The Committee of the Huddersfield Club on Saturday added to the bewildering variety of nationality represented in their players by securing the signatures of two of the Australian Northern Union players. The Fartown team, despite its general excellence, has shown the want of a wing three-quarter and another good forward, and these have now been secured in A.A. Rosenfeldt (sic) and Patrick Walsh respectively. The former is a well-built player on the small side, and an excellent runner. He played at Fartown on Saturday and created a good impression as outside-half, but he is able to play at either outside position, and he will operate in the three-quarter line when he turns out with Huddersfield. Walsh was not playing against Huddersfield but he has made a big reputation during the tour as an effective forward.'

Rosenfeld played in victories over Merthyr Tydfil and Lancashire at Leigh, the final tour fixture on 8 March. Four days later he embarked for Australia with twenty-eight of his fellow tourists on the SS *Suevic*. Five tourists, Paddy Walsh (Huddersfield), Syd Deane and George Anlezark (Oldham), and Andy Morton and Jimmy Devereux (Hull), remained in England to play out the season for their new clubs. Five others – Rosenfeld, Mick Bolewski (Leigh), Dan Frawley and Larry O'Malley (Warrington), and Tom McCabe (Oldham) – would later also return to England.

Albert Rosenfeld had more reason than the others to return. He had fallen in love with a Huddersfield girl and intended to marry her.

The tourists, their return fares to Australia paid for by the Northern Union, who also gave them pocket money for the voyage, were welcomed home on 1 May at a reception given by the NSWRL. The Kangaroos played a couple of games against the Rest of New South Wales before Rosenfeld played for Easts again. He represented New South Wales, running in four tries and landing a goal, in a 26-21 triumph over the New Zealanders in Sydney on 5 June. Two days later he scored a try and a goal as NSW beat the Kiwis again 27-20. The improvement in his play was noticed by J.C. Davis, of *The Referee*, who later noted, 'Short and thick-set, he had great strength, real bounce and speed. He cultivated intuition, became a rare judge of position, and when I saw him on his return from England he had so developed his skill that he was fit to rank with the best all-round three-quarters, either centre or wing, one ever saw.' Albert played his last game for Easts on 17 July 1909 at the Agricultural Ground in a 15-24 loss to Balmain.

By August 1909 Albert was back in Huddersfield and ready for his great adventure to begin. It began by the removal of the 't' from the end of his name, although it did sometimes re-emerge in programmes and match reports, and the abandonment of the Australian diminutive of his name 'Alby'. Henceforth, to rugby followers at least, he was Albert, Abe or even Little Abe but, most affectionately and simply, 'Rozzy'. Apparently he was known among the Kangaroos as 'Issit'.

Huddersfield's season began on 4 September with a 17-3 win at Bramley but Albert was missing, having picked up a minor knock while playing in a practice match on 25 August. He made his debut on the right wing, outside Edgar Wrigley, on 11 September scoring twice in a 36-0 home thrashing of Broughton Rangers. The Huddersfield programme notes reported that 'all the backs were in great form, Rosenfeld being wonderfully agile in snapping up chances, and Wrigley obliged with some of his unique long-range goals'. The *Huddersfield Daily Examiner* was equally happy, saying, 'There need be little anxiety as to his fulfilling expectations. A pocket Hercules, with some pace, he combines dash with cleverness, and is always on the look-out for something to do.' He scored again in the next game, a 15-14 win at Leeds – a match which Walter Goldthorpe, the Leeds centre, described as 'the best and hardest game he had ever played in'. That must have been some game as Goldthorpe had been playing top-grade rugby since 1892!

In his first season at Fartown, Rozzy only played on the wing eight times. Instead, he was a big hit at centre. The prodigious Harold Wagstaff suffered serious illness and missed practically the whole season and it was the little Australian who stepped into his place at left centre. In two of the big games of the season, against Warrington and Hull on 27 and 28 August during the local holiday known as the Honley Feast week, the Fartown followers were treated to a taste of his brilliance as a mid-field player. He had to move to scrum-half during the 10-2 victory over Warrington and drew the following notice in the *Huddersfield Examiner*, 'Rosenfeld, at inside-half, in Holroyd's absence, got the ball an astonishing number of times, and he and Davies at half were a very hot pair, and suggested big possibilities with a short experience of each other's play'. The following afternoon, Hull were downed 21-8 and 'Rosenfeld and the ball were close companions all the afternoon. No player could have worked more splendidly for his side, and his centre play was a revelation. I hope he may sustain this form and fill the gap made by the deeply regretted absence of our clever, youthful centre, Wagstaff.'

Huddersfield were about to launch on their pot-winning frenzy in 1909 under skipper Billy Kitchin, a Cumberland and England wingman. The other wing was generally shared by locals Eddie Sykes and Harry Wilson, but towards the end of the season a third local, Stanley Moorhouse, began to make a name for himself on the flank. There was therefore no rush to see what Rozzy could do on the wing. Within three months of arriving at Fartown he had earned his first winners' medal. In fourteen years of Northern Unionism, Huddersfield had not won a solitary trophy but the Yorkshire Cup of 1909 broke that drought. Albert played a blinder in the 33-5 first round defeat of Hull KR, scoring two tries and helping Kitchin to four. Hunslet were defeated 12-4 in the next round and the semi-final drew a record crowd of 28,608 to Fartown for a 20-2 hammering of Halifax. The final at Headingley on 27 November was equally easy, Batley perishing by 21-0 before a crowd of 22,000. Rozzy and the other three three-quarters got a try each but stand-off Jim Davies was sent off along with Batley forward Fozzard. Albert's fifteen-carat gold medal would be the first of many.

Huddersfield finished a creditable eighth in the league but when they had visited table-toppers Oldham in the first round of the Challenge Cup and left with a 2-0 victory, there were serious hopes of lifting a second trophy. An even greater shock occurred in the second round, however, when Ebbw Vale won 8-3 at Fartown. Rosenfeld had, nonetheless, experienced a successful first season in English rugby. He had scored 22 tries – just five fewer than Kitchin – and no one had made more appearances than his 36. A local critic wrote, 'Rosenfeld may be instanced as our most dependable back and has often played under difficulties, but the plucky way he has gone through in several matches should be an object lesson to players who are too ready to retire to the touchline'.

The 1910/11 season much resembled the previous campaign. Huddersfield rose one place in the league to seventh, reached the Yorkshire Cup final again and were ousted early from the Challenge Cup. For Rozzy the season was not quite so similar. With the return of Harold Wagstaff, his days as a centre were numbered and a place on the right wing became the natural order of things. Now his penchant for try-scoring was given full rein. The side that was to become legendary as 'The Team of All the Talents' had been more or less assembled by 1910. It consisted of Jack Bartholomew or Major Holland at full-back; Rozzy and the Kiwi Edgar Wrigley on the right flank, with Wagstaff partnering Kitchin, and latterly Moorhouse, on the left; Welshmen Jim Davies and Tommy Grey a mesmeric half-back pairing; a forward selection from, New Zealanders Bill Trevarthen and Con Byrne, the Australian Paddy Walsh, Welshman Ben Gronow, Cumbrian Douglas Clark and Tykes such as Wimpenny Brook, Elijah Watts, Arthur Swinden, Arthur Sherwood and Willie Higson.

Rozzy played twice for a Colonial XIII against the returning 1910 Lions – his only representative matches in his English career. At Headingley on 19 September the Colonials beat the weary, just-arrived-home tourists 31-15, Rozzy being one of six of the 1908 Kangaroos in the team. The Colonials lost the second game, at Wigan on 27 December, 22-40 but Rosenfeld had the satisfaction of scoring his first hat-trick on English soil. A few weeks earlier, on 3 December he had figured in his second Yorkshire Cup final against Wakefield Trinity at Headingley. The Fartowners lost 2-8 and Albert had to settle for a runners-up medal. On 11 February he registered his first hat-trick for Huddersfield in a 39-2 home win against Bradford Northern, when he also landed the first of only two goals he would kick for the club.

The following week he grabbed a try at Wigan in the Challenge Cup first round but there was a furore when referee Frank Renton ruled out a crucial touchdown by Little Abe – despite being twenty yards behind the play. Huddersfield lost 13-18. There is little doubt that he would willingly have traded several, if not all, of the five tries he scored in a 70-5 massacre of Keighley seven days later for that disallowed effort. By the close of the season he had amassed 35 tries for Huddersfield, four fewer than Kitchin. The redoubtable Kitchin had finished as the league's leading try-scorer with 41 in all matches. Rozzy's total of 38 left him in third place behind Wigan's Joe Miller on 40. It was, however, going to be an awful long time before anyone would head the little Aussie flyer in the try-scoring charts again.

The 1911/12 season saw Huddersfield flourish as never before. The team reached heights of excellence that no other club side had ever approached and they were to maintain and even better these soaring standards over the succeeding years. For his part, Albert Rosenfeld began to score tries at a rate no one before or since has ever matched, not even the great Brian Bevan. In the next four seasons Rozzy piled up 269 tries in only 158 games. Bevan is the only man who came near to emulating such a total over four English seasons, his best figure being 258. The only others to have topped 200 tries in such a period are Tom van Vollenhoven (231), Lionel Cooper (227), Johnny Ring (207) and Billy Boston (206).

A postcard celebrating Huddersfield's first trophy in Northern Union rugby. Albert Rosenfeld is on the second row, third right. Harold Wagstaff, in England jersey, is on the front row, second left.

Of course, there had been wonderful wingers before Rosenfeld. Oldham had had Sam Williams, who topped the league's try-scorers in three consecutive seasons at the turn of the century, climaxing with a record 47 tries in 1900/01. He had been followed by the legendary Jackie Fish at Warrington, a man built on similar lines to Rozzy himself, if somewhat heavier. Fish's undoubted genius had brought him 215 tries for the Wire. Rozzy's own colleague, Billy Kitchin, had scored a club record 211 tries for Huddersfield by the time he retired in 1913. The most prolific scorer of all, however, had been Jim Leytham, captain of Wigan, who amassed 314 tries from 1901 to 1912. The record for tries in a season stood at 49 and was jointly held by Wigan's England winger, Joe Miller, and Halifax's Welsh international, Billy Williams, who both performed the feat in 1908/09. Albert Rosenfeld would smash all their records to smithereens in an unimaginably short time.

It might seem incongruous that such gigantic feats emanated from such a diminutive figure. Rozzy had apparently grown a bit in England. He was now half an inch taller at 5ft 5½ins and his weight had risen to 11st 10lbs, although Harold Wagstaff would later insist that he was 12st at his best. Whatever his vital statistics, Albert was sturdily built and made of the right stuff. He could certainly run and was the fastest of all the Huddersfield players with a time of 10.5 seconds for the 100 yards – slightly faster than Stanley Moorhouse on the other wing. Dinny Campbell described him thus, 'He was a dapper little figure … He had a beautifully moulded frame, with a swarthy complexion that had been bronzed by Bondi's sun in his youth. He was on the end of a great three-quarter line but he added to its greatness by the manner in which he finished off the play of the famous men in Huddersfield's ranks. His speed was his greatest asset – he was a professional runner of some note – but added to that he had perfect hands, a neat sidestep, a deceptive swerve and a

Some of Bennett's Nuts.

Huddersfield greats in unusual guise. From left to right, back: Bill Ellis. Standing: Douglas Clark, Wimpenny Brook. Front: Fred Longstaff, Harold Wagstaff, Albert Rosenfeld.

bewildering change of pace. Near the goal-line he was so full of grit that only a brick wall would stop him.'

Rozzy was a tough little beggar, hardly missing a game through injury in his pomp, and he was peppery enough to have got himself sent off at least twice, both times against Bramley. Although Huddersfield were also dubbed the team that did not kick, two of their main attacking ploys did involve kicking. Rozzy became a past master at the chip-over kick when faced with a defender and little room in which to work. He had to develop the art by constant practice – he could not kick at all, according to Wagstaff, when he arrived at Fartown. He was so poor at it that the ball would sometimes go back over his own head. Eventually he was able to punt the ball over an opponent and catch it before it landed. Many tries ensued from this move. Rozzy also got plenty of tries from Moorhouse's cross kicks, as did the Fartown forwards.

Of course, it helped that he was a member of a sublime team, which had developed passing into an art form. In addition, many of the team's set moves, initiated by Jim Davies and Wagstaff, gravitated to the right flank. Having two great centres alongside him also contributed heavily to his effectiveness. His first centre partner was Edgar Wrigley, ex-All Black and All Gold, who was a real handful at about 5ft 9ins and around 14st. He was a bull of a man, who knew how to use his weight and power but was also an intelligent footballer. He was succeeded by Tommy Gleeson, a fellow Australian, who had played for Glebe and New South Wales. Gleeson was smaller but quicker than Wrigley and had an almost equally acute nose for a try as Rosenfeld. Of the two, Rozzy preferred Gleeson as his partner. As a finisher, Albert Rosenfeld had few, if any, peers.

In 1911/12 Rosenfeld broke records for fun. In 40 games for Huddersfield he scored 78 tries to make the previous tries-in-a-season record of 49 look anaemic. On Boxing Day he claimed eight tries, his best ever return, in a 62-5 victory over Wakefield Trinity at Fartown. He scored five tries on four occasions, four tries on three occasions and three hat-tricks. Huddersfield were practically irresistible. The Yorkshire Cup was won on 29 November, Rozzy grabbing one of six tries in a 22-10 victory over Hull KR at Wakefield. The following week, before a crowd of 17,000 at Fartown, he scored again in a 21-7 beating of the touring Australians – the worst defeat the Kangaroos suffered on tour.

New Year's Day 1912 was a special occasion for Albert. Huddersfield won 9-3 at Broughton Rangers, the wingman scoring two excellent tries. His centre that afternoon was his brother, Percy, who was never to play another game for the Fartowners. On 13 January Rosenfeld registered his 100th try for Huddersfield when he scored the first of five in a 56-5 home drubbing of Bradford Northern. The Challenge Cup campaign began on 17 February with a 30-0 romp against Swinton. It brought Rozzy his 50th try of the season and a new try-scoring record. He had drawn level with Joe Miller's and Billy Williams's old record of 49 by scoring twice at Coventry the previous week. The only blot on Huddersfield's season came on 23 March when they were ousted from the Cup at Oldham by a solitary goal by Alf Wood. On 8 April Rozzy was missing from the side that beat Broughton Rangers 14-6 at Fartown but he had the pleasure of watching Stanley Moorhouse become the second man in history to score 50 tries in a season. Stanley bagged 54, including seven in representative games.

Huddersfield went on to lift the Yorkshire League and won the Championship, Rozzy running rings round Hunslet in the semi-final with five out of seven tries in a 27-3 canter. He claimed his 78th try of the season in the 13-5 Championship final defeat of Wigan at Halifax.

The 1912/13 season was as successful as the previous season for Huddersfield – top of the league again and three trophies being captured. Only the Yorkshire Cup eluded them, Hull KR beating them 11-3 in the first round at Craven Street. Huddersfield won their first nineteen league games and were not beaten in the league until 18 January 1913, once again on Humberside, Hull succeeding 8-2. By then Rozzy had plundered 33 tries, including hauls of five against York and Bramley.

Huddersfield had still never won the Northern Union Challenge Cup. Victories at St Helens and Batley carried them into the third round and an away tie with their closest rivals, Wigan, on 29 March. A ground record crowd of 33,000 witnessed an epic encounter. Wigan had not been beaten at Central Park all season, had won the Lancashire Cup and League and were challenging Huddersfield for the league leadership. At half-time Huddersfield led 3-2, but early in the second half Rozzy gave Huddersfield the edge. A reporter wrote, 'Nothing could have been finer than the way Rosenfeld went for the line and opened the scoring in the second half. Possibly he overdoes the short punt trick, but his running is a picture, and his tackling superb.' Huddersfield pulled away to win 14-5. Their football was breathtaking, one correspondent declaring, 'Then we saw the real Huddersfield, the Huddersfield full of dash and daring, the Huddersfield of clockwork precision in their passing, the Huddersfield of irresistible attack and unfailing defence'.

Ten days later Rozzy scored twice at Wigan but Huddersfield were hammered 31-10 in the last league game of the season. On 12 April, three days after that disaster, Huddersfield swept Wakefield Trinity aside 35-2 before 22,000 spectators at Halifax in the Challenge Cup semi-final, Rozzy and Moorhouse each collecting hat-tricks. The following Saturday, Rozzy was missing when Huddersfield smashed Dewsbury 30-3 at Fartown in the Championship semi-final. Huddersfield therefore had an opportunity to perform the league and cup double for the first time.

The Challenge Cup final at Headingley on 26 April pitched them against Warrington, who had finished eighteenth in the table. It was supposed to be an easy thing but Warrington fought tooth and nail. They led 5-0 at the break, and it took a fine hat-trick from Moorhouse to give Huddersfield a hard won 9-5 victory and so take the Cup to Fartown for the first time. On 3 May, Wigan gave Huddersfield an equally hard time in the Championship final at Wakefield but only for 40 minutes. At the interval Huddersfield led 3-2 but the second half saw them in imperious form. Douglas Clark scored three tries from the pack and it was not until Huddersfield had stretched away to 21-2 that Rozzy finally scored, running over for two tries in the closing minutes. Somewhat facetiously, 'The Veteran' wrote, 'Rosenfeld, in the last few matches, has hardly been as dangerous as usual, and his straight dashes for the line have been superseded by cutting in or cross-kicking. Perhaps he has got tired of scoring tries'. Well, he had only scored 56 tries that season – 13 more than Stanley Moorhouse, the runner-up to Little Abe in the try-scoring chart! The campaign of 1913/14 was to prove that he had not got tired of scoring tries. He rewrote the record books again – almost certainly permanently.

Huddersfield finished top of the league for a third season running and lifted the Yorkshire Cup and Yorkshire League, but on occasions proved unnervingly mortal. Rozzy got the season off to a flying start with four tries at York, and five in a 31-10 rout of Leeds at Fartown, the third of which brought up his 200th try for the club. The Yorkshire Cup campaign was a stroll. Rozzy scored twice in the 67-0 first round massacre of Bramley and twice again in an unbelievable 39-0 win at Halifax in the second round, which was watched by a Thrum Hall record crowd of 29,122. His first touchdown broke Billy Kitchin's club record of 211 tries. He snatched three when Dewsbury were smashed 37-0 in the semi-final. Amazingly, Bradford Northern, who finished next to bottom of the league, restricted Huddersfield to a 19-3 score-line in the final at Halifax and Rozzy had to settle for a solitary try.

He set a new record by claiming tries in 14 consecutive games between 18 October and 26 December (totalling 33 tries). The feat was not superseded until Leeds's Eric Harris scored in 17 consecutive games (1935/36).

Huddersfield for a time seemed vulnerable on their trips to Lancashire. Rochdale Hornets (seventh) and Warrington (eleventh) beat them and St Helens (nineteenth) held them to a draw, while Wigan blitzed them 35-3 at Central Park on 8 November. They had ample revenge, however, on 21 February 1914 at Fartown. The famous Labour politician Keir Hardie had come to watch the game, along with a large party from Merthyr, and was observed smoking a cigar and enjoying himself at the front of the main stand in the reserved seats. Huddersfield certainly put on a show for the new ground record crowd of 30,125, winning 46-10. Moorhouse went over for four tries and Rozzy for three. His combination with Gleeson really took the eye, 'Rouge' writing, 'The way these two worked together was glorious and, if asked

The Team of All the Talents – Huddersfield 1914/15. From left to right, back row: -?-, Lodge, -?-, Lockwood, Sir C. Sykes. Standing: Bennett (trainer), Lee, Higson, Banks, Jones, Heyes, Longstaff, Clark, Swinden, Sutcliffe. Seated: Habron, Holland, Moorhouse, Wagstaff, Gleeson, Todd, Gronow. Front: Ganley, Rosenfeld, Rogers.

for the most thrilling try of the match, how many would reply, the try scored by Gleeson after passing and re-passing with Rosenfeld. Rozzy, like all the rest, was at his best. His first two tries were typical of the man, and his dart over in the second half was made when most wings would have regarded the chance as practically hopeless. But with Rozzy it is not his fault if he does not get through a whole team if he is near the line.'

The following Saturday Huddersfield and Rosenfeld ran riot against amateurs Swinton Park at Fartown in the Challenge Cup. The Fartowners smashed all records in winning 119-2. Rozzy scored seven tries and Gleeson five. Full-back Major Holland booted 18 goals. The second round posed more of a problem at Hull KR, where a record crowd of 18,000 paid receipts of £601 – £200 more than any previous game at Craven Street. Huddersfield won 17-2, one of Rozzy's two tries being a stupendous 100-yard interception. Widnes were beaten 21-10 in the third round on 21 March. Four days later, Rozzy's fifteenth hat-trick of the season against Keighley brought him a record-equalling 78th try. On 28 March he broke the record with a try in a 29-5 win against Hull KR at Fartown. He claimed his 80th two days later but Huddersfield fell, disbelievingly, 5-8 at Bradford Northern.

There was more disappointment on 4 April when Hull evicted Huddersfield from the Challenge Cup with an 11-3 success at Headingley in the semi-final. On 20 April, Huddersfield had revenge when they beat the Boulevarders 23-5 in the Championship semi-final but another inexplicably poor performance in the final at Headingley saw them lose 3-5 to a heroically determined Salford.

Albert Rosenfeld's scoring of 80 tries in a season was a truly monumental achievement. It remains the record no one expects to be beaten. It could have been a few more too had

Rozzy scored in any of his last three games and not missed a further two as the season ended. A measure of just how wonderful that Huddersfield three-quarter line must have been is reflected in the league's five leading try-scorers for the campaign. It read: Rosenfeld 80, Gleeson 47, Lewis Bradley (Wigan) 39, George Todd (the Huddersfield reserve winger) 33, Moorhouse 31. Harold Wagstaff scored a mere 17. In 44 games, the Huddersfield three-quarter line amassed 206 tries. Full-back Major Holland created a league record by landing 131 goals (128 for Huddersfield).

By the time the 1914/15 season began, Britain had been at war for a month. The Northern Union carried on as normal, however, and Huddersfield did too. This time they made a clean sweep of all the four major trophies – setting themselves alongside Hunslet, who had achieved the distinction in 1907/08. However, the difference in class between Huddersfield and their rivals was more pronounced than ever, although the Fartown three-quarters' try tally fell to 198 in 46 games. In the entire season Huddersfield lost only twice – 12-13 at home to Warrington and 8-18 at Barrow, both league fixtures.

Rozzy topped the try-lists for the fourth year running, his 55 in 40 games being three better than Hull's Jack Harrison's and nine ahead of Moorhouse. The fact that 14 of his appearances were in the centre probably limited his chances. He scored in all four rounds of the Yorkshire Cup, including the final in which Hull were humbled 31-0 at Leeds, playing brilliantly at centre alongside Wagstaff. Hull put up a better show at Fartown on Christmas Day, losing 10-20. Unusually the game was played on the cricket ground because the rugby pitch was frozen, Rozzy scoring one of Huddersfield's four tries. On 30 January he grabbed half a dozen tries, as did Moorhouse, in a 79-0 victory over Bramley, his sixth being his 300th for Huddersfield. Another major milestone was passed on 27 March 1915 when Salford were expelled from the Cup 33-0 in the third round at Fartown. Rozzy scored his 41st try of the season and in so doing broke Jim Leytham's record of 314 tries. He had become the greatest try-scorer in the game's history.

The business end of the season saw him in prime form. In the Challenge Cup semi-final at Hunslet on 10 April, 18,000 saw him torment Wigan with four tries in a 27-2 win. The following Saturday it was the turn of Rochdale Hornets, who lost 2-33 in the Championship semi-final at Fartown, Rozzy claiming five tries. The finals of the two major competitions were virtually no-contests, Leeds succumbing 2-35 in the Championship final and St Helens 3-37 in the Challenge Cup.

The Great War rumbled horribly on and Rozzy joined the Royal Army Service Corps with several of his colleagues and became a member of Major Stanley's phenomenally successful Grove Park rugby union XV. Eventually he was sent to Mesopotamia (Iraq), where he saw out the hostilities. After the war he played on for Huddersfield, figuring at centre in their 14-8 Yorkshire Cup final victory over Dewsbury at Leeds on 17 May 1919. He enjoyed Huddersfield's final great season, 1919/20, bagging 31 tries and picking up another Yorkshire Cup winners' medal, when he scored his last try in a major final as Leeds were beaten 24-5 at Halifax. The Yorkshire League provided another winners' medal, as did the Challenge Cup, Wigan losing 10-21 at Headingley – a game Rozzy missed. It looked likely that Huddersfield would repeat their All Four Cups-winning feat when they faced Hull at Leeds on 24 April 1920 but the lack of five Australasian tourists proved too much. Rozzy captained the side but was robbed of a further slice of immortality when Billy Batten's 75th-minute try gave Hull a 3-2 victory.

Above: *A cartoon depicting the opening of Hull KR's Craven Park ground on 2 September 1922. Albert Rosenfeld spoiled Rovers' party by scoring the only try in Wakefield Trinity's 3-0 win.*

Below: *An extremely rare image – Albert Rosenfeld scoring a try.*

Albert Rosenfeld in caricature, 1937.

As the great team broke up Albert was transferred to Wakefield Trinity in 1921, spending two years there before playing a final year at Bradford Northern. He scored his last try, the only one he ever scored for Northern, on 26 January 1924 in a 12-8 home win against Wigan Highfield.

Albert Rosenfeld's final career try tally was 386. It remained a record until Wigan's Johnny Ring broke it and extended his own total to 415 (1922-33). His compatriot Lionel Cooper eventually broke Rozzy's club record of 366 tries, finishing with 420 (1947-55).

Albert had been a corporation van driver in private life but was still working in a Huddersfield dye house well into his seventies. In his fifties he was still playing in workshops cricket and bowling, while his major interest outside sport was mending wirelesses. When he died on 4 September 1970, aged eighty-five, he was the last of the 1908/09 Kangaroos.

JAMES SULLIVAN

Jim Sullivan with the Championship trophy, 1934

WIGAN

Debut: 27 August 1921 v Widnes (h)
Last game: 23 February 1946 v Batley (a)

	A	T	G	P
1921/22	39	1	99	201
1922/23	44	9	157	341
1923/24	40	1	151	305
1924/25	33	2	132	270
1925/26	44	3	127	263
1926/27	42	7	128	277
1927/28	38	3	92	193
1928/29	39	2	93	192
1929/30	39	2	88	182
1930/31	42	4	115	242
1931/32	40	5	114	243
1932/33	39	5	138	291
1933/34	37	6	159	336
1934/35	43	6	161	340
1935/36	44	3	109	227
1936/37	42	6	114	246
1937/38	37	3	107	223
1938/39	45	4	119	250
1939/40	27	5	57	129
1940/41	1	1	3	9
1941/42	-	-	-	-
1942/43	12	4	42	96
1943/44	4	-	7	14
1944/45	-	-	-	-
1945/46	3	1	5	13

CAREER RECORD

	A	T	G	P
Wigan	774	83	2317	4883
Dewsbury*	27	2	84	174
Keighley*	3	-	8	16
Bradford N*	1	-	5	10
Tests	25	-	64	128
Wales	26	3	60	129
Other Nat.	6	-	22	44
England	3	-	14	28
Glam & Mon	12	2	33	72
Represent	14	2	54	114
1924 Tour**	13	-	72	144
1928 Tour**	9	3	40	89
1932 Tour**	15	1	94	191
TOTALS	928	96	2867	6022

* War-time guest
** Excluding tests

TESTS (25)

Great Britain	22	Australia	3	1924	Sydney (5 goals)
Great Britain	5	Australia	3	1924	Sydney (1 goal)
Great Britain	11	Australia	21	1924	Brisbane (1 goal)
Great Britain	31	N Zealand	18	1924	Dunedin (5 goals)
Great Britain	28	N Zealand	20	1926	Wigan (5 goals)
Great Britain	21	N Zealand	11	1926	Hull (3 goals)
Great Britain	32	N Zealand	17	1927	Leeds (4 goals)
Great Britain	15	Australia	12	1928	Brisbane (3 goals)
Great Britain	8	Australia	0	1928	Sydney (1 goal)
Great Britain	21	Australia	14	1928	Sydney (4 goals)
Great Britain	13	N Zealand	17	1928	Auckland (2 goals)
Great Britain	13	N Zealand	5	1928	Dunedin (2 goals)
Great Britain	6	N Zealand	5	1928	Christchurch
Great Britain	9	Australia	3	1929	Leeds (3 goals)
Great Britain	0	Australia	0	1930	Swinton
Great Britain	3	Australia	0	1930	Rochdale
Great Britain	8	Australia	6	1932	Sydney (1 goal)
Great Britain	6	Australia	15	1932	Brisbane
Great Britain	18	Australia	13	1932	Sydney (3 goals)
Great Britain	24	N Zealand	9	1932	Auckland (3 goals)
Great Britain	25	N Zealand	14	1932	Christchurch (5 goals)
Great Britain	20	N Zealand	18	1932	Auckland (4 goals)
Great Britain	4	Australia	0	1933	Manchester (2 goals)
Great Britain	7	Australia	5	1933	Leeds (2 goals)
Great Britain	19	Australia	16	1933	Swinton (5 goals)

INTERNATIONALS (35)

Wales	16	Australia	21	1921	Pontypridd (1 goal)
Wales	7	England	12	1922	Herne Hill (2 goals)
Wales	13	England	2	1923	Wigan (2 goals)
Wales	11	England	18	1923	Huddersfield
Other Nat.	23	England	17	1924	Leeds (4 goals)
Wales	22	England	27	1925	Workington (2 goals)
Wales	14	England	18	1925	Wigan (3 goals)
Other Nat	11	England	37	1926	Whitehaven (1 goal)
Wales	22	England	30	1926	Pontypridd (1 try, 2 goals)
Wales	34	N Zealand	8	1926	Pontypridd (1 try, 4 goals)
Wales	8	England	11	1927	Broughton (1 goal)
Wales	12	England	20	1928	Wigan (3 goals)
Wales	15	England	39	1928	Cardiff (3 goals)
Other Nat.	20	England	27	1929	Leeds (4 goals)
Wales	10	Australia	26	1930	Wembley (2 goals)
Other Nat.	35	England	19	1930	Halifax (4 goals)
Other Nat.	18	England	31	1930	St Helens (3 goals)
Wales	18	England	23	1931	Huddersfield (3 goals)
Wales	2	England	19	1932	Salford (1 goal)
Wales	13	England	14	1932	Leeds (2 goals)
Other Nat.	27	England	34	1933	Workington (6 goals)
Wales	19	Australia	51	1933	Wembley (5 goals)
England	13	Australia	63	1933	Paris (2 goals)
England	19	Australia	14	1934	Gateshead (5 goals)
England	32	France	21	1934	Paris (7 goals)
Wales	11	France	18	1935	Bordeaux (4 goals)
Wales	41	France	7	1935	Llanelli (3 goals)
Wales	17	England	14	1936	Hull KR (4 goals)
Wales	3	England	2	1936	Pontypridd
Wales	9	France	3	1936	Paris
Wales	7	England	6	1938	Bradford (2 goals)
Wales	18	France	2	1938	Llanelli (1 try, 3 goals)
Wales	17	England	9	1938	Llanelli (3 goals)
Wales	10	France	16	1939	Bordeaux (2 goals)
Wales	16	England	3	1939	Bradford (5 goals)

COUNTY GAMES (12)

Glam & Mon	12	Yorkshire	20	1927	Hunslet (3 goals)
Glam & Mon	18	Cumberland	12	1927	Pontypridd (3 goals)
Glam & Mon	12	Lancashire	7	1927	Pontypridd (3 goals)
Glam & Mon	5	Cumberland	15	1928	Whitehaven (1 try, 1 goal)
Glam & Mon	10	Lancashire	25	1928	Leigh (2 goals)
Glam & Mon	17	Yorkshire	22	1929	Cardiff (1 try, 4 goals)
Glam & Mon	9	Australians	39	1929	Cardiff (3 goals)
Glam & Mon	13	Yorkshire	6	1930	Hunslet (2 goals)
Glam & Mon	3	Lancashire	29	1930	Warrington
Glam & Mon	14	Lancashire	10	1930	Salford (4 goals)
Glam & Mon	19	Cumberland	12	1931	Whitehaven (5 goals)
Glam & Mon	12	Yorkshire	33	1931	Halifax (3 goals)

JAMES SULLIVAN
Peerless Jim

'Britain is a country in which great sportsmen have always abounded. From the archery contests of the Middle Ages to the highly professional games of today each century has thrown up a sporting genius who has stamped his skill and personality on his chosen field for all time. Jim Sullivan was such a genius … He was the greatest rugby player of all time.'

Cliff Webb, 1977

Cliff Webb, the rugby league reporter for the *Wigan Observer*, penned the above eulogy when Jim Sullivan passed away. He may well have been biased, and his opinion is open to challenge. On the other hand, he may have been right. Plenty of good judges would agree – Dinny Campbell, for example, who said (even while Sullivan was still playing in around 1937), 'His uncanny anticipation, his faultless catching and his accuracy and length in kicking earned him the title, the Greatest Roman of them all. Jim Sullivan at his best had everything a footballer needs – height, weight, speed, elusiveness, power, courage and brains. And, with the lot, he has personality – the personality that commands respect from his team and his opponents, and the goodwill of the crowds … I have seen George Nepia of New Zealand, Otto Nothling and Alec Ross of New South Wales, all rugby union players. They were great full-backs, measuring up to world standard but none of them will take Jim Sullivan's place in my estimation. I always felt that Sullivan's very presence in a team won matches without his amazing skill. He inspired men more than any other full-back captain I ever saw.'

Gus Risman, one of the greatest of the greats, wrote in 1957, 'Few men can ever have loved their sport more than Jim. He simply lived for it, and it was, perhaps, this passionate love for the game which made him such a remarkable player. So many full-backs are either good in defence or good in attack. Hardly any are good in both departments. Yet Jim Sullivan … was simply brilliant at both. He weighed fourteen and a half stones and yet he could move forward with his three-quarters and take part in all their passing movements. He was at his most dangerous when he came forward at tremendous speed on the blind-side to take a pass from the half-back and dart through before anyone had realized the danger. He was incredible in those attacks, and once he had started to move it was well-nigh impossible to stop him. But that was Sullivan, a master tactician, a great student of the game, and perhaps the most brilliant captain the game has ever known. With Sullivan in command you were playing under a general who was quite willing to do as much work as the private. He had that happy knack of keeping morale high, no matter how tough the situation, and many a rugby league player has said that with Sullivan against you, you could never be sure of victory, no matter how comfortable your lead might look. Jim Sullivan's greatest glory was won with his kicking. It didn't matter whether it was a punt, a drop kick or a place kick, Sullivan was always a model of accuracy. He had timing, direction and strength, and what is more he had the cunning of a fox.'

Jim Sullivan was born on 2 December 1903, at 35 Elaine Street, Cardiff. He was the son of Cornelius and Mary (née Dobbin). Cornelius was a labourer at an ironworks at the time of Jim's birth, but had been a shoemaker when he had emigrated from Ireland, probably in the 1870s.

Jim began playing rugby as a nine-year-old at St Alban's school but took up soccer for some years, rugby having been abandoned at school during The Great War. During the summers he played baseball, ultimately becoming a Welsh international. He reverted eventually to rugby with St Alban's Old Boys. When he was fifteen, London Irish took a fancy to Jim after watching him in a game at Aberavon and invited him to play full-back for them at Abertillery.

Emboldened, Jim applied for a trial with Cardiff and attended with a huge number of other hopefuls, all older than him. He was selected to play for the reserves and after a handful of games was promoted to the firsts, much to his surprise. Still only sixteen, he made his debut at Neath on 16 October 1920. On Christmas Day he was in the Cardiff XV which beat the Barbarians 6-5 and the following afternoon turned out for the Barbarians, who lost 0-39, at Newport. Sullivan remains the youngest player to have represented the Babas, being 17 years and 26 days old. He played again, placing a conversion, for Cardiff when they lost to the Barbarians 5-10 later in the season. Jim was so impressive for Cardiff that he was given a Welsh Trial at Pontypool, played magnificently and landed half a dozen goals. Placed on stand-by, he would have won a Wales cap at seventeen had not Ossie Male recovered from injury in time to play against France at Swansea.

Jim's performances were being closely monitored by several Northern Union clubs, who knew a star in the making when they saw one. Hull, Huddersfield and Wakefield Trinity were all keen but it was Wigan who struck lucky. Jim was given £750 and a twelve-year contract – not bad for an apprentice boiler-maker with little prospect of a job. His match fees were set at £5 a win, £4/15/- a draw and £4/10/- a defeat. These were phenomenal figures for a mere boy, but then Jim Sullivan was a phenomenal talent.

One big regret Jim had on leaving rugby union was not receiving the Cardiff cap to which he was entitled. He had played more than twice as many games as were necessary to earn that cap. In the official Cardiff RFC history (1975), Danny Davies wrote, 'There were two … notable debuts, that of Tom "Codger" Johnson … and Cardiff-born Jim "Buller" Sullivan, a young but powerfully built full-back, who played 35 matches and gained a First XV cap … Had he remained an amateur he would most probably have become Cardiff's greatest of all full-backs'. Not receiving that coveted cap really rankled with Jim. As late as 1950 he remarked, 'I played in Cardiff with rugby union internationals who travelled from the north, but asked for expenses as though they had come from the North Pole. If a young man asked me for advice regarding rugby union and rugby league, I would most certainly tell him to become a professional. I have made many friendships in both codes. Everything I have earned in rugby league I have received, but I am still waiting for the Cardiff rugby union cap I once won.'

Jim settled in immediately at Central Park. Wigan had ambitions to take over Huddersfield's pre-eminence in the game. Before the First World War they had been locked in a struggle for supremacy in Lancashire with an equally ambitious Oldham, but neither had been able to reach the excellence of Huddersfield. In the inter-war years Wigan's enterprise in seeking out the best players knew no bounds. They recruited from all parts of England, Australia, New Zealand, South Africa, Scotland, and, particularly, from Wales. Consequently, the game's followers came to expect spectacular, entertaining rugby from Wigan teams, which were always awash with expensive, talented stars. Wigan were a major attraction in the game in this period but they were not as successful as they should perhaps have been, when it came to taking the major trophies, the Challenge Cup and the Championship.

Jim made his debut for Wigan on 27 August 1921 in a 21-0 home win against Widnes. Ten of the Wigan team had been signed from Welsh RU clubs. It was the young full-back who took the eye, however, as he potted five goals to launch a career which would shred the record books. One of Jim's goals was kicked after he had claimed a mark, by then a fairly unusual occurrence. The goal from a mark was abolished within a year. In his seventh game for Wigan, on 15 October, he booted three goals in a 6-14 defeat by the Australians, watched by 24,308. The Australians would not get much change out of him in future. They would see him again soon, however, for when Huddersfield's Gwyn Thomas, Jim's predecessor at Wigan, dropped out of Wales's team to met Australia at Pontypridd on 10 December Sullivan took his place. Wales lost a close game 16-21 with Jim kicking a penalty although Ben Gronow, then regarded as the greatest kicker in the game, landed four goals. Sullivan had celebrated his eighteenth birthday just eight days before his international debut. He would go onto make 26 appearances for Wales – a record which has never been broken. He played a record eighteen years for Wales (1921-39), missed only one game in that period and still holds the scoring records with 60 goals and 129 points.

In his debut season Wigan finished a distant second in the league to Oldham but surprised most pundits by beating them 13-2 in the Championship final at Broughton on 6 May 1922. A crowd of 26,000 saw a well-contested final but Wigan were clearly the better team. They led 6-0 at half-time, Jim having kicked a penalty and another goal from a mark, while centre Tommy Howley had dropped a goal. Three minutes into the second half Oldham's Reg Farrar replied with a goal from a mark (the last such goal in history). After 63 minutes, Wigan's Welsh centre Jerry Shea made a sweet interception and swerved away for the game's only try, which Sullivan converted. He also landed a late penalty, his 100th goal of the season, and Wigan claimed only their second Championship. The play by both full-backs was exceptional, 'Centre' reporting, 'Finer full-back play could not be wished for. Knapman … was cool and calculating in all he did, giving nothing away, and saving his forwards much work by his judicious use of the touch-line. Sullivan was more dashing, but just as safe – a really great full-back'.

By the close of his first campaign Jim had a Welsh cap and a Championship winners' medal. He had also broken Wigan's goals-in-a-season record, previously set at 83 by his compatriot Johnny Thomas in 1913/14. He had passed Thomas's mark on 15 April in a 5-2 win at St Helens Recs and finished with 99 for the club. His goal in the international had raised his total to 100 and enabled him to finish as the game's leading kicker, 17 ahead of Ben Gronow.

Astonishingly, Sullivan would land at least 100 goals in every season between 1921/22 and 1938/39, a feat never remotely challenged. He was the first player from a Lancashire club to claim a century of goals in a season. His position as the league's leading goal-kicker in this period was usurped only twice, by fellow Wales international Joe Thompson, in 1927/28 and 1929/30. In 14 of those 18 seasons Jim was also the game's top points scorer.

Jim Sullivan's propensity for kicking goals was simply staggering. He had spent endless hours as a boy at kicking practice to develop an unerring accuracy, which, allied to his power and technique, also gave him a tremendous range. His achievements are all the more astounding when it is remembered that he had to kick with a much bigger, less uniform ball than modern players. In bad conditions leather balls soaked up water and weighed pounds more than when they started the match. Some clubs were so wary of Sullivan's marksmanship that they were alleged to have deliberately knocked balls out of shape or readjusted the air pressure to try to thwart him. Additionally pitches tended to be heavier more often and penalty kicks had to be taken ten yards back from where the offence occurred. None of which seemed to bother Sullivan, however. He just carried on belting them over – *ad nauseam*, if you were an opposition player or supporter. To add insult to injury, by the 1930s he had stopped practising, asserting that too much kicking hardened his legs and slowed him down.

In some other respects, too, he was a law unto himself. He knew what he should eat as a player but admitted that most of the things he enjoyed were supposed to be bad for athletes. He decided that players should work out what diets suited them and that was fine. His sweet tooth did not make him put on weight and he could more or less eat anything he fancied. Having said that, Jim, just a shade short of six feet tall, started at Wigan weighing around 12 stones, had reached 13st 5lbs by 1936 and weighed over 14 stones by the time his career ended. His fitness was never in doubt, he trained hard, he neither smoked nor drank and he was active in other sporting pursuits. Apart from being an international baseballer, he was a 4-handicap golfer, a good soccer player, an adept cricketer (who once took a hat-trick) and a fine exponent of billiards and snooker. In short, he was a natural games player.

In 1922/23, Jim added to his medals tally when Wigan won the Lancashire League and the Lancashire Cup, kicking four goals in the final of the latter, when Leigh were despatched 20-2 at Salford. His goal-kicking during the campaign was awesome. The previous record for the Northern Union was held by Ben Gronow, who had scored 148 goals and 332 points in 1919/20. Jim rattled up 161 goals, including 4 for Wales, and 349 points. There was a general feeling that the game had never seen a better goal-kicker. On 7 March 1923 Wigan overran Halifax 64-0, Welshmen scoring 61 of the points. Jim equalled the club record by landing 11 goals and added a couple of tries, which gave him a tally of 28 points, thereby breaking John Blan's club record of 26 set in 1919. Jim's club-mate, Johnny Ring, the ex-Aberavon and Wales RU winger, enjoyed his own first season by topping the try-scoring lists with 41. Jim's scoring feats were marked by the club, who gave him a gold hunter watch bearing the inscription, 'Presented to James Sullivan by the Wigan Football Club to commemorate his feat of kicking 172 goals during season 1922/23 – a world's record'. The extra 11 goals were presumably claimed in friendly matches. Two of the directors presented him with a beautiful solid gold miniature rugby ball, while the Supporters Club gave him a silver rose-bowl.

Season 1923/24 was a crucial one in Sullivan's career. Wigan had a successful year, finishing top of the league, retaining the Lancashire League title and contesting the Challenge Cup and Championship finals. Meanwhile, Jim continued dismantling records. On 22 March 1924 he broke the club record when he kicked 12 in a 57-5 defeat of Rochdale Hornets. He also came within a handful of beating his own record by landing 158 goals in the season, finishing 78 goals ahead of his nearest challenger, Hull KR's Laurie Osborne.

The highlight of the year was unquestionably the Challenge Cup, a competition Wigan had never won. Their progress to the final was via Leigh (home) 7-5, Broughton Rangers (home) 49-0, Hunslet (away) 13-8 and Barrow 30-5 at Salford in the semi-final, Jim contributing 15 goals in the process. Their opponents in the final at Rochdale on 12 April were Oldham, who finished third in the league. The game was expected to be a battle between Wigan's brilliant backs and Oldham's tremendous pack. The final was Jim's 110th consecutive match for Wigan. He had not missed a game since 17 December 1921, when he had made his Welsh debut.

The final was played out amid chaotic scenes. A record crowd for a rugby league match in England of 40,786 had descended on the Athletic Grounds and the stadium could not cope. Spectators spilled over the fences, onto the cycle track around the pitch and onto the playing field itself. A hailstorm broke before play started and ambulance men were busy before a ball was kicked. Mounted police were summoned and patrolled the touch-lines but the crowd remained almost on the field of play throughout. Stoppages occurred at regular intervals and the referee, Reverend Frank Chambers, did not bother with half-time, merely changing the players round to avoid more pandemonium. A chap in the crowd with a bugle caused much mirth when he sounded 'The Retreat' but the milling mob took no notice.

The conditions were a nightmare for the players, particularly the full-backs, who were disorientated when kicking to touch as they could not see the lines. Oldham took the lead on 14 minutes with a penalty from Knapman but within a minute the Wigan forwards smashed a way through for Fred Roffey to score near the flag. The crowd had to be cleared to allow Sullivan to take the conversion. Unsurprisingly, he missed. As the first half ended the newest Wigan pin-up, South African winger Attie van Heerden, swiftly followed up a kick, which bounced wickedly near a policeman whose horse was prancing near touch. Attie stole the ball from under the noses of the horse and two defenders and careered to the posts for Sullivan to convert. Oldham responded with a penalty goal from Albert Brough and at half-time Wigan led 8-4. Oldham, however, were already beaten, their vaunted forwards subdued by Wigan's inspired pack. Tommy Parker, skipper Jack Price and Johnny Ring, from an interception, all scored tries. Jim converted the last and landed a penalty and Wigan took the Cup for the first time with a 21-4 score-line.

'Forward', in *The Athletic News*, wrote, 'Sullivan was perhaps not so unorthodox as under less exacting conditions he would have been. He fielded well, kicked a great length, and if his touch direction was somewhat faulty, he could reasonably plead that finding touch with half a dozen mounted police parading up and down the touch-line was a difficult task.'

Three weeks later Wigan failed to pull off the league and cup double when they lost 7-13 to Batley in the Championship final at Broughton. Jim Sullivan was not there, nor were four of his colleagues – Danny Hurcombe, Johnny Ring, Tommy Howley and Jack Price. They had all sailed for Australasia with the 1924 Lions. Jim had felt that he may not have been picked for the tour – why exactly, no one has ever explained. His form and ability were not in doubt, at least not by the public. He had strong opposition for the two full-back berths, particularly from Leeds's England full-back, Syd Walmsley, who had played a stormer against Jim at Huddersfield, when Wales were beaten earlier in the season, and Oldham's Ernest Knapman. Jim was so concerned at his possible exclusion that he seriously considered joining Herbert Chapman's Huddersfield Town and had fixed up terms, if the worst came to pass. He need not have worried. On 20 February he played in the second tour trial at Central Park, played beautifully opposite Walmsley and landed seven goals in Whites' 38-15 win against Reds. Walmsley made the selectors' decision even easier when he declared he could not tour as his employers – he was a teacher – would not give him leave of absence.

Sully, as he was now popularly known, took Australia and New Zealand by storm. He began by booting six goals in the opening game, a 45-13 beating of Victoria at Melbourne on 24 May and finished it on 16 August with seven in a 47-10 victory over Canterbury. He played and scored in 17 tour fixtures, amassing 84 goals and 168 points (both records). His test debut against Australia at the Sydney Cricket Ground on 23 June was sensational. The gates were closed two hours before kick-off with 50,005 fans inside. Sir James Joynton Smith, the Governor-General, kicked off and, as normal, a scrum was ordered at the centre. Before the ball even entered the scrum Australia were penalized for off-side and Jim was called upon to kick for goal. The crowd hooted in disbelief, for under the penalty laws he had to take the ball eight or ten yards back into his own half. It was his first action in test rugby but the ball flew straight and true and the crowd was nonplussed. A few minutes later he landed another difficult goal and by the close had kicked five in a 22-3 triumph, including a touchline conversion of a try by skipper Jonty Parkin.

Five days later at the same venue but in dreadful conditions Britain secured the Ashes with a 5-3 win. Six minutes from time they trailed 0-3 but Jim's conversion of another Parkin try brought victory. Australia won the third test 21-11 at Brisbane, Jim landing a drop goal from halfway. The New Zealand section of the tour was disappointing for Jim, who had a throat problem that caused him to miss the first two tests – which were lost. He reappeared in the third at Dunedin, however, and popped over five goals in a 31-18 success.

On his return to England Jim Sullivan was still not twenty-one, yet he had won all the medals open to him, attained international and test status and racked up all manner of records. He carried on where he had left off. On 1 November he sauntered past Johnny Thomas's club career record of 440 goals, when he scored seven in a 44-4 home rout of Warrington. The previous week he had put 11 over in a 58-0 thrashing of Wigan Highfield. These were small beer, however, compared to his performance on St Valentine's Day 1925, when Wigan met Cumberland amateurs Flimby & Fothergill in the first round of the Cup. Wigan won 116-0, just short of Huddersfield's record of 119-2 against Swinton Park in 1914. Jim broke all records, however, in collecting 22 goals – still a record for a first-class match. His 44 points in the match also remains a Wigan record. Johnny Ring established a club record with seven tries. A report of the game noted, 'A remarkable feature of the match was that Sullivan … kicked the ball only once, except when taking shots at goal … The difficulty of recording Wigan's score on the board when the hundred was reached was overcome by the third figure being placed on the visitors' side of the board.' Wigan were third in the league at the season's close and for the first time Jim did not gain any medals. He did have a new experience, though, on 15 October 1924 at Headingley when he made his debut for Other Nationalities, who beat England 23-17, his contribution being four goals.

In 1925/26 Jim eclipsed the legendary winger Jim Leytham's Wigan career record of 1,304 points and augmented his haul of medals, when table-toppers Wigan beat Warrington 22-10 in the Championship final, took the Lancashire League title and were runners-up to Swinton in the Lancashire Cup final. On 12 April 1926, Jim had the thrill of captaining Wales for the first time. A crowd of 22,050 saw him strive manfully to hold his injury-riddled team together against England at Taff Vale Park, Pontypridd, in a game which was the precursor to establishing a rugby league team in the town. England won 30-22. Jim brought the house down when he ran 75 yards for a try.

Jim Sullivan played for Glamorgan & Monmouthshire in 12 of the 13 games of their existence (1927-31). This team group is probably the Welsh Counties team which lost 17-22 to Yorkshire on 15 April 1929. Sullivan is seated centre (with ball).

The following season was a barren one in terms of trophies for Wigan but that did not prevent Sully becoming the most prolific goal-kicker in the game's history. Hull KR's Alf 'Bunker' Carmichael had held the record with 814 goals (1904-19), a figure Jim would more than treble before he retired. The New Zealanders made their second tour of Britain in 1926/27 and Jim had the pleasure of meeting them five times as a winner. On 4 December he scored 11 points in Wales's 34-8 defeat of the tourists at Pontypridd and a week later Wigan beat the Kiwis 36-15. Jim had an off-day, converting only three of ten tries, two of which he scored, however. He played in all three tests, which were won 28-20 at Wigan (5 goals), 21-11 at Hull (3 goals) and 32-17 at Leeds (4 goals). The latter test was his first as captain, Jonty Parkin dropping out. On 30 April 1927 he skippered Glamorgan to an 18-14 defeat of Monmouthshire at Pontypridd, the only time such a fixture has ever taken place.

Glamorgan & Monmouthshire were admitted to the County Championship in 1927/28 and played for four seasons. Jim missed only one of the thirteen games contested by the twin counties, scoring two tries and 33 goals and captaining the side each time. Another trophy-less season for Wigan ensued, although they were runners-up in the Lancashire Cup and, for the first time, Jim failed to top the league's goal-kicking list. However, towards the end of the season he registered his 1,000th goal and this time there was absolutely no doubt that he would be selected for his second Lions tour. By this time in his working life, Jim had entered the butchering trade.

Jim had a superb tour. He played in 15 fixtures, failing to score in only one, totalling 113 points (3 tries, 52 goals). He played in all six tests, both Australia and New Zealand being beaten 2-1 – all the tests being close run affairs. Because of captain Jonty Parkin's misfortunes on tour, Jim led the Lions in the first and third tests against Australia and in the first and second tests in New Zealand. On the way home the Lions played two exhibition games in Canada at Vancouver and Montreal, when teams representing Wales and England met. Wales lost 17-30 and 18-21, Sullivan landing four goals in each encounter.

The 1928/29 campaign was one of the most memorable of Sullivan's career. Wigan fought their way to the Lancashire Cup final on 24 November, when they met Widnes at Warrington. On the morning of the game, Jim was married at St John's RC church, Wigan. The wedding had been a closely kept secret and there was no general knowledge of it until after the final. Johnny Ring was Jim's best man. The game was a hardfought affair but Wigan prevailed 5-4, with a last gasp try from Lou Brown, and Jim received his first trophy as Wigan's captain before decamping for Somerset on honeymoon.

The RFL had decided that the 1929 Challenge Cup final was to be staged at Wembley, thereby lifting the game's profile immeasurably and beginning a tradition that captivated everyone connected with the sport. Jim Sullivan was going to write his name large at the start of rugby league's love affair with the Empire Stadium. Wigan summarily despatched Batley 25-0 and Hunslet 16-0 in the first two rounds at Central Park. The third round created enormous interest as, for the first time since 1897, they were drawn against St Helens, away. Unusually, it was a boiling hot day and a ground record of 28,000 was set with thousands more locked out. Saints led with a penalty after 25 minutes but Sullivan equalized seven minutes later and there was no more scoring. The replay drew 31,000 to Central Park and Wigan made no mistake with a 25-5 victory.

The semi-final produced another replay for Wigan, who drew 7-7 with St Helens Recs at Swinton before another 31,000 crowd. The replay at Leigh, attended by 21,940, was another cliffhanger, Wigan scraping through 13-12. The big day at Wembley was 4 May 1929 and there was a very satisfactory attendance of 41,500 for this novel experiment. Dewsbury, ten places below Wigan in the league, were opposition Wigan were expected to beat. They gave Wigan a hard game, however, even if the final was not the spectacle for which people had hoped. Newspapers had warned the southern audience to watch out for Jim Sullivan. One described him as 'The greatest full-back playing today. His play will be a treat to watch.' Jim immediately stamped his mark in history by registering the first points at Wembley when he kicked a third-minute penalty. Stand-off Syd Abram tore through to score the first try and at half-time Wigan led 5-2. Second half tries from Lou Brown and Roy Kinnear, the latter converted by Jim, gave Wigan a 13-2 victory and allowed Sullivan to become the first recipient of the Cup at Wembley. Lord Daresbury presented the trophy. 'Centre' wrote, 'Sullivan confined himself strictly to defence. He made no attempt to achieve the spectacular and his powerful kicking was a decisive factor.' Jim played twice again at Wembley for Wales but 1929 was his solitary Cup final there and the last time he would raise the venerable trophy as a player.

The 1929 Kangaroos offered Great Britain a serious challenge and it was with considerable amazement that followers greeted the news that Jim Sullivan had been disregarded for the first test at Craven Park, Hull, on 5 October. Jim Brough, a wonderful player, was selected in his place but he withdrew injured. Incredibly, Sullivan was overlooked again and another Welshman, Oldham's Tommy Rees, was preferred. Australia pasted Britain 31-8 and the selectors were jolted back to reality. They made ten changes for the second test at Headingley on 9 November. It was a wise move. On a glutinous pitch, Britain were not convincing but they won 9-3, the difference being Sullivan's three penalty goals, all awarded for off-side – one of them being a monstrous 50-yarder, which stunned the crowd of 31,402.

That test was the start of a ten-week period in which Jim played sixteen games, eight against the Kangaroos. On 4 December he converted three tries at Central Park, where a Northern League XIII beat the Aussies 18-5. A week later he kicked three goals at Cardiff, as the Kangaroos overwhelmed Glamorgan & Monmouthshire 39-9. On 18 December he led another Northern League XIII against the tourists at St James' Park, Newcastle, hoofing another five goals in a scintillating match, which was lost 22-32. Having played three league games over the Christmas period, he turned out for Wigan against the Kangaroos on 28 December, potting another three goals before torrential rain caused the game to be abandoned ten minutes early with Wigan losing 9-10.

On 4 January 1930 the third test at Swinton failed to produce any score, as the only 0-0 draw in test history left 34,709 spectators bemused and drained. It did, however, produce one of the sport's most contentious no-try decisions. Australia's scrum-half 'Chimpy' Busch claimed a try at the corner with two minutes remaining. Everyone on the ground, except one touch-judge, believed it was a fair try. Loose-forward Fred Butters had clattered into Busch as he touched down and ripped his own ear in doing so. Everybody went down and so did the corner flag. Whether Butters's bleeding ear was a result of hitting the flag or copping a blow from Busch's boot remained a mystery. Australia had deserved the Ashes but the touch-judge had thwarted them. A massive attempt to drop a goal by Sullivan had earlier shaved the Australian goalpost but it would have been unjust had it succeeded.

Uniquely, a fourth test was arranged at Rochdale for Wednesday 15 January, Jim Sullivan captaining Britain. An equally close tussle occurred with Britain scoring the only points of the game in the 74th minute, when winger Stan Smith shot over for a try. Jim thus enjoyed his third consecutive Ashes-winning series. He played his final game against Tommy Gorman's Kangaroos three days later when Wales lost 10-26 at Wembley.

Jim enjoyed a benefit in 1930/31 which raised about £475. Wigan lost in the Lancashire Cup final to St Helens Recs 3-18 and they also appeared to have lost the knack of winning big games. Jim was made player-coach but 1931/32 was also trophy-less. His form never faltered, however, and he was made captain of the 1932 Lions. The tour was a triumph. Jim broke all records by scoring 223 points (one try, 110 goals) in 21 matches. His leadership was remarkable, the Ashes being won 2-1 and the New Zealanders beaten 3-0. The Australians were appreciative of his powers but heartily sick of losing. They would have to suffer once more, however. Jim was still in charge when the 1933 Kangaroos contested the Ashes in England. It was Sully's matchless goal-kicking which again won the Ashes. His side won 4-0 (Sullivan two goals) at Belle Vue, Manchester, 7-5 (two goals) at Leeds and 19-16 (five goals) at Swinton. That was the end of Jim's test career. He had played 25 tests, 15 as captain, and kicked 64 goals – all record figures in 1933. He had set standards of excellence that many regarded as unattainable. In 1936 he was selected as captain of the Lions for an unprecedented fourth tour but declined.

His career with Wales, however, continued until 1939. When France entered the world of rugby league in 1934, Jim played in many of the games which helped to establish the game there and he was skipper of the Welsh teams which won the European Championship in 1935/36, 1936/37 and 1937/38. His final tally of 60 internationals/tests remains a record

Above: *Jim Sullivan preparing to kick at goal.*

Left: *Jim Sullivan, appearing as a guest player for Keighley in 1941/42.*

Below: *Coach Jim Sullivan, approaching 54 years of age, relaxes with Tom van Vollenhoven, shortly after the South African signed for St Helens in 1957.*

today, as does his 160 goals and 329 points at that level. In representative rugby he amassed 925 points (11 tries, 446 goals) and he captained Wales, England, Other Nationalities, the Lions and the British Empire XIII.

The latter part of his club career at Wigan saw Sully amassing even more records. In 1933/34 he smashed his own records in piling up 194 goals and 406 points in all games. He broke the Wigan record with 159 goals but extended it to 161 in 1934/35. He led Wigan to Lancashire Cup finals in 1934, 1935, 1936 and 1938, all against Salford, but only the last was won, when he kicked five goals in a 10-7 victory. Jim had also led Wigan to a surprise victory over Salford (who had finished 11 points clear of them) in the 1934 Championship final at Warrington. Jim hit two conversions and a drop goal in a comprehensive 15-3 success, E.G. Blackwell reporting, 'Wigan possessed a great general in Sullivan, and well as Osbaldestin played, he was eclipsed by the Wigan captain, whose catching and kicking were superior'.

Between 1940/41 and 1944/45 Jim played only 48 games (149 goals, 7 tries), a mere 17 of which were for Wigan. He guested for Bradford Northern and Keighley but mostly for Dewsbury, where Eddie Waring was offering extremely good terms, appearing in the 1941 Yorkshire Cup final – which was lost 5-15 to Bradford Northern at Huddersfield. In 1942, however, Wigan refused to allow him to turn out for Dewsbury and he returned to Wigan. Typically, on his reappearance against St Helens on 7 November he kicked seven goals in a 32-11 home win. Bizarrely, the game was a second leg, second round Yorkshire Cup tie, Saints having won the first leg 21-8. In 1943/44 Wigan reached the Challenge Cup and Championship finals, both played over two legs. Jim figured in the first leg of the Cup final, Bradford Northern being beaten 3-0 at Wigan, but missed the return, a 0-8 defeat at Odsal. He had better luck, ironically, against Dewsbury, in the Championship. He missed the first leg 13-9 home victory but kicked three goals in a 12-5 win at Dewsbury. Wigan took the Championship 25-14 on aggregate, twenty-two years after Jim's first appearance in a Championship final.

Jim finally bowed out on 23 February 1946 in Wigan's 2-13 defeat at Batley. It was his 928th game – a record which will surely never be broken. His goal was his 2,867th – probably another unattainable target. Only one player, Neil Fox, has ever scored more than Jim's 6,022 points. Having broken all records as a player, Jim went on to break a lot more as a coach. He created two fabulous teams, at Wigan (1946-52) and St Helens (1952-59), nurturing future Hall of Famers Vince Karalius, Alex Murphy and Tom van Vollenhoven at the latter. Jim briefly coached Rochdale Hornets but heart troubles caused his retirement. Jim died on 14 September 1977. Fittingly, his ashes were scattered over Central Park.

Fellow Hall of Famer Vince Karalius accorded Jim Sullivan the following eulogy, 'The most important ingredient Sully looked for in a player was courage and it was this part of his own make-up that showed when he was partially paralysed some sixteen years ago. He was a fighter who fought to the end and never moaned – a man with a great sense of humour who loved rugby league and Wigan very dearly. I was privileged to be under his wing at St Helens and I have some wonderful memories which I shall always treasure. His wife, Eve, said when he was great he was humble and when he was humbled he was great. There could be no better epitaph for Sully.'

KAREL THOMAS
van **VOLLENHOVEN**

ST HELENS

Debut: 26 October 1957 v Leeds (h)
Last game: 27 April 1968 v Hull KR (a),
Championship semi-final

	A	T	G	P
1957/58	30	38	-	114
1958/59	44	62	-	186
1959/60	42	54	-	162
1960/61	45	59	-	177
1961/62	38	45	-	135
1962/63	37	33	-	99
1963/64	35	22	-	66
1964/65	22	11	-	33
1965/66	39	18	-	54
1966/67	39	27	-	81
1967/68	38	23	-	69

CAREER RECORD

	A	T	G	P
St Helens	409	392	-	1176
Represent	4	3	-	9
TOTALS	413	395	-	1185

KAREL THOMAS VAN VOLLENHOVEN
The Flying Springbok

'They will talk in Yorkshire for a long time about the Vollenhoven try, which set the Saints eating up (4-12) arrears with an appetite that could only have one result. For eighty yards or so Vollenhoven raced, beating four men before touching down and at no stage of the run was he given any sort of breathing space. How he squeezed between men and the touch-line baffles description, but then few if any men in the game's history, have been gifted with Vollenhoven's ability to wriggle through the minimum sized opening, like putting thread through the eye of a needle'

Horace Yates, 1959

Tom van Vollenhoven was born on 29 April 1935. His birthplace – perhaps appropriately enough for the many who hero-worshipped him – was Bethlehem, in the Orange Free State. Of Dutch ancestry, Afrikaans was his first language. His father was an engine driver and Tom had three brothers, Carl, Pieter and Andre, and a sister, Carry. As a child Tom was regarded as frail and suffered from chest problems. He did not play rugby until he was eleven, which was unusual in the South African context, and then he began as a forward. In his later teens, however, he began to acquire pace and represented Orange Free State Under-19s as a centre.

At seventeen Tom went to Pretoria Police College and progressed through the various police teams, gaining a big reputation as a swift and powerful centre. In 1953 he represented Northern Transvaal in their 27-11 victory over the Wallabies at Pretoria. His all-round athletic ability was reflected in his prowess at hockey, long jumping and sprinting. His best time for the 100 yards was 9.8 seconds, putting him in the first rank of South African sprinters.

It was, however, as a rugby union player that Tom van Vollenhoven was to become a household name in South Africa. On 6 August 1955 he made his test match debut for South Africa. He played centre against the British Isles at Ellis Park, Johannesburg, in a game which created all kinds of records. At twenty Tom was the youngest man in the South African team and was one of nine new caps. He was listed in records as 5ft 9½ins tall and weighed 11st 8lbs. A world record crowd for a rugby union match of 95,000 witnessed a match which was regarded as one of the most thrilling ever seen in the country. The Lions won 23-22 after trailing 3-11 and then racing to lead 23-11 with half an hour to play. Agonizingly, South Africa's full-back, Van der Schyff, a former crocodile hunter, failed to convert a last-minute try, which would have brought victory. The aggregate of 45 points was the largest in any test South Africa had ever played and the Lions' score was the biggest ever conceded in a test by the Boks.

For the second test at Newlands, Cape Town on 20 August, Tom was moved to the left wing. His replacement at centre was Wilf Rosenberg, a rabbi's son who had spent eleven years of his childhood in Sydney. Wilf would later earn a big reputation in English rugby league with Leeds and Hull. A crowd of 46,000 saw a very different game from the one at Johannesburg, as South Africa triumphed 25-9. Vollenhoven was the star, Vivian Jenkins reporting, 'He scored three tries, two of them mainly opportunistic, but one which will be remembered as a great one. It was his third, nine minutes after half-time, and it had a decisive effect on the run of the game. At that stage South Africa were leading by only 6-3 and the British team were still in the picture … Vollenhoven took a ball near the halfway line, beat O'Reilly with an inside cut and then hared off towards Cameron. Another lightning side-step and Cameron was left floundering while the wing ran over half-way out.' Vollenhoven had become a national hero. No one had ever scored three tries in a test match in South Africa. Moreover, it had been a genuine hat-trick – all three tries scored consecutively.

A week later Tom scored Northern Transvaal's only try before a Pretoria crowd of 35,000 as the Lions snatched a dramatic 14-11 victory, when Jeff Butterfield scored a miraculous 80-yard, 77th-minute try, holding off Vollenhoven in a desperate race for the line. On 3 September it was back to the Loftus Versfeld Stadium, Pretoria, for the third test, the first ever on that ground. 45,000 South Africans went home deflated as the Lions ground out a 9-6 win. Vollenhoven got few chances in general and no change in particular out of Gareth Griffiths, who had swapped wings with Tony O'Reilly to mark him. The final test took place at Port Elizabeth on 24 September with 37,000 in attendance. South African national pride was at stake. No South African team had lost a test series since 1896 and so the relief which greeted the Springboks' 22-8 victory, which squared the series, was almost palpable. Vollenhoven put himself among the try-scorers when he went down the blind-side of a scrum 15 yards out and dived over the British scrum-half to touch down at the flag.

That 1955 series is still regarded as one of rugby union's greatest and Vollenhoven's name still reverberates in the sport almost half a century later. The series was notable in that both sides contained three future rugby league converts. The Springboks included Vollenhoven, Rosenberg and Tommy Gentles, the tiny scrum-half, who joined Wigan and later went to Leeds. The Lions provided centre Pat Quinn, who won at Wembley with Leeds in 1957, Russell Robins, a Welshman who also joined Leeds, and the tour captain, Irishman Robin Thompson, who joined Warrington.

Tom Vollenhoven's Springbok career continued apace and in 1956, along with Gentles and Rosenberg, he toured Australia and New Zealand, playing in both tests against Australia at Sydney and Brisbane, both of which were won 9-0. At Brisbane he dropped a late goal. The series against New Zealand was lost 1-3 and Tom only played in the third test, a 10-17 loss, at Christchurch. He was the leading try-scorer on tour, however, with 16 in 19 appearances.

Tom's exploits had not gone unnoticed in rugby league circles. Warrington had been first in the field for him in 1956 but had not pursued matters very vigorously. Wigan became extremely keen and made him an initial offer of £2,000, the bid reportedly rising to £4,000 as St Helens also entered the race. It was a massive news event when he eventually signed for St Helens in October 1957. In total his signing cost Saints £7,230 – easily the biggest fee yet paid for a player, either from rugby union or through a transfer between league clubs. It was later reported that Wigan had been prepared to go to £8,500 to sign Vollenhoven and had consequently gone out and paid £9,500 to Huddersfield for their test winger Mick Sullivan.

Tom's contract provided him with winning pay of £9 and losing pay of £5, and an extra £1 for games at Barrow, Whitehaven, Workington and in Yorkshire. There was a huge expectation attached to his signing. If he failed to make the grade at that cost, there would be much egg on many faces. No one need have worried. 'Pin' McMillan, a South African centre, who had just signed for Hull, but who never made the first team, told Eddie Waring, 'Vollenhoven will be in his glory. The crowds will love him.'

Tom made his debut on 26 October 1957 at Knowsley Road against the Cup-holders Leeds. A crowd of 23,000 paid £2,181 in receipts (compared to £1,272 for the last home game against Whitehaven) – that £7,230 would be quickly recouped. While all eyes were on the South African, the stars of the show were half-backs Ray Price and Alex Murphy, who scored a hat-trick. Tom had the misfortune to allow Pat Quinn, his old adversary from 1955, to score an early try for Leeds, when he failed to boot the ball dead. However, a minute from time, Price suddenly ruptured Leeds's defence and veered to the right wing before releasing Tom on a breathtaking 40-yard burst to the line, leaving the Leeds chasers floundering in his express wake. The 'Voll' had arrived. That try was the first of 392 he would register for St Helens over the next eleven seasons.

Leeds were beaten 36-7 and Tom was able to say, 'St Helens have the best club side I have ever seen. I have no misgivings about turning professional and I shall soon settle down … I felt rather nervous at the start, but the crowd were with me and my colleagues so helpful. The terrific cheer that greeted my try was a wonderful experience … The tackling was heavier than I expected.' His wife, Leonie, declared, 'Rugby league is rougher than South African rugby union and the difference in the rules was confusing to me. So it must have been a little difficult for Tom.' Saints' coach, Jim Sullivan, was in no doubt about Tom's prospects, 'I'm a Dutchman if Van does not turn out to be a stunner. Any team that gives him a yard will be lost. He is also a great tackler.' Sullivan decided to play Tom in the reserves the following week. A crowd of over 8,000 rolled up to see him scintillate in scoring two tries in a 33-23 win over Whitehaven 'A'. Thereafter, the reserves would see no more of Tom.

On his arrival in rugby league, Vollenhoven was hailed as 'the new Boston' or 'the new Bevan', and especially at St Helens as 'the new Ellaby'. Of course, he was not. There was only one Billy Boston, one Brian Bevan and one Alf Ellaby. Equally, there was only one Tom van Vollenhoven. All four were quite fabulous in their own ways. Tom was as quick as anyone in the game and he ran like a deer. He had instant acceleration and even when seemingly running at full pelt he would suddenly find an extra zip, which completely disconcerted would-be tacklers. He was deceptively strong – Billy Boston regarded him as one of his most powerful opponents – and had a magnificent swerve. Given any space he was gone and there was no point chasing him! In 1959, barely more than a year into Tom's rugby league career, Eddie Waring wrote, 'Few recruits have created such a speedy sensation … as Tom van Vollenhoven. Some experts rank the St Helens Springbok as the best ever! The test of a really great winger is whether he can score from any blade of grass, wherever the opposition might be. Vollenhoven, like Bevan at his peak, can pass this test, which qualifies him for a place among the great wingers of all time. "The Van", like Mike Sullivan, can score tries when they are hard to get and when they are badly needed. Is there a flaw in the Vollenhoven make-up? So far he seems to have all the requirements of the perfect winger – speed, side-step, ability to seize openings, an excellent tackle. Perhaps his greatest test has still to come. Wherever he plays from now on he will be a marked man, just as Alf Ellaby was in his palmy days.'

In his second first-team appearance, a 43-11 home win against Swinton, Voll scored his first hat-trick. He registered another in a 25-7 win over Barrow a month later and, on 21 December 1957, he proved that he was going to be every bit as effective as Alf Ellaby had been in the inter-war years. Saints walloped Wakefield Trinity 52-5 and Tom equalled the club record of six tries held jointly by Ellaby and Steve Llewellyn, whose place Tom had usurped. Phil King (*The Sunday People*) wrote, 'Vollenhoven was over inside two minutes when he crashed through Lockwood's tackle wide out. His second try, after 26 minutes, was a remarkable affair. Lockwood sliced his kick from the dead-ball line and Vollenhoven plucked it out of the air like lightning to touch down. His third and fourth tries were only formalities after concerted passing. He picked up a loose ball to register his fifth. But the try which brought the St Helens house down was the winger's sixth. "VV" intercepted on his own "25" line and cantered 75 yards with an all-out Lockwood chasing him in vain.'

Two weeks later Tom ripped the Rochdale Hornets defence to shreds, scoring five in a 51-0 romp at Knowsley Road, and mesmerized Hunslet in bagging four at Parkside on 4 April. On 16 April he represented a Rugby League XIII against France at Headingley. Unfortunately for Tom, and for the paying public, he arrived in English rugby league at the wrong time to play in representative games, the famous Other Nationalities international side having been disbanded two years previously. He therefore had no chance to win rugby league international honours. The game at Leeds drew a crowd of 13,714 to watch such luminaries as Voll, on the left wing, partnered by Lewis Jones, and Brian Bevan on the right wing. They saw plenty of biff and malice as the game boiled over frequently, the French losing 8-19. It was Voll who turned the game in scoring two sizzling tries, sheer speed undoing the French. Bevan scored the other try and full-back Garfield Owen booted five goals.

By the season's close he had claimed 38 tries in 30 matches for Saints, who, however, had failed to gather any silverware, having finished second in the league and been beaten at home in the Championship semi-final by Workington Town.

St Helens' signing of Vollenhoven had ignited the flames of envy in many clubs' administrations. They all wanted a Vollenhoven! Scores of South Africans and Rhodesians were brought to England in the next few years. South Africa was seen as a new hunting ground for talent, after the international transfer ban precluded clubs from bringing over star Australians and New Zealanders. There had been South Africans in rugby league before but they had been thin on the ground. In the 1920s Wigan had some success with South Africans, the most notable capture being the Springbok winger and international hurdler, Attie van Heerden, while George 'Tiny' van Rooyen, a gigantic forward, had also made a big impression with Hull KR, Wigan and Widnes. The early post-war years saw a handful of South Africans playing in England, the most notable probably being Jack Pansegrouw, who signed for Leeds and went to Wembley with Halifax in 1949. When Vollenhoven signed, Hunslet already had a strong-finishing South African winger in Ron Colin but there were no others anywhere.

From 1958 onwards 'a new Vollenhoven' seemed to be signed every few weeks. Some turned out to be very good, many were serviceable but a lot were not. Saints themselves entered the market in the hope of cloning Voll. Among their captures was Jan Prinsloo, a 1958 Springbok, who was, at least on the track, faster than Tom, a really good class winger/centre and a prolific try-scorer. Jan later moved on to Wakefield Trinity for a fee of

Another try for Voll as he glides past Workington Town's renowned half-backs Harry Archer and Sol Roper.

Apart from being a master try-scorer, Tom van Vollenhoven was an exceptionally good defensive winger. Here, he deals with a Widnes attacker as Alex Murphy rushes to help.

£9,000 but died at the tragically early age of thirty-one in 1966. They also signed Johnny Gaydon, another good wingman, full-back Percy Landsberg and forward Ted Brophy, all of whom moved on fairly rapidly to other clubs.

Tom was fortunate in his first two seasons to be paired with former test centre Duggie Greenall. Greenall was already thirty when the two joined forces. His reputation went before him for, despite his lack of poundage, Duggie was one of the most feared men in the game. Not too many players would take liberties with Voll, if they had to contend with Duggie as well. Combativeness apart, Greenall was a good winger's centre and Voll thrived alongside him. The Saints team of 1958/59, his first full season, was arguably one of the best the game has seen. Great names abounded – Glyn Moses, Austin Rhodes, Alex Murphy, Frank Carlton and Greenall were all past, present or future test backs. Abe Terry, Alan Prescott, Dick Huddart, Brian Briggs, Tom McKinney and Vince Karalius were all Great Britain forwards. The reserve strength was also immense. By the season's end they had amassed 1,005 points in league matches – the first team to achieve that feat.

The campaign started well. Voll ran in 16 tries in the first 12 matches. Included were two against Rochdale Hornets, one against Leigh and one against Barrow in the first two rounds and semi-final of the Lancashire Cup. The final against Oldham on 25 October was Tom's first major final. A crowd of 38,780 assembled at Swinton for a clash of giants. On the day Oldham proved too strong, winning 12-2. Voll hardly got a chance to run and was well policed by his opposite, John Etty.

He got plenty of chances to run in the following league fixtures, though, careering over for 13 tries in 5 games, including hat-tricks against Rochdale at home and at Featherstone and four in a 32-3 thumping of Swinton at Knowsley Road. In amongst his Saints duties he had another appointment for a Rugby League XIII against the French on 22 November 1958. He did not have far to go, however, as the fixture was hosted by Knowsley Road. It was just as well because neither he nor Brian Bevan got any worthwhile chances to shine in a game that was played in the best of spirits but dominated by the French, who won 26-8. The 16,000 spectators enjoyed some superb rugby from the French pack and admired the prowess of the French wings Maurice Voron and Andre Savonne, alias 'The Bison of Vaucluse', who scored three tries between them. Jack Paul (*Sunday Express*) wrote, 'Trouble was the League pack had neither power nor pace. Their leaden-footed lumbering allowed the fleet-footed Frenchmen all the time in the world to cover. And it was painful to see the League forwards consistently turning the ball back into the ruck as Brian Bevan and Tom van Vollenhoven gasped for it. These two match-winning wingers didn't get one decent running chance between them.'

St Helens reinforced their position as league leaders with victories over Leigh (10-6, away), Wigan (13-9, home) and Oldham (22-6, home) on 25, 26 and 27 December. Almost 70,000 watched the three games – 12,000 at Leigh, 29,465 for the Wigan derby and 28,000 for the clash with Oldham, who were pressing hardest for the leadership. Voll scored only two tries, against Wigan, in those three games but they were both crucial. For the first Tom Ashcroft (*The St Helens Newspaper*) reported, 'In the fourteenth minute St Helens took the lead in glorious fashion, smart passing and a final hard flung transfer from Greenall to Vollenhoven giving the winger his chance. He caught Sullivan in two minds, passed him on the outside and beat Griffiths for speed into the corner. It was a brilliant try.' His second try was less

Test winger John Stopford (Swinton) gets to grips with Tom van Vollenhoven but fails to prevent him passing to Alex Murphy.

Featherstone Rovers winger Gary Jordan feels the weight of a Vollenhoven hand-off.

spectacular but displayed his great strength, when he forced his way through Griffiths' tackle to give Saints an 8-5 half-time lead. With ten minutes remaining Wigan led 9-8 only to succumb to a fearsome charge from Prinsloo, who dived over at the corner to win the match for Saints. All three tries for the winners had gone to South Africans and another, Fred Griffiths, had scored all the losers' points. Tom Ashcroft was so enthralled that he wrote, 'It was a match which will be talked about long after a thousand others are forgotten ... The forward exchanges were terrific and the tackling was the toughest I have ever seen.' The clashes between the four wingmen – Voll, Prinsloo, Billy Boston and Mick Sullivan – were riveting. Both Saints wingers brought off miraculous tackles on their illustrious opposites, which did as much as anything to secure the victory.

St Helens' play in the league matches bordered on the incredible in 1958/59. Their attacking play was sublime for they had brilliant, instinctive players throughout the side. The main strike force, however, was Tommy Voll. Typical of his displays was one at Hull, the reigning champions, on 7 February 1959. Saints won a humdinger 19-9. Phil King reported, 'Star of the show was the great van Vollenhoven, who brought the house down with two match-winning tries in the 15th and 28th minutes. The prancing Springbok's brilliant efforts – both from his own half – received amazing ovations from the partisan Hull fans. It was the Boulevard roar in reverse.'

The following Saturday Saints crushed Barrow 71-15. Voll grabbed five tries and Greenall got three, while left centre Peter Fearis equalled the club record with 13 goals. There appeared to be no stopping Vollenhoven in this period and by the end of the season he had obliterated Alf Ellaby's club record of 50 tries set back in 1926/27. His own 50th try of the season was his second of four in a 46-11 home win against Blackpool Borough. His final tally of 62 remains a record at St Helens. Voll finished as the league's leading try-scorer, pushing those two other legends of the game, Bevan and Boston, into joint second place, eight touchdowns behind.

Although St Helens ended the season five points ahead of Wigan at the top of the league, Tom had still not earned a winners' medal in any competition. Wigan had snatched the Lancashire League title, a point ahead of Saints – a drawn game at Workington on 18 October effectively having cost St Helens the trophy. Their Challenge Cup hopes had vanished for the second successive season at Featherstone Rovers, who had won well, 20-6, in the third round. All that remained now was the Championship, via the top four play-offs.

In the final game of the league campaign on 27 April Saints had gone to Oldham and lost 14-15 before a 19,000 crowd. Voll had scored two tries but had suffered a severe thigh strain. The injury caused him to miss the Championship semi-final five days later, when Saints gained immediate and cruel revenge by despatching Oldham 42-4 at Knowsley Road in front of 22,000 fans.

The Championship final was staged at Odsal on 16 May and Hunslet, who had surprisingly won 22-11 at Wigan in the semi-final, were the opposition. It was Jim Sullivan's last game as St Helens coach and, ultimately, his team did him proud. Tom van Vollenhoven presented his usual figure – blond, crew-cut, 5ft 10ins tall and 12st, collar turned up and scraping his ears. There was a difference, however, for his left thigh was heavily strapped. He was not really sure that he should be playing at all. The club chairman, Harry Cook said after the game, which was witnessed by 52,560 in summery conditions, 'Tom's leg 'went' after his second try. We

Tom van Vollenhoven has blazed a trail of destruction in Blackpool Borough's ranks, but they have finally bundled him into touch. Ken Large is the other Saints player.

took a big risk playing him, but he had set his heart on it. We knew he could win the game for us – and he did. Who else could have done what he did?'

All the headlines in the evening sports editions, the Sunday and Monday papers were paeans of praise to Vollenhoven, who turned the game and ensured that he at last got that winners' medal he coveted. Hunslet had rocked St Helens by racing into a 12-4 lead. On 24 minutes the whole complexion of the game changed, when Vollenhoven scored one of the sport's most celebrated tries. Lewis Jones, the scorer of many an improbable try himself, wrote, 'It was Vollenhoven's great try – the first of his three – that put St Helens on the victory path. I doubt whether there had ever been a better one. In various parts of the world I've seen some great wingers make some tremendous efforts, but this beat the lot'.

Jack Nott (*News of the World*) reported, 'V for Van Vollenhoven; V for Victory. St Helens's star winger turned the Championship final in his side's favour with a wonder try ... St Helens were trailing 12-4. Hunslet had their measure, and were hurling them back on all fronts. Then Doug Greenall flung out a desperate pass to his partner and called, "Do your best with it, Tom". The winger had 75 yards to travel, a couple of feet in which to work and a clutch of Parksiders were moving in. A change of pace left three defenders pawing at nothing ... a change of direction had another flying into the crowd ... a hand-off sent a fifth sprawling to the ground ... and the Springbok with the academic feet was behind the posts for a miracle touchdown.'

The trackside crowd engulfed the South African saint and then the Saints engulfed Hunslet. By half-time they led 24-12, Murphy and Prinsloo scoring magnificent tries before Voll got his second just before the interval, when Greenall drew the Hunslet cover and flicked the ball inside for Voll to touch down. Two minutes into the second half, Alan Prescott wafted a long pass out to the flying winger, who swiftly cut inside to shred the defence for his third try. A fabulous game ended in a 44-22 win for St Helens and Voll was chaired across the field by wildly elated fans. Only two other men had ever scored three tries in a Championship final – Douglas Clark (Huddersfield) in 1913 and Wigan's Johnny Ring in 1926. Voll's wonder try had been his 100th in first class rugby league, while his third try had been his 100th for St Helens in only his 74th game.

Captain Alan Prescott took over from Jim Sullivan as Saints' coach for 1959/60 and little seemed to have changed. Saints again topped the league, five points clear of Wakefield Trinity and Tom received his first Lancashire League Championship winners' medal. However, there was still disappointment as Saints' overwhelming dominance in league matches did not translate into winning more trophies. Tom repeated his feat of the previous year by scoring tries in all the rounds of the Lancashire Cup, except the final, when Saints were beaten by a contentious try by Brian Bevan at Wigan. A pulsating game went to Warrington by 5-4. There was much hand-wringing too, when Wakefield Trinity went to Knowsley Road and beat Saints 15-10 in the first round of the Challenge Cup. The last and cruellest cut of all, though, was a 9-19 home loss to arch rivals Wigan in the Championship semi-final. Voll scored his 54th try of the season in that match, to again top the try-scoring lists, ahead of Boston (47) and the thirty-five-year-old Bevan (40). His form was as good as ever, even though his centre partnership with Greenall came to an end in December 1959. His new partner was Ken Large, another comparative lightweight, but who was almost as fast as Voll.

Season 1960/61 saw a great deal of personnel change at Knowsley Road. Duggie Greenall finally left for Bradford Northern. Frank Carlton went to Wigan and Jan Prinsloo to Wakefield. Incoming backs included Tom's fellow countrymen, Percy Landsberg and Johnny Gaydon, and in January 1961 Saints shelled out a world record £11,000 for Wigan's test winger Mick Sullivan. Abe Terry, Huddart and Karalius still formed the nucleus of the pack, but major signings were Don Vines (Wakefield Trinity) and Cliff Watson (Dudley Kingswinford RU), while Jim Measures, Bob Dagnall and Fred Leyland were establishing themselves in a no-nonsense, hard-working unit.

In contrast to previous seasons, Saints dropped down the table to fourth but excelled in the cup competitions. Two hard games in the Lancashire Cup were provided at Widnes, where Saints won 19-17, and in a tense 7-4 home victory over Wigan. The semi-final on 17 October took Saints to Leigh. Prior to the semi-final, Tom had only scored 8 tries in 11 games – a poor return by his standards – and after half an hour the game was deadlocked. Don Vines then created enough room for Tom to fly. Tom took off near halfway and swerved and side-stepped his way to the line for what was described as 'the try of the season so far'. He went on to score all three tries in a 15-2 victory. Five days earlier, Saints had encountered the 1960 Australian World Cup team. They won a famous 15-12 victory, even though they were without their own World Cup men, Karalius, Rhodes and Murphy. Voll was involved in a couple of incidents which incensed the 12,250 baying Saints fans, once when he was robbed of the ball, which was played forward to an offside Aussie, who proceeded to score a try which put the Kangaroos into a 10-2 lead. Then he was denied a try by the touch-judge's flag. The crowd was finally appeased when Voll snapped up a loose Australian pass, disposed of his tackler and shot to the corner for a try that heralded a mighty Saints surge to victory.

The Lancashire Cup final, a 15-9 victory over Swinton at Wigan, broke Tom's duck in the competition. He would collect another five winners' medals. It was Tom who set his side on the way to victory, finishing off some inspired play by Murphy in the 11th minute. Saints' reward for taking the trophy was a £40 pay packet. Tom's try in the final sparked an absolutely wonderfully prolific period, when his play reached the nearest thing to perfection anyone had ever seen at Knowsley Road. Between 29 October 1959 and 25 March 1960, he scored 39 tries in 22 games, including five against Widnes, three four-try hauls and a couple of hat-tricks.

His form spilled over into Saints' Challenge Cup campaign. He was the only try-scorer in a 5-5 draw with Widnes in the first round, and scored two in a 29-10 win in the replay at Naughton Park. It was his class, and another couple of tries, which saw off a spirited Castleford 18-10 at Wheldon Road in the next round. Swinton were ousted 17-9 in the third round before a 24,407 crowd at Knowsley Road and 42,074 turned up at Odsal for the semi-final against Hull. It was Voll who swung the game Saints' way in the 36th-minute. Hull led 4-2 when, according to Arthur Brooks, 'Vollenhoven took a snappy Don Vines pass – the only real pass the "Van" got in the whole of the drama-packed match – and set off like a bomb for the line. Then he ran into big trouble. A try looked out of the question. But Vollenhoven was superb as he casually turned his back on two burly Hull men and beat both with a side-step on a sixpence. Then he shrugged his way out of three more tackles. And he was over Hull's line from a pass that he collected three inches inside the touch-line! That sizzling try knocked the stuffing out of Hull.'

Saints won 26-9 and qualified for what was deemed 'the dream final', against Wigan at Wembley on 13 May – the most important Saints-Wigan derby ever played (at least, until 1961). Saints went into the game on the back of a 4-11 defeat at Leeds in the Championship semi-final the previous Saturday. Voll's first appearance at Wembley could hardly have been more special. The temperature was in the 80s and there was a near-capacity crowd of 94,672 (mostly red and white bedecked) Lancastrians. It might not have been a great game, but it was an exciting and close affair. Around the hour mark Saints led 5-4 – a Murphy try and a Rhodes goal to two Griffiths penalties. At that point Wigan were attacking under Saints' posts but lost the ball. Huddart fell on it, played it back to Murphy, who sent it right to Karalius. Karalius shipped it to Large, who swerved and accelerated between Frank Collier and Frank Carlton. One of the tries of the century was unfolding. Large shot away and straightened out about ten yards inside the touch-line with Voll flying outside him. Voll took his pass and accelerated through an attempted tackle by Griffiths, who sailed helplessly into touch. Tom returned the ball to Large as he approached halfway, the pair flying on parallel paths. Wigan's long-striding captain Eric Ashton was flying on his own diagonal path of destruction from the opposite wing and bearing down on Large, who by then had crossed the Wigan '25'. Fifteen yards out Ashton clattered Large to the grass, the momentum taking both to the goal line, but not before Large had served Voll, who raced past the corner flag and straightened out to run along the deadball line, passing a dumbfounded photographer and

A magnificent study of Tom van Vollenhoven escaping a tackle from Swinton's Bob Fleet in the Lancashire Cup final of 1961. Saints won 25-9.

a boy scout along the way. He plonked the ball down one-handed as Billy Boston arrived too late to make any difference and was swallowed up by his ecstatic team-mates.

The whole sublime passage of play took less time than it took the reader to read this description but for those who were there, the image will be forever treasured in the mind's eye, and for those who were not there ... well, we have all seen it on television and video so often that we can imagine being there. Saints took the Cup, 12-6.

If he had only scored this Wembley try and his spellbinder against Hunslet in 1959, Vollenhoven's lasting fame would have been assured. Those who were lucky enough to watch him regularly will know they were only the tip of the iceberg.

Tom finished as leading try-scorer for 1960/61 with 59. Runner-up was his old Springbok colleague, Wilf Rosenberg, with 44. He thus became the first post-war player to top the lists in three consecutive seasons. In three-and-a-half seasons with Saints he had amassed 213 tries in 161 games. There were 179 more to come but at a slower rate – 248 games (which was still a lot quicker than most top-rated wingers).

Saints won the Lancashire Cup in 1961 beating Swinton 25-9 in the final, Voll claiming a try. However, no more trophies were won as the team dropped to ninth in the table. Tom played twice for Rugby League XIIIs. On 20 September they beat the New Zealanders 22-20 at Manchester's White City Stadium and on 12 October they lost 20-21 to France at Paris's Parc des Princes. It was Tom's first trip to France. The game was played under rugby union laws regarding playing the ball. Consequently, the League side was filled with ex-union players, including six South Africans. The game was a mess but Tom provided the highlight, scoring after a dazzling 75-yard touchline run. It was his last appearance in representative rugby. Another highlight of his season was when he equalled the club record by claiming six tries against Blackpool on 23 April.

In July 1962, Tom, Fred Griffiths, Wilf Rosenberg and Ted Brophy were invited to join Wakefield Trinity on a six-match promotional tour of South Africa, taking in Johannesburg,

The referee seems to be getting in Tom van Vollenhoven's way as he touches down for a try against Huddersfield at Knowsley Road in 1962. Huddersfield winger Ken Senior is well beaten.

Bloemfontein, Durban, Benoni and Pretoria. On returning to St Helens he found that they had signed another match-winning South African winger in Len Killeen, whose speciality, however, was goal-kicking. Between them they were to dominate Saints' scoring for the next five years.

In the latter part of Tom's career, Saints continued to figure in the challenge for honours and although his speed declined, his experience and nous increased. His reading of the game and his defensive capacity, which had always been good, became even better. He played in winning Lancashire Cup finals in 1962, when he scored the only try in a 7-4 success against Swinton, 1963 and 1967, but missed the 1964 final through injury. He was skipper of the team that took the trophy in 1967, beating Warrington in a replay. Saints won the Lancashire League in 1964/65, 1965/66 and 1966/67 and took the short-lived Western Championship in 1963/64, accounting for luckless Swinton 10-7 in the final. Another first was an appearance in the inaugural BBC2 Floodlit Trophy final on 14 December 1965, when Castleford ground out a 4-0 win at Knowsley Road.

There were also a couple of Championship finals to add to Voll's *curriculum vitae*, but both ended in disappointment, Halifax beating Saints 15-7 in 1965, when Tom played at centre. In 1967 he captained the side against Wakefield Trinity in a 7-7 draw, the replay ending in a 9-21 defeat at Swinton, where Voll scored his last try in a major final. The season between

St Helens, 1965/66. From left to right, back row: Coslett, Sayer, Dagnall, Watson, Warlow, Mantle, A. Barrow, Hitchen. Front row: Halsall, Benyon, Bishop, F. Barrow, Vollenhoven, French, Harvey, Prosser, Killeen.

those defeats, 1965/66, had been one of Saints' greatest. They had won the Cup, hammering Wigan 21-2 at Wembley, and completed the double by over-running Halifax 35-12 in the Championship final, although injury kept Tom out of that game. They had also lifted the Lancashire League and taken the League Leaders Trophy.

Tom's career ended in 1968. He was made captain in his last season, which was also his testimonial year. He received a record £2,800 but it was not Knowsley Road which witnessed his finale. Tom was invited to play for the Great Britain World Cup team in its final preparatory game on 3 May 1968, against Halifax before leaving for the Antipodes. It was low-key game but a high-key gesture from the RFL. Voll went out how he should – in style, with a hat-trick.

HAROLD
WAGSTAFF

HUDDERSFIELD

Debut: 10 November 1906 v Bramley (a)
Last game: 23 March 1925 v Oldham (a)

	A	T	G	P
1906/07	21	6	8	34
1907/08	24	2	-	6
1908/09	35	11	1	35
1909/10	5	1	-	3
1910/11	30	14	2	46
1911/12	40	21	1	65
1912/13	34	22	-	66
1913/14	30	16	-	48
1914/15	38	34	-	102
1918/19	1	1	-	3
1919/20	34	13	-	39
1920/21	27	6	-	18
1921/22	35	15	-	45
1922/23	18	3	-	9
1923/24	35	8	-	24
1924/25	29	2	-	6

CAREER RECORD

	A	T	G	P
H'field	436	175	12	549
Tests	12	2	-	6
England	9	7	3	27
Yorkshire	15	4	-	12
Represent	4	-	-	-
1914 Tour*	9	11	4	41
1920 Tour*	9	10	-	30
TOTALS	494	209	19	665

* Excluding tests

Note: The records for the 1914 and 1920 tours of Australasia are incomplete.

TESTS (12)

Great Britain	10	Australasia	19	1911	Newcastle
Great Britain	11	Australasia	11	1911	Edinburgh (2 tries)
Great Britain	23	Australia	5	1914	Sydney
Great Britain	7	Australia	12	1914	Sydney
Great Britain	14	Australia	6	1914	Sydney
Great Britain	16	N Zealand	13	1914	Auckland
Great Britain	4	Australia	8	1920	Brisbane
Great Britain	8	Australia	21	1920	Sydney
Great Britain	19	N Zealand	3	1920	Christchurch
Great Britain	11	N Zealand	10	1920	Wellington
Great Britain	6	Australia	5	1921	Leeds
Great Britain	6	Australia	0	1922	Salford

INTERNATIONALS (9)

England	14	Australia	9	1909	Huddersfield
England	39	Wales	13	1910	Coventry (1 try, 2 goals)
England	27	Wales	8	1911	Ebbw Vale (1 try, 1 goal)
England	6	Australasia	11	1911	Fulham (1 try)
England	31	Wales	5	1912	Oldham (1 try)
England	40	Wales	16	1913	Plymouth (1 try)
England	16	Wales	12	1914	St Helens (1 try)
England	33	Other Nat.	16	1921	Workington (1 try)
England	2	Wales	13	1923	Wigan

COUNTY GAMES (15)

Yorkshire	30	Cumberland	0	1908	Huddersfield
Yorkshire	0	Lancashire	13	1908	Salford
Yorkshire	3	Lancashire	17	1910	Wigan
Yorkshire	13	Cumberland	16	1911	Millom
Yorkshire	12	Lancashire	13	1912	Halifax
Yorkshire	19	Cumberland	5	1912	Hull KR (1 try)
Yorkshire	20	Lancashire	8	1912	Oldham (2 tries)
Yorkshire	3	Cumberland	8	1913	Workington
Yorkshire	5	Lancashire	15	1919	Broughton
Yorkshire	25	Cumberland	9	1919	Hunslet (1 try)
Yorkshire	27	Cumberland	6	1920	Maryport
Yorkshire	8	Australians	24	1921	Wakefield
Yorkshire	9	Cumberland	4	1922	Maryport
Yorkshire	11	Lancashire	11	1922	Hull KR
Yorkshire	5	Lancashire	6	1923	Oldham

HAROLD WAGSTAFF
The Prince of Centres

'There were famous men in the Huddersfield and England teams in those days, but Waggy was the most famous of all.'
George M. Thomson, the *Yorkshire Observer*, July 1939

Like his great contemporary Billy Batten, Harold Wagstaff came from humble origins. He was born on 19 May 1891 at Underbank, Holmfirth, a small picturesque Pennine village a few miles from Huddersfield, which has now been immortalized as the setting for the long-running television comedy *Last of the Summer Wine*. His father Andrew had been born in Underbank but in the 1870s had moved to Rochdale to work as a millhand and married a local girl, Hannah Rhodes, who was also a millhand. Two of Harold's older siblings, Ann Eliza and Arthur, had been born in Rochdale but the family's return to Underbank around 1881 meant that Harold and two other brothers, Young and Norman, were native Tykes. Andrew Wagstaff's occupation changed eventually from millhand to painter's labourer, so the Wagstaff household never enjoyed times of plenty. Harold's mother died in 1904 when he was not yet thirteen.

By that time Harold was rugby mad, having begun to play the game as a child with an old yeast bag stuffed with rags for a ball. He graduated to being a member of the Pump Hole Rangers, a team of youths who met at the village pump in Holmfirth and played against other groups of lads from the surrounding districts, often in farmers' fields without goals or pitch markings. He was a big lad for his age but many of his playing colleagues and opponents were three or four years older. The game they played was Northern Union football, for the old rugby union game had been virtually wiped out in the area since the Great Schism of 1895. Even so, Harold Wagstaff later recalled that the feats of the 1905/06 New Zealand All Blacks had a profound effect upon him and his play-mates, even though none of them ever saw the All Blacks in action. The vibrant reports of their matches and the descriptions of their revolutionary tactics, which placed utter reliance on handling and team-work linked to an unprecedented athleticism in the work of the forwards, strongly influenced the young three-quarter's philosophy on how the game should be played. Another major influence on him was the open style of play employed by the Broughton Rangers team in the early years of the twentieth century.

However, the young Wagstaff's primary ambition was to play for Underbank Rangers, who joined the Western Division of the Bradford & District League in 1906, after previously being a member of the Huddersfield & District League. Such was the fever for football in those times that the Rangers would draw crowds of a thousand and more to their Bank End ground for the visits of teams such as Hebden Bridge, Salterhebble, Rastrick, Brighouse St James, Marsden, Birkhouse Rangers, Slaithwaite Juniors, Thrum Hall and the reserve teams of Huddersfield and Halifax. By March 1906 Harold had achieved his aim and made his debut for Underbank a couple of months before his fifteenth birthday.

The start of the 1906/07 season saw the birth of an essentially new game. The Northern Unionists reduced teams from fifteen to thirteen-a-side, the knock-on law was modified, direct kicking into touch was banned and the play-the-ball was transformed into a defining feature of the game. Harold Wagstaff's first taste of the new rugby came on 8 September 1906 and he found it delicious. Underbank beat Huddersfield St Joseph's 26-5 at Bank End with Harold scoring the first try for Underbank under thirteen-a-side laws. He also kicked the first goal when he converted forward Arthur French's try and finished the match with three tries and two goals. The *Holmfirth Express* noted, 'The new game is one of life and activity, and full of incident. Too many games in the past have ended with both sides nil. Under the new rules, tries and goals should be plentiful. Sheer strength will be at a discount, and speed with staying powers will count.'

Although he was still only fifteen, Harold was attracting a great deal of attention. On 20 October he starred in Underbank's 10-2 victory at Birkhouse Rangers in the second round of the Halifax Charity Cup, scoring two tries and two goals. The referee George Dickenson, a former Halifax captain and Yorkshire forward, approached Harold after the game and asked him if he would like to join Halifax. Harold was keen enough but Halifax did not come back to him. Apparently, Dickenson told the Halifax committee of the youngster's talents the following morning but on hearing that he had barely passed fifteen, they did not care to risk signing him – one of them famously (but foolishly) declaring, 'We want men, not boys'. Huddersfield heard of Halifax's *faux pas* and Joe Clifford, of the football committee, displayed more sense, persuading Harold to sign for the Fartowners. The deal was done at Harold's uncle's pub, the Druid's Hotel in Underbank, and the signing-on fee was 5 gold sovereigns.

Having exchanged the red jersey of Underbank for the new-fangled claret and gold hoops of Huddersfield, Harold Wagstaff made his first-class debut for the Fartowners at Bramley on 10 November 1906. He was aged 15 years and 175 days. Only Bramley's Harold Edmondson, at 15 years and 81 days old, when he appeared against Bradford Northern in 1919, has ever played at senior level at a younger age than Wagstaff. Coincidentally, Edmondson and Wagstaff were to be team-mates at Fartown in the post-Great War period.

Harold Wagstaff retained vivid memories of his debut at the Barley Mow, particularly of his direct opponent in the centre. Harold at that time weighed almost 11 stones but opposite him was the famous veteran Albert Hambrecht, capped 18 times by Yorkshire between 1895 and 1901, under both rugby union and northern union auspices, a formidably hard-running player who topped 13 stones. Wagstaff recalled, 'The first time that I went to tackle Hambrecht – I can feel the bump now when I think of it! If ever a youngster felt that he had been under a steamroller, I did. In junior football, if one looked hard enough at a man he would pass the ball. I tried the same trick with Hambrecht, and, when he made it clear that he was not going to be intimidated, I went in to tackle in, I am afraid, a somewhat half-hearted sort of way. One knee hit me under the chin, the other whizzed past my face. I went down with a foot on my chest, and I realized at once that the making of a tackle in senior football was a vastly different thing from the making of a tackle in junior football. Someone said, "Get him sideways. Don't face him." Whenever I had to tackle again that afternoon I dived at Hambrecht's ankles.'

Jim Davies, Wagstaff's co-centre, chided him for not holding one of his bullet passes and informed him that football was not a game for babies. However, the portents were good.

Huddersfield won 28-11 and Harold scored a second half try, with a delightful cut through to the posts. The *Leeds & Yorkshire Mercury* reported that 'he played finely and gave promise of becoming a capital centre'. The *Huddersfield Daily Examiner* was more verbose: 'The other centre position was given to the new recruit from Underbank, who, I should say, is one of the youngest, if not the youngest player, who has ever represented the club. His handling of the ball was a long way from perfect, which, I imagine, was the result of nervousness, as he improved considerably as the game wore on. Apart from this, I was very favourably impressed by him. He was always in the right place, whether on the attack or defence, he is already distinctly speedy, kicks well, tackles well, and all the way through displayed a considerable knowledge of the game, and, when he gets over the weakness he showed on Saturday, will make a really first-class player with luck, or I shall be much disappointed, for he has the build and physical attributes, and, what is more important still, he evidently possesses brain, and I fully expect him to go a long way.' Wagstaff did not appear in reserve team rugby until he was near retirement in 1925, but he was allowed to turn out in a few more games for Underbank. On 22 December 1906 he played in the centre alongside his brother in a 3-10 loss to Halifax 'A' at Bank End in the semi-final of the Halifax Charity Cup and on Christmas Day he made his last appearance for his native club, playing brilliantly and 'kicking some good goals' in Underbank's 47-0 rout of Marsden.

In 1906 Huddersfield had high aspirations and a ground at Fartown prestigious enough to host county matches and major finals. They had been one of the aristocrats of rugby union in the north but since the formation of the Northern Union they had won precisely nothing. In Wagstaff's first season they finished nineteenth of 26 in the league table – which represented an improvement for in 1904/05 they had finished fifth in the old second division and only been saved from further degradation when the two division system had been abandoned for 1905/06, when they attained eleventh place. The potential at Huddersfield was nonetheless enormous and crowd support would boom if a successful, attractive team could be assembled. By the time Harold Wagstaff became a Fartowner the seeds of success had been planted but it would take a few years for fruit to appear. When those fruits ripened Wagstaff was, as it were, the head gardener.

On his arrival at Fartown the club possessed some real talent. Jim Davies, a Welsh centre, who later became a great stand-off in the glory years, and Cumbrian winger-centre, Billy Kitchin, a future England cap, were the star men. There were others, such as the veteran scrum-half Percy Holroyd and the elusive young full-back from Morecambe Jack Bartholomew (uncle of comedian Eric Morecambe), and a couple of rising forwards in Ike Cole, an international at 19, and Arthur Swinden. Many more, however, were needed to make Huddersfield a real force.

In the meantime, Harold Wagstaff continued to blossom. The training regime at Fartown quickly drove his weight up to 12 stones – he always maintained his best playing weight was 12st 4lbs. The extra poundage to his 5ft 11ins frame, he averred, went onto his hips and thighs so he never looked as heavy as he was, retaining a slim waist. With that shape he maintained he was able to swerve and sway away from defenders more effectively than if he had been more heavily built. Under skipper Fred Charlesworth the 1907/08 season saw Huddersfield rise four places in the league to fifteenth. Harold's progress was faster than the team's. Crucially, his views on the game were reinforced by his encounter with the New Zealand All Golds at Fartown on 12 October 1907. Albert Baskerville's tourists were breaking new ground as the first overseas visitors and their impact was immeasurable. Huddersfield lost 8-19 and Harold's eyes were opened wide as he watched and tried to counter the machinations of Lance Todd, who scored two stunning tries, Edgar Wrigley, George Smith and the wonderful Australian Dally Messenger, alias 'The Master'. The young centre was confirmed in his belief that the Northern Union game produced too much kicking and not enough passing, that teamwork and support play were prerequisites for success and that forwards should be capable of joining in the open play.

The 1908/09 season was a turning point for both Huddersfield and Harold Wagstaff. The team shot up to fifth in the table under new captain Billy Kitchin, who topped the try-scoring with 32. A major signing was that of Edgar Wrigley, the New Zealand All Gold, who partnered Wagstaff in the centres, while the forward pack, still adept in dribbling, became renowned for its ability to handle. Its inability to win the scrimmages, however, was its Achilles heel.

His development had been so swift that he was chosen to play in a Yorkshire trial at Dewsbury on 6 October 1908. Remarkably, he decided that he would adopt a policy of not kicking at all, whatever the others did. It certainly worked. His team, the Possibles, beat the Probables 20-13 and Wagstaff's performance 'captivated the crowd'. He was duly selected to play for Yorkshire against Cumberland on 17 October on his home ground at Fartown. Cumberland were despatched 30-0 and Wagstaff did sufficiently well to retain his position in the Roses Match at Salford a fortnight later. A 0-13 defeat was the result but experience against men like George Smith, the New Zealand All Black and All Gold, and the celebrated Welshman Bert Jenkins – an incongruous centre pairing for Lancashire – was invaluable.

Wagstaff's county debut caused a stir. Many of those who saw it could not believe that Wagstaff was as young as it was claimed. His physique and maturity of play belied his youth. So much controversy over the issue arose that a facsimile of his certificate of baptism was reproduced in the *Northern Union News* on 14 November 1908. The fact was that he had made his county debut at the tender age of 17 years and 141 days – a record which still stands for Yorkshire. His county career ultimately encompassed 15 caps and did not end until 1923. The fact that there were no county games between 1913 and 1919 clearly robbed him of many more caps. His county cap was presented to him by Harry Lodge, a Huddersfield committeeman and former club captain, on 5 December 1908 in the saloon of the railway carriage by which the Huddersfield team was conveyed to their match at Hunslet.

Within a month of that presentation, Waggie was elevated to a higher plane. The first Australian touring team had journeyed to Britain and were to play England in an international at Fartown on 2 January 1909. Their tour had been disappointing in many ways but the team had not been defeated in representative fixtures, having beaten Yorkshire, Lancashire and the Northern Rugby League and three weeks earlier had drawn the first Ashes test match against the Northern Union. Wagstaff and Huddersfield half-back Percy Holroyd were chosen to make their international debuts. Again Wagstaff was setting records for at 17 years and 228 days old he became, and remains, the youngest English international of all time.

The game was a robust and bustling affair, which hung in the balance until the final minutes. The star of the match was Harold's centre partner, James Lomas, the English captain. Lomas was here, there and everywhere and played himself almost to a standstill – he was the benchmark for all aspiring centres in Edwardian England. Waggie had a good game too, showing many touches of brilliance. Australia led 9-8 at the interval but a tremendous dribble by Wagstaff was capped when Percy Holroyd scored the try that gave England the lead. A further late try gave England a 14-9 victory.

The season continued to go well for Wagstaff, whose centre partnership with the aggressive, bull-like but clever Wrigley became a sore trial to other teams. The duo were the main cause of Huddersfield's 5-3 victory over the Australians on 20 February 1909, the local paper reporting, 'It is getting quite monotonous to say that Wagstaff and Wrigley were the pick of the home backs. They again stood out by themselves, and one or the other was responsible for the opening out of almost every movement in which the home backs took part, while they were both insatiable in their search for work and their grand defence it was that made the Australians' attack look weak on so many occasions.' A few weeks later Huddersfield were looking a good bet for a place in the Challenge Cup final but were held to a 10-10 draw by Wigan at Fartown in the third round, played before a ground record crowd of 28,053. The game was reckoned to be one of the best ever seen on the arena, but Huddersfield were well beaten, 16-3, in the replay at a mud-bound Central Park.

The team was certainly developing on the right lines – two tourists, Albert Rosenfeld and Paddy Walsh, had been signed following the Kangaroos' game at Fartown and, during the 1909 close season, that forward of forwards Douglas Clark threw in his lot with Huddersfield. Other fine forwards in Bill Trevarthen, a 1907 All Gold, and Elijah Watts (Leeds) added to the club's burgeoning staff. These were men who could make a difference and Waggie was raring to go for the following season, when the first Lions tour of Australasia would surely be an attainable goal for the new international centre.

Sadly, his dream was shattered. Having played in the first three games of the season (all victories) Harold was taken gravely ill. He had grazed his knee in the opening fixture at Bramley and must have picked up some soil-born infection. The knee turned septic and general blood poisoning followed. He was taken to Leeds Infirmary and Huddersfield announced, 'There is every hope of his ultimate recovery but his illness, we are afraid, will be a long and tedious one'. So it was, and to make matters worse, he contracted mild diphtheria and was transferred to Seacroft Isolation Hospital. By January 1910 he was back in training but suffered another leg injury and was not able to return to action until the end of March. Ironically, Huddersfield had lifted their first major trophy, the Yorkshire Cup, back in November and he had missed the historic event. By the time he returned to the playing ranks the Lions touring team had been selected and his hopes of touring had vanished. His club-mates Jim Davies and Jack Bartholomew had earned places, however.

It was not the end of the world. Wagstaff was still only nineteen and he was to prove almost injury free in the coming years – although he did periodically suffer severe illnesses. Huddersfield had reinforced their side even more. John Willie Higson, a member of Hunslet's 'Terrible Six' in their Four Cups side of 1907/08, the great Welsh second-rower Ben Gronow and Con Byrne, yet another All Gold, added massively to the forward strength. Tommy Grey, a superb Welsh scrum-half, had been signed from Halifax and Wagstaff had a new partner on the left wing in Stanley Moorhouse. The two would terrorize opponents for many years to come. Even so, Huddersfield still flattered to deceive. They did reach the final of the Yorkshire Cup on 3 December and Waggy made his first appearance in a major final but a dismal display ended in a 2-8 defeat by Wakefield Trinity at Headingley.

There was talk in the papers of a lack of 'esprit de corps' at Fartown and attendances fell, while some of the spectators who did turn up were proving unruly. The turn of the year, however, proved the making of the team. The last 15 league games ended in victories, several of massive

Harold Wagstaff in 1909, resplendent in his England jersey and Yorkshire cap. He remains the youngest player to represent England, making his international debut against Australia on 2 January 1909 at the age of 17 years and 8 months, while he first played for Yorkshire at 17 years and 5 months.

proportions. Towards the close of the season the club made Harold Wagstaff – still not yet twenty – captain, a position he was to hold, except for one season, until he retired in 1925. His own form through the season was tremendous. He won back his England place and confirmed his prodigious talent at Coventry on 10 December 1910, scoring a try and landing two conversions in a 39-10 drubbing of Wales. In the return at Ebbw Vale on April Fools Day 1911, he partnered Billy Kitchin, who went over for two tries, while he scored a try and a goal himself in a 27-8 triumph. His display brought forth the following eulogy from the *Athletic News*, 'Wagstaff by sheer skill and resource completely baffled such experienced defenders as Willie Thomas and Bert Jenkins. He was perfectly unorthodox and passed either inside or outside in a manner which made him the hero of the match … Never have I witnessed more perfect centre three-quarter back play, and the last try was a fitting termination to a game which will, I think, be regarded as Wagstaff's.'

The 1911/12 season brought another Kangaroo touring team to Britain. Harold's test career began in a 10-19 loss against them in the first test at Newcastle on 8 November and he scored the only two tries of his test career in the second at Edinburgh on 16 December in an 11-11 draw. Injury kept him out of the final test, which was lost 8-33. The 1911/12 tourists were a much more successful team than their predecessors and Wagstaff was in losing teams on three other occasions against them, for England and twice for Northern Rugby League XIIIs. He had better luck with Huddersfield, however, helping his winger Stanley Moorhouse to a hat-trick in a 21-7 win at Fartown on 2 December 1911.

This was the point at which everything finally clicked. Major Holland established himself at full-back and Fred Longstaff bolstered the pack. Wagstaff had the men to do the job and what a job they did under their inspiring leader. They won everything except the Challenge Cup, going down 0-2 at Oldham in the third round. The Yorkshire Cup, the Yorkshire League and the Championship were all lifted and only 4 league games out of 36 were lost.

Wagstaff had decided views about how he wanted his team to play. Huddersfield became known as the team that will not kick. Wagstaff had long been convinced that good passing was the most effective way of winning games. Kicking away possession, particularly on attack, was pointless. With good teamwork and constant support play, the ball could be taken forward without recourse to kicking for position. He had a collection of players of outstanding individual qualities but he knew that teamwork and team spirit were paramount virtues. Somehow he induced his band of extreme talent to subsume their individualistic tendencies for the good of the team. Result – brilliant football, big crowds, shoals of cups and championships, everlasting fame. Of course, the players had to be fit and trainer Arthur Bennett, who had been at Fartown since 1886, was a huge asset to the club. The importance of team spirit could not be overestimated. Wagstaff made sure no one missed team meetings, when 'operational talks', as the players termed them, were delivered. He wanted a disciplined team but a happy one, in which all could depend on their colleagues. In his later career he was a leading light in the formation of a Players' Union. On the field, Wagstaff was like a beacon to his team. Everyone on the ground knew that his force of personality dominated proceedings.

There was no doubt that he was a brilliant leader. He thought deeply about the game, could pinpoint teams' and individuals' strengths and weaknesses and was able to adapt tactics to any given situation. Albert Rosenfeld summed things up succinctly when he said, 'All the players looked up to him. That's half the battle for a captain.' Dinny Campbell, an Australian contemporary of Waggy and a superb centre for Leeds, believed he was the best captain the game had known, lauding him as 'the greatest tactician I ever played against. His personality was dynamic.' The journalist V.A.S. Beanland was somewhat more poetic when he wrote in 1945, 'He was the pivot of one of the finest scoring combinations I have ever seen ... He was never afraid of bustling methods when those methods were demanded, but it was his scheming brain that made him the great player that he was. He could fit in perfectly with any combination and was a master of the art of adapting his play to that of his colleagues ... If you watched him closely you would realize how perfectly he blended with his colleagues, how obviously he was the "god in the machine", how deep was his knowledge of the weakness of the opposition, and how amazing was his intuition as to the right thing to do at the right moment.'

To all intents and purposes Wagstaff had no weaknesses as a player. He had a robust physique, was a graceful runner with an exceptional swerve and could sidestep as well as most three-quarters. His passing was wonderfully accurate and effective and he was a master at changing the direction of attack. He was totally unselfish, never gave his colleagues a ball unless they were better placed to progress than he. For a winger he was the ideal partner, his straight running giving the man outside him maximum opportunities and he would always take the bump rather than expose the winger to damage. He hardly ever dropped the ball, either in passing or in fielding kicks and his tackling was exemplary. Wagstaff often decried himself as one of the slowest men in Huddersfield's team, declaring some of the forwards were faster. His time over 100 yards was 11.5 seconds but to onlookers he appeared quicker than he claimed. A career total of 209 tries indicate that he was no slouch. While he eschewed kicking, he was adept at it when necessary and his skill at dribbling was outstanding. Early in his career in a game against Leigh in very heavy conditions a ball was thrown to him from a scrum on his own '25'. It dropped at his feet and he dribbled it 75 yards, never attempting to pick it up, to score a sensational try. No Leigh player even touched the ball!

Always an innovative player, Wagstaff constantly sought different ways of breaking down defences. Towards the end of his first season as Huddersfield captain, he and Jim Davies devised a most famous manoeuvre – the standing pass. The move produced innumerable tries, invariably on or towards the right wing. Wagstaff was a left centre and the move always followed a scrum. Grey would fire the ball to Davies at stand-off, who in turn passed to Wagstaff, who was already in motion when the ball arrived. He then ran dead straight to come up level with the scrum, which had not yet broken up. This four-yard dash was the vital element. Davies meanwhile had run to the outside of Waggy and was going full pelt. Waggy would then pass in an orthodox manner or ship the ball over his shoulder to him, depending on where the opposing tackler was coming from. If it was the opposite centre he turned to meet the impact of the tackle with his right hip. If the tackle came in from the other side, he faced it and took the bump on his left hip. Opponents used to call the move scientific obstruction but, as Waggy asked, who was he obstructing? The only person suffering in the transaction was himself. He would later write, 'It cost me a great deal of pain. I have come out of matches with my hips so sore that I could not put my hands on them, with hips so sore that the weight of my clothes seemed to hurt and sleep that night was almost an impossibility.'

The 1912/13 and 1913/14 seasons produced almost unalloyed success to Wagstaff's Team of All the Talents. In 1912/13 only the Yorkshire Cup eluded them and in 1913/14 the Yorkshire

Cup and League were both won, although defeat in the Championship final by Salford was most unexpected. The team had added Johnny Rogers, the fastest scrum-half of his generation, and the fiery Australian centre Tommy Gleeson, to the back division, while Jack Chilcott and Aaron Lee had found places in the pack. Waggy himself had prospered. By 1914 he had become captain of England and when the second Lions team to Australasia was selected for that summer, he was the first man to receive an invitation. He was also awarded the captaincy. He celebrated his twenty-third birthday just four days before the first tour fixture and remains the youngest man to lead a Lions tour to Australia and New Zealand.

The 1914 tour was the occasion of his supreme triumph. At extremely short notice (and unilaterally) the Australian authorities decided to stage all three Ashes tests within a week. The British tour managers protested, cabled home for instructions and were directed by the Northern Union, half the world away, to make the best of a bad job. The outcome was the most celebrated test in history. On 27 June Britain routed Australia 23-5 at the Royal Agricultural Ground in Sydney. Two days later at the Sydney Cricket Ground a 12-7 win by Australia levelled matters. The deciding test, on 4 July, also took place at the SCG. Britain had six players on the injured list and cock-a-hoop Australia fielded the team which had won the second test. Within minutes Lions winger Frank Williams twisted a knee and later had to retire. Douglas Clark broke his thumb but carried on until a dislocated collar-bone forced him off. In the second half centre Billy Hall was taken off concussed. Despite being reduced to ten men, Harold Wagstaff marshalled his depleted forces so adroitly that they established a 14-0 advantage. The Australians managed to pull back to 14-6 but the gallant British held on to win the test and the Ashes. The game was dubbed 'The Rorke's Drift Test' in remembrance of the heroic action of a small British force against an overwhelming Zulu army in 1879.

J.C. Davis wrote in *The Sydney Referee*, 'I have never seen the bulldog tenacity, the courage and heroic skill of the Englishmen that afternoon surpassed on the football field. That day, Wagstaff, the English captain, played with inspiration that left upon my memory that it was the most wonderful game any man has ever played in the face of colossal odds. Wagstaff, always a great player, that day became *the ubiquitous*, and the King of the game … Here, there and everywhere, all the time he was doing the work of half-a-dozen men. Wagstaff the Great.'

'Arawa', in *The Sydney Morning Telegraph*, eulogized: 'They say Inkermann was a soldiers' battle. So was this. For individual desperation no great match seen in Australia, or, perhaps, anywhere else, has equalled it. And standing out clear of all as the hero of his side and the day was the English captain, Wagstaff. Fine-looking, with an athlete's model frame, he was in everything, was everywhere, until at last he had the same effect on the Australian imagination as did Richmond on the distorted mind of Richard III. What a captain! He haunted the Australians. It was not Harold Wagstaff, the footballer, but Wagstaff, the Englishman, with his mind on a pole star. Never before has he played like this. One moment he was actually seen crashing into the scrum, to give his tired, hard-pressed vanguard a helping hand. Anon he was heading a desperate sortie on the left. A moment later he had come up in the centre, and then he was seen on the right supporting a forward who had broken away and fallen, dog-tired, by the way. Once, alone, he wormed, wriggled, twisted through half a dozen of them – a choice piece of work. And always he took the ball like an artist.'

Wagstaff's men went through New Zealand unbeaten in six matches but within days of the last fixture matters of greater import were on all minds. The Great War had commenced. It

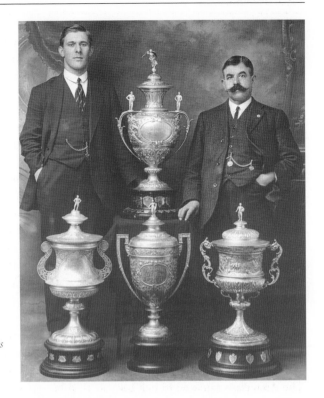

Harold Wagstaff with All Four Cups won by Huddersfield in 1914/15. He is accompanied by Arthur Bennett, the Fartown trainer.

would claim the lives of three of the tourists – Walter Roman, Billy Jarman and Waggy's club-mate, Fred Longstaff.

The Northern Union carried on as normal in 1914/15, apart from abandoning representative fixtures. Waggy and Huddersfield also carried on as normal. For the fourth consecutive campaign Huddersfield topped the table, losing only twice in the league. They swept all before them, at last emulating Hunslet's feat of taking All Four Cups in a season. They did it in far more style, however. Some have argued that it was easier for Huddersfield as the war took away many men at other clubs while the Fartowners only lost Jim Davies, who joined up straightaway. Whatever the case, Huddersfield were untouchable. After losing at Barrow in the league on 10 October they were undefeated in the succeeding 39 matches. Even in the three finals, they simply annihilated their opposition – Hull by 31-0 in the Yorkshire Cup, Wigan 27-2 in the Championship and St Helens 37-3 in the Challenge Cup. After the latter game at Oldham, the *Yorkshire Observer* stated, 'No club, in any age or any clime, has ever placed a team in the field which is comparable to the present Huddersfield combination, which has brought such lustre to the game'.

The following season, however, the Northern Union abandoned competitive rugby. Wagstaff was a motor driver in civilian life and had married Ann Battye, a local Holmfirth girl, in January 1915 but now his world changed completely. In 1916 he was drafted into the Army Service Corps (ASC), seeing service in Egypt and Palestine (1917-18), where he played some soccer as a full-back. The ASC, which played out of Grove Park, was a top rugby union playing unit from 1915 to 1917 and Waggy became its shining light as it became the most successful team in Britain. It could hardly have been otherwise, containing as it did

The great ASC team which swept all before it in services and club rugby union during the First World War. Many of its personnel were Northern Union players. From left to right, back row: Mellor, Jones, Holbrook, L. Coral, Clark. Middle row: J. Corsi, Gabrielle, Alexandra, Gronow, Pavine, Brown. Front row: Ware, Cockell, Neal, General Burn, Major Stanley, Wagstaff, Nixon.

Action photographs of Harold Wagstaff seem to be practically non-existent. Ironically, this poor quality image is of Harold actually playing rugby union for the Army Service Corps. It appeared in an article in The Tatler on 28 March 1917, entitled 'Corp. H. Wagstaff, the star threequarter'.

Huddersfield's Albert Rosenfeld, Douglas Clark, Ben Gronow and Bill Trevarthen, as well as several other Northern Union stars.

When peace returned Huddersfield remained the team to beat. In 1919/20 they topped the league and came within five minutes of lifting All Four Cups again. The Yorkshire League, the Yorkshire Cup and the Challenge Cup were all safely tucked away and the Championship final against Hull was to take place at Leeds on 24 April. By that time, however, Wagstaff and four of his team-mates were en route for Australia. Huddersfield led Hull 2-0 only for a 75th-minute try from Billy Batten to wrest the final accolade from them.

Wagstaff had again been selected as captain of the Lions. Although New Zealand were defeated 3-0, Britain lost the first two Ashes tests and Harold missed the 23-13 victory in the final test. By his own standards, his tour had not been quite up to scratch. Even so, he continued to play representative rugby until 1923. One of his greatest satisfactions was his leadership of the team which won back the Ashes in the home series of 1921/22. His final test match was the decider against those Kangaroos at Salford on 14 January 1922. The conditions were appalling, snow and straw being the main ingredients of the pitch. Waggy never played in, and most of the onlookers never saw, a more strenuous match. Britain won 6-0 and Wagstaff was carried in triumph from the field by a mass of invading fans but not before his mud-covered white jersey had been ripped to pieces by idolators seeking a relic of the great man's last test.

In 1923 Harold underwent an operation for a duodenal ulcer – he had suffered from stomach problems for several years – and subsequently always played in a corset to protect his abdomen. He played on until 1925, making his last appearance in a first-class fixture in the unaccustomed role of full-back in a 0-16 defeat at Oldham on Monday, 23 March. A couple of months earlier

The programme cover for Harold Wagstaff's benefit match. Huddersfield beat Rochdale Hornets 22-8 on 31 January 1920 in front of a crowd of 15,888. Wagstaff's benefit realised a massive £926/19/2. A few months later, Billy Batten's benefit match (Hull v. York on 3 April 1920) produced £1,079/13/8. Harold was apparently never paid more than £6 per match, whereas Billy reputedly earned £14 per match in his pomp at Hull.

The 1920 Lions power brokers. From left to right: John Wilson (tour manager and secretary of the Rugby Football League, 1920-46), Harold Wagstaff (tour captain), Sydney Foster (tour manager) and Gwyn Thomas (tour vice-captain).

he had become licensee of the Boar's Head in Halifax. In 1925/26 he became coach at Halifax but his tenure was brief and unsuccessful and he joined the committee instead, serving on the football and finance committees. In 1931 he returned to Huddersfield to take over the Royal Swan Hotel. He dallied again with coaching when he took over the reins at Broughton Rangers in 1935/36 but it was a short-lived dalliance. His last association with the game was as a committeeman at his beloved Fartown.

Harold Wagstaff died on 19 July 1939, aged only forty-eight. On the day of the funeral Westgate, in the centre of Huddersfield and the street on which Wagstaff's hotel stood, was lined by hundreds of people, who made the thoroughfare almost impassable for fully half an hour, a squad of police officers having to direct traffic. At the funeral service at Holmfirth Parish Church, the vicar, the Revd T.H. Cashmore echoed the feelings of the congregation when he said, 'Holmfirth was rightly proud of a man who, in his own sphere, had carried her name far beyond their hills and valleys. He had great qualities of heart and mind and body that won for him the confidence and admiration of thousands.'

Eight of Waggy's old playing comrades bore the coffin – Douglas Clark, Wimpenny Brook, Hartley Hirst, Stanley Williams, Ben Gronow, Billy Kitchin, George Todd and Major Holland. On the coffin lay two wreaths – a cross from his widow and son, and a model of a rugby ball made of golden lilies and claret carnations, which bore the inscription, 'From the boys of the Fartown football team'.

Right: *Harold Wagstaff shakes hands with his 1914 Lions stand-off Stuart Prosser of Halifax, probably in the 1922/23 season.*

Next page: *This* All Sports Illustrated Weekly *cover from 1921 is illustrative of the esteem Harold Wagstaff generated in the wider world of sport.*

The Yorkshire team, captained by Harold Wagstaff, for the drawn 11-11 Roses Match of 1922 at Craven Park, Hull. From left to right, back row: Major Cass, Betteridge, Marshall, Wild, Brown, Batten, Gallagher. Seated: Clements, Lyman, Wagstaff, Brittain, Turnbull. Front: Binks, Osbourne.

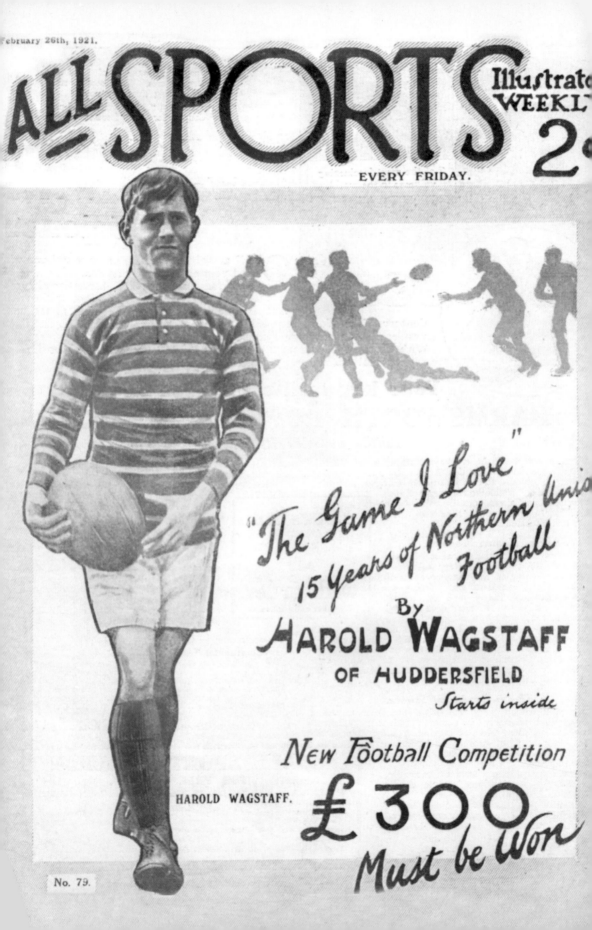